W9-AAP-785

THE ULTIMATE ADULT ONLY JOKE BOOK

HB
HINKLER
BOOKS

HINKLER
BOOKS

Ultimate Adult Only Joke Book
Published in 2005 by Hinkler Books Pty Ltd
45-55 Fairchild Street
Heatherton VIC 3202 Australia
www.hinklerbooks.com.au

© Hinkler Books Pty Ltd 2005

10 9 8 7 6 5
10 09 08 07

All rights reserved. No part of this publication may be reproduced,
stored in a retrieval system, or transmitted in any way or by any
means, electronic, mechanical, photocopying, recording or otherwise,
without the prior written permission of the copyright holders.

ISBN 1 7415 7017 4
Cover design: Sam Grimmer
Editor: Ben Ripley

Printed and bound in China

CONTENTS

Introduction	1
And so, to the beginning . . .	2
A . . . walks into a bar	5
Aeroplanes and flying	19
Animals	21
Blondes	34
Battle of the sexes	52
Rejected Dr Suess books	74
The sanctity of marriage	76
Cultural diversity	83
Signs collected by a flight attendant along her travels	94
Business is business	98
Signs you have had too much of modern life	103
Believe it or not	104
Deserted islands	113
Government	115
Religion	118
Schooldays	146
You're a shocker!	149
The innocence of kids	170
Lawyers	176
Law enforcement	186
Courtroom capers	190
Making music	193
10 reasons why chocolate is better than sex	204
On the farm	205
Hunting and fishing	209
University life	212
Doctors and nurses	215
Why did the chicken cross the road?	233
Eating out	235
Growing old gracefully	239

Death and dying 247
You know you're having a bad day when . . . 249
A load of old balls 252
30 things *not* to say during sex 269
Laughing at disabilities 271
Hard drives and floppies 274
Accountants and their ilk 281
It's all in the mind 283
The banking sector 285
Funny signs seen in Great Britain 288
The military 290
The moral of the story is . . . 296
How many . . . does it take to change a light bulb? 299
We wish you a merry Christmas 302
Miscellaneous 305
Jail vs work 327
Country folk 329
The 80s! 331
Domestic tips 333
Education 337
Employment 342
Ethnicity 346
Families 352
Fishing 356
Office, business and technology 364
Politics 370
Quotes 387
Rednecks 390
Riddles 393
Telephone tales 395
Toilet humour 398
Mummy! 407
Confucius say . . . 408
Best jokes in the world . . . debatable! 411

INTRODUCTION

I n this day and age, it's common practice for books to have lengthy introductions in which the author, editor or compiler explain the motivation behind the contents. But this is a joke book for Christ's sake. And whether you've bought, borrowed or pinched this book, you really only want to read the jokes.

So let's get on with it.

AND SO, TO THE BEGINNING . . .

You know you're in a redneck hotel when you phone the front office and say, 'I've got a leak in the sink.' And they say, 'Go ahead!'

What's grosser than gross?
Two Siamese twins connected at the tongue.

What's even grosser than that?
When one of them throws up.

Dean saw an advertisement for a blow-up doll called Life-Like Tina which claimed she was 'so realistic you can't tell the difference!' As Dean had not had a girlfriend for a long time he ordered one, and waited in anticipation.

The supplier got the order from Dean, and the bloke who was mailing it couldn't believe how realistic 'Life-Like Tina' looked. When no one was around he decided to blow her up. He then thought that as she was inflated he might as well give her a bit of a test run. He had sex with the doll, meticulously washed it afterwards, packaged it up and posted it out to Dean.

A month later Dean rang the supplier.

'You know that "Life-Like Tina" blow up doll? I can't tell you how happy I am.'

'That's great!' said the supplier.

'It was a totally unbelievable experience,' enthused Dean.

'Realistic then?' asked the supplier.

'So realistic . . . I got syphilis.'

A farm boy accidentally overturned his wagonload of corn. A farmer who lived nearby heard the noise, saw the mess, and yelled over to the boy, 'Hey Jimmy, forget your troubles. Come in and visit with us. I'll help you get the wagon up later.'

'That's mighty nice of you,' Jimmy answered, 'but I don't think Pa would like me to.'

'Aw come on boy,' the farmer insisted.

'No, Pa –'

'Forget about your Pa. You been working so hard, it was bad luck when that wagon fell over, so you come inside and set a spell and rest up.'

'Well OK,' the boy finally agreed, and added, 'but Pa won't like it.'

After a hearty dinner, Jimmy thanked his host. 'I feel a lot better now, but I know Pa is going to be real upset.'

'Don't be foolish!' the neighbour said with a smile. 'He's a very understanding man, your father. By the way, where is he?'

'Under the wagon.'

Frank works hard at the factory. His only joy is to spend most evenings bowling or playing basketball at the gym. His wife thinks he is pushing himself too hard, so for his birthday she takes him to a local strip club.

The doorman at the club greets them and says, 'Hey, Frank! How ya doin?'

His wife is puzzled and asks Frank if he's been to this club before.

'Oh no,' says Frank. 'He's on my bowling team.'

When they are seated, a waitress asks Frank if he'd like his usual VB.

His wife is becoming a little uncomfortable and says, 'You must come here a lot for that woman to know you drink VB.'

'No, darling, she's also in the Ladies Bowling League on Wednesday nights. We share lanes with them.'

Then, a stripper comes over to their table and throws her arms around Frank. 'Hi, Frankie,' she says, 'Want your usual table dance?'

Frank's wife, now furious, grabs her purse and storms out of the club. Frank follows and sees her getting into a cab. Before she can slam the door, he jumps in beside her and she starts going ballistic, screaming at him.

The cabby turns his head and says, 'Hey, Frankie, looks like you picked up a real doozie this time!'

One fine morning in Eden, God was looking for Adam and Eve, but couldn't find them. Later that day, God saw Adam and asked where he and Eve were earlier.

Adam said, 'This morning Eve and I made love for the first time.'

God said, 'Adam, you have sinned. I knew this would happen. Where is Eve now?'

Adam replied, 'She's down at the river, washing herself out.'

'Damn,' said God, 'now all the fish will smell funny.'

A . . . WALKS INTO A BAR

It's easy to see why so many jokes are set in bars.
Bars offer warmth. Bars offer solace. Bars offer companionship.
But more than that, bars offer alcohol.

Three mice are sitting at a bar in a pretty rough neighbourhood late at night, trying to impress each other with how tough they are.

The first mouse sinks a shot of Scotch, slams the glass onto the bar, turns to the second mouse and says, 'When I see a mousetrap, I lie on my back and set it off with my foot. When the bar comes down, I catch it in my teeth, bench press it twenty times to work up an appetite, and then make off with the cheese.'

The second mouse orders up two shots of sour mash, sinks them both, slams each glass onto the bar, turns to the first mouse, and replies, 'Yeah, well when I see rat poison, I collect as much as I can, take it home, grind it up to a powder, and add it to my coffee each morning so I can get a good buzz going for the rest of the day.'

The first mouse and the second mouse then turn to the third mouse.

The third mouse lets out a long sigh and says to the first two, 'I don't have time for this bullshit. I gotta go home and screw the cat.'

A sexy woman in a bar walks up to the counter and motions the bartender over. She starts to run her fingers through his hair and asks to speak to the manager.

The bartender says, 'He isn't here but I can do anything the manager can do for you.'

By this time the woman is running her fingers down his face and into his mouth and is letting him suck on her fingers. She says, 'You're sure he isn't here?'

The bartender says, 'Yes, I'm very sure.'

The woman says, 'Well, I just wanted to tell him there's no toilet paper or soap in the women's toilet.'

A man is sitting outside a bar enjoying a quiet drink when a nun starts lecturing him on the evils of alcohol.

'How do you know alcohol is evil?' asks the man. 'Have you ever tasted it?'

'Of course not,' answers the nun.

'Then let me buy you a drink and, afterwards, if you still believe that it's evil, I promise I'll never touch another drop.'

'But I can't possibly be seen to be drinking,' says the nun.

'Right. Well, I'll get the bartender to put it in a teacup for you.'

The man goes inside and asks for a beer and a vodka.

'And would you mind putting the vodka in a teacup?'

'Oh no,' says the bartender. 'It's not that bloody nun again, is it?'

A drunk rolls into a bar, but the bartender refuses to serve him. 'You've had too much to drink,' he says. 'I'm not serving you.'

Five minutes later, the drunk comes in again. The bartender stands firm.

'There's no way I'm serving you more alcohol. You've had more than enough already.'

Five minutes later, the doors open and the drunk lurches in once more.

'Look,' says the bartender, 'I'm not serving you. You're too drunk.'

The drunk nods. 'I guess I must be,' he says. 'This is the third place in a row that's refused to serve me.'

Two flies walk into a bar, order drinks and sit down for a chat.

First fly: How was your trip down here?

Second fly: It was so cold I rode in a biker's moustache. How was yours?

First fly: I was warm all the way. I rode in a biker chick's pussy. You ought to do it next year.

A year later, the same two flies meet in the same bar.

First fly: Did you travel down like I told you?

Second fly: Yes. But somehow I still showed up in a biker's moustache.

A man walks into a bar with a dog. He puts the dog on the bar and says to the bartender, 'This is the smartest dog in the world. I bet you $5 that he can answer any question you ask him.'

The bartender agrees and asks the dog, 'What's the cube root of 81?'

'Three,' the dog answers immediately.

'That's amazing,' says the bartender, handing over $5.

At this point, the dog owner has to go to the toilet. He asks the barman to look after the dog, and puts the $5 in the dog's collar.

While the man is in the toilet, the barman says to the dog, 'If you're so smart, go down the road and get me a newspaper.'

So the dog leaves. When the man comes out of the toilet he goes ballistic.

'Where's my dog?' he shouts.

The barman calms the man down and tells him about the newspaper. The man immediately leaves the bar to search for his dog. He eventually finds the dog in an alley, screwing a poodle.

'What are you doing?' the man shouts. 'You've never done this before.'

'I've never had $5 before either.'

A bar has a sign up that reads Pianist Wanted. So this guy walks in and tells the owner that he's a great pianist. The owner tells the pianist to play a couple of songs and if he's as good as he claims, then the job is his. So the pianist sits down and plays a song that nearly has the owner in tears.

'What a beautiful song! What's it called?' the owner asks.

'It's called, *The dog's shagging the cat and my wife's doin' my brother.*'

'Um, well, how about playing one more tune.'

So the man plays another tune and this time the manager does break down in tears.

'What do you call that song?' he asks, wiping his eyes.

'*The elephant's taking a shit while the lion's licking his balls.*'

The bar owner tells the pianist that he has the job on one condition. He must not tell the customers the names of the songs he is playing. So the pianist starts playing that night. After every song he gets a standing ovation. After about two hours of solid playing, he announces he is going to have a break. He goes to the toilet to take a piss.

On his way out a man passing says, 'Hey mate, do you know your fly's undone and your cock's hangin' out?'

'Of course I know it. I wrote it!'

A guy is sitting at a bar feeling sorry for himself because his wife just kicked him out. A woman comes up and sits beside him and orders a drink. She looks as depressed as he does.

'Is there something wrong?' the guy asks her.

'My husband just left me. He said I was too kinky.'

The guy says, 'What a coincidence. My wife just kicked me out as well because I was too kinky.'

The woman has an idea. 'Why don't we go back to my place and get kinky together?'

'Sounds perfect,' the guy replies. When they get to her house, she tells him to make himself comfortable while she goes to change. She goes to her room and takes off her clothes. She puts on a leather G-string, a leather bra, black stockings, big, black leather boots and gets out her whip. When she's ready, she goes out to the living room and finds the guy putting his coat and boots back on.

'Where are you going?' she asks. 'I thought we were gonna get kinky together.'

The guy replies, 'I screwed your dog and shat in your purse, how much kinkier can I get?'

A confident man walks into a bar and takes a seat next to a very attractive woman. He gives her a quick glance, then looks down at his watch for a moment.

The woman notices this and asks, 'Is your date running late?'

'No,' he replies. 'I just bought this state-of-the-art watch and I was testing it.'

'A state-of-the-art watch? What's so special about it?'

'It uses alpha waves to telepathically talk to me,' he explains.

'What's it telling you now?'

'Well, it says you're not wearing any panties . . .'

The woman giggles and replies, 'Well it must be broken then because I am wearing panties!'

The man explains, 'Damn thing must be an hour fast.'

A struggling bar owner decides that he needs a gimmick to bring more people into his bar. After wracking his brains, he comes up with the idea of holding a competition to find the toughest man in town. He puts up posters around town and advertises in the local newspaper. On the appointed day, his bar is full. The first contestant is a huge man, holding a snapping turtle. The man jumps up on the bar, unzips his pants and whips out his large penis. The man then picks up the snapping turtle and holds it right in front of his dick. With unbelieving eyes, the onlookers gasp as the turtle bites down on the man's penis.

The big man let's go of the turtle and starts swaying his body. The turtle bounces from side to side off the man's hips. After about thirty seconds of this, the man pokes the turtle in the eyes, and the turtle drops to the floor.

'Now,' shouts the big guy. 'Is there another son of a bitch in here that thinks he is tough enough to do that?'

A timid hand at the back of the bar is raised, 'I'll do it, if you promise not to poke me in the eyes.'

A huge muscular man walks into a bar and orders a beer. The bartender hands him the beer and says, 'You know, I'm not gay but I want to compliment you on your physique, it really is phenomenal! I have a question though, why is your head so small?'

The big guy nods slowly. He's obviously fielded this question many times.

'One day,' he begins, 'I was hunting when I got lost in the woods. I heard someone crying for help and finally realised that it was coming from a frog sitting next to a stream. So I picked up the frog and it said, "Kiss me. Kiss me and I will turn into a genie and grant you three wishes." So I looked around to make sure I was alone and gave the frog a kiss. Suddenly, the frog turned into a beautiful, voluptuous, naked woman.

She said, "You now have three wishes."

I looked down at my scrawny body and said, "I want a body like Arnold Schwarzenegger."

She nodded, whispered a spell, and abracadabra there I was, so huge that I burst out of my clothes and was standing there naked.

She then asked, "What will be your second wish?"

I looked hungrily at her beautiful body and replied, "I want to make sensuous love with you here by this stream."

She nodded, lay down, and beckoned to me. We then made love for hours!

Later, as we lay there next to each other, sweating from our glorious lovemaking, she whispered into my ear, "You know, you do have one more wish. What will it be?"

I looked at her and replied, "How about a little head?"'

A drunk gets up from the bar and heads for the bathroom. A few minutes later, a loud, blood-curdling scream is heard coming from the bathroom. A few minutes later, another loud scream reverberates throughout the bar. The bartender goes to the bathroom to investigate why the drunk is screaming.

'What's all the screaming about in there?' he says. 'You're scaring my customers!'

'I'm just sitting here on the toilet and every time I flush something comes up and squeezes the hell out of my balls!'

With that, the bartender opens the door, looks in and says, 'You idiot. You're sitting on the mop bucket.'

A businessman enters a tavern, sits down at the bar, and orders a double martini on the rocks.

After he finishes the drink, he peeks inside his shirt pocket and orders another double martini. After he finishes that one, he again peeks inside his shirt pocket and orders a double martini.

The bartender says, 'Look, buddy, I'll bring ya martinis all night long. But you gotta tell me why you look inside your shirt pocket before you order a refill.'

The customer replies, 'I'm peeking at a photo of my wife. When she starts to look good, then I know it's time to go home.'

Joe walks into a bar. With him is a little guy a foot tall. Joe walks up to the bar and the little guy walks over to the piano and starts playing it and singing. The bartender, amazed at the sight of this little guy playing the piano and singing, moves over to Joe and talks to him.

'Hey,' he says, 'that little guy's really good. Where did you find him?'

Joe replies, 'I got him from my genie.'

'You've got a genie?' The bartender asks. 'Do you mind if I borrow him for a little while? I could really use some money.'

'No problem,' Joe says. 'Wish away.'

Whoosh! The genie appears.

'Wow,' gasps the bartender. 'I wish for a thousand bucks!' With a bright flash and a crash of thunder there appears in the bar a thousand ducks.

'Wait a minute,' cries the bartender. 'I asked for a thousand bucks not a thousand ducks!'

'Well,' says Joe, 'do you think I asked for a twelve-inch pianist?'

A man walks into a bar with a steak-and-kidney pie on his head. He walks over to the bartender and says, 'Can I have a beer please?'

The bartender gets him his beer but he can't stop staring at the pie on the man's head. Finally the bartender can't bite his tongue any longer.

'Excuse me Sir, but why do you have a steak-and-kidney pie on your head?'

The man replies, 'I always have a steak-and-kidney pie on my head on a Thursday.'

The bartender says, 'But it's Wednesday today.'

'Oh I must look like a right prick then.'

A really drunk woman walks into a bar. She sits down at the bar and yells, 'Heyyyy tenderbar, give me a tinimar, with a pickle on top.'

The bartender gives her a drink, she drinks it down, and then goes, 'Ahhh, heartburn.'

Again, the drunk woman says, 'Heyyyy tenderbar, give me a tinimar, with a pickle on top.'

Again, she drinks the drink and says, 'Ahhh, heartburn.'

This goes on a couple more times when, finally, the bartender gets fed up. The drunk woman tries to order another drink, but the bartender says, 'Look lady, it's not tenderbar, it's bartender; it's not a tinimar, it's a martini; it's not a pickle, it's an olive; and its not heartburn you have, your left tit is hanging in the ashtray!'

A bear walks into a bar. He goes up to the barman and says, 'Can I have a large gin and . . . . tonic please?'

The barman replies, 'Sure, but what's with the big pause?'

'I'm a bear,' says the bear, holding his palms up.

Four men are telling stories in a bar. One man leaves for a bathroom break. Three men are left. The first man says, 'I was worried that my son was gonna be a loser because he started out washing cars for a local dealership. Turns out that he got a break, they made him a salesman, and he sold so many cars that he bought the dealership. In fact, he's so successful that he just gave his best friend a new Mercedes for his birthday.'

The second man says, 'I was worried about my son, too, because he started out raking leaves for a realtor. Turns out he got a break, they made him a commissioned salesman, and he eventually bought the real estate firm. In fact, he's so successful that he just gave his best friend a new house for his birthday.'

The third man says, 'Yeah, I hear you. My son started out sweeping floors in a brokerage firm. In fact, he's so rich that he just gave his best friend a million in stock for his birthday.'

The fourth man comes back from the toilet. The first three explain that they are telling stories about their kids, so he says, 'Well, I'm embarrassed to admit that my son is a major disappointment. He started out as a hairdresser and is still a hairdresser after fifteen years. In fact, I just found out that he's gay and has several boyfriends. But I try to look at the bright side–his boyfriends just bought him a new Mercedes, a new house, and a million in stock for his birthday.'

A mangy looking guy goes into a bar and orders a drink. The bartender says, 'No way. I don't think you can pay for it.'

The guy says, 'You're right. I don't have any money, but if I show you something you haven't seen before, will you give me a drink?'

The bartender says, 'Only if what you show me ain't risqué.'

'Deal,' says the guy and reaches into his coat pocket and pulls out a hamster. He puts the hamster on the bar and it runs to the end of the bar, down the bar, across the room and up onto the piano, jumps on the keyboard and starts playing Gershwin songs. And the hamster is really good.

The bartender says, 'You're right. I've never seen anything like that before. That hamster is truly good on the piano.' The guy downs the drink and asks the bartender for another.

'Money or another miracle, or else no drink,' says the bartender. The guy reaches into his coat again and pulls out a frog. He puts the frog on the bar, and the frog starts to sing. He has a marvellous voice and great pitch – a fine singer. A stranger from the other end of the bar runs over to the guy and offers him $300 for the frog.

The guy says, 'It's a deal.' He takes the $300 and gives the stranger the frog. The stranger runs out of the bar. The bartender says to the guy, 'Are you some kind of nut? You sold a singing frog for $300? It must have been worth millions. You must be crazy.'

'Not so,' says the guy. 'The hamster is also a ventriloquist.'

A Scottish farmer walks into the neighbourhood pub, and orders a whiskey.

'Ye see that fence over there?' he says to the bartender. 'Ah built it with me own two hands! Dug up the holes with me shovel, chopped doon the trees for the posts by me ownself, laid every last rail! But do they call me "McGregor the Fence-Builder?" No.'

He gulps down the whiskey and orders another. 'Ye see that pier on the loch?' he continues, 'Ah built it me ownself, too. Swam oot into the loch to lay the foondations, laid doon every single board! But do they call me "McGregor the Pier-Builder"? No.'

'But ye screw just one sheep . . .'

A panda walks into a bar, sits down and orders a sandwich. He eats the sandwich, pulls out a gun and shoots the waiter dead. As the panda stands up to go, the bartender shouts, 'Hey! Where are you going? You just shot my waiter and you didn't pay for your sandwich!'

The panda yells back at the bartender, 'Hey man, I'm a panda! Look it up!'

The bartender opens his dictionary and sees the following definition for panda: 'A tree dwelling marsupial of Asian origin, characterised by distinct black and white colouring. Eats shoots and leaves.'

A mouse and a lion walk into a bar, and they're sitting there chugging away at a few ales when a giraffe walks in.

'Get a load of her,' says the mouse. 'I fancy that!'

'Well, why not try your luck?' says the lion.

So the mouse goes over to the giraffe and starts talking to her, and within five minutes they're out the door and gone into the night.

Next day, the lion is in the bar drinking away, and the mouse staggers in. He is absolutely stuffed.

The lion helps his pal up on to a stool, pours a drink down his throat and says, 'What the hell happened to you? I saw you leave with the giraffe, what happened after that? Was she all right?'

The mouse says, 'Yeah, she was really something else – we went out to dinner, had a couple of glasses of wine, and she invited me back to her place to spend the night. And oh, man! I've never had a night like it!'

'But how come you look like you're so exhausted?' asks the lion.

'Well,' says the mouse, 'between the kissing and the screwing, I must have run a thousand miles.'

On the top of a tall building in a large city, there is a bar. In this bar, a man is drinking heavily. He asks the bartender for a shot of tequila, then walks out to the balcony and jumps off. Minutes later, he appears in the elevator and repeats the whole process. Another guy in the bar watches this happen a number of times until curiosity gets the better of him.

Finally, he goes up to the man and asks, 'Hey, you keep drinking, then jumping off the balcony. And yet, minutes later, you're back again. How do you do it?'

'Well, the shot of tequila provides buoyancy such that when I get near the ground, I slow down and land gently. It's lots of fun. You should try it.'

The guy, who is quite pissed, thinks to himself, Hey, why not? So he goes to the bar, drinks a shot of tequila, then walks out to the balcony and jumps off. *Whoooooooooooooo . . . SPLAT!*

The bartender looks over at the first guy and says, 'Man, you're an arsehole when you're drunk, Superman.'

A young man sits down at the bar.
'What can I get you?' the bartender inquires.
'I want six shots of vodka,' says the young man.
'Six shots? Are you celebrating something?'
'Yeah, my first blowjob,' the young man answers.
'Well, in that case, let me give you a seventh on the house.'

'No offence, Sir. But if six shots won't get rid of the taste, nothing will.'

Three women, all with boyfriends named Leroy, are at a bar when one of the women says, 'I'm tired of getting my Leroy mixed up with your Leroy, and her Leroy mixed up with your Leroy. Why don't we all name our Leroys after a soft drink?'

The other two women agree, and the first woman says, 'OK, then, let me go first. I name my Leroy 7-UP.'

The other two women ask her, 'Why 7-UP?'

'Because my Leroy has seven inches and it's always UP!'

All three women holler and hoot and slap each other on the back.

Then the second woman says, 'OK, I'm next, and I name my Leroy Mountain Dew.'

The other two women ask, 'Why Mountain Dew?'

'Because my Leroy can Mount and Dew me anytime.'

All three women holler and hoot and slap each other on the back.

The third woman then stands back and starts thinking and says, 'You know, those two Leroys were good, but I'm gonna name mine Jack Daniels.'

The other two women shout in unison, 'Jack Daniels? That's not a soft drink – that's a hard liquor!'

The third woman shouts, 'That's my Leroy!'

While a man at a bar savours a double martini, an attractive woman sits down next to him and orders a glass of orange juice.

The man turns to her and says, 'This is a special day. I'm celebrating.'

'I'm celebrating, too,' she replies, clinking glasses with him.

'What are you celebrating?' he asks.

'For years I've been trying to have a child,' she answers. 'Today my gynaecologist told me I'm pregnant!'

'Congratulations,' the man says, lifting his glass. 'As it happens, I'm a chicken farmer, and for years all my hens were infertile. But today they're finally fertile.'

'How did it happen?'

'I switched cocks.'

'What a coincidence,' she says, smiling.

A very shy guy goes into a bar and sees a beautiful woman sitting at the bar.

After an hour of gathering up his courage, he finally goes over to her and asks, tentatively, 'Um, would you mind if I chatted with you for a while?'

She responds by yelling, at the top of her lungs, 'No! I won't sleep with you tonight!'

Everyone in the bar is now staring at them. Naturally, the guy is hopelessly and completely embarrassed and he slinks back to his table.

After a few minutes, the woman walks over to him and apologises.

She smiles at him and says, 'I'm sorry if I embarrassed you. You see, I'm a graduate student in psychology, and I'm studying how people respond to embarrassing situations.'

To which he responds, at the top of his lungs, 'What do you mean $200?'

AEROPLANES AND FLYING

Q: What's the difference between a skydiver and a golfer?
A: A golfer goes 'WHACK . . . Oh shit!' A skydiver goes 'Oh shit! . . . WHACK'

NASA planned a mission that involved keeping three astronauts in space for two years. Because of the extended duration of the trip, each was allowed to take 100kg of baggage.

The first astronaut decided to take along his wife. The second decided to take along tapes so he could learn how to speak Arabic. The third astronaut decided to take along 800 packets of cigarettes.

Two years later, when the space shuttle landed, there was a big crowd waiting to welcome them home. Out came the first astronaut and his wife, each with a baby in their arms. Next, came the second astronaut speaking fluent Arabic. They both gave their speeches and got a rousing applause.

Suddenly out came the third astronaut with a cigarette in his mouth. He walked up to the podium and snarled at the crowd, 'Has anyone got a match?'

A military cargo plane, flying over a populated area, suddenly loses power and starts to nose dive. The pilot tries to pull up, but with all their cargo, the plane is too heavy. He yells to the soldiers in the back to throw things out to make the plane lighter. They throw out a pistol.

'Throw out more!' shouts the pilot.

So they throw out a rifle.

'More!' he cries again.

They heave out a missile. The plane stabilises and the pilot regains control. With a sigh of relief they land safely at the airport.

They unload the plane and head off home. Pretty soon they meet a boy on the side of the road who's crying. They stop and ask why he is crying.

'I was riding my bike and out of the sky a pistol hit me on the head!'

They drive a little further, and meet a boy who's crying even harder. Again they stop and ask why the boy crying.

He says, 'I was walking to the shops when from nowhere a rifle hit me on the head!'

They apologise and keep driving until they come across a boy who is crying hysterically. They stop and ask him what the matter is.

'Nothing,' the boy replies, 'I'm crying from laughter – I just farted and a house blew up!'

A student was heading home for the holidays. When she got to the airline counter, she presented her ticket to Houston.

'I'd like you to send my green suitcase to Hawaii, and my red suitcase to London,' she told the agent.

The confused agent said, 'I'm sorry, we can't to that.'

'Really? I am so relieved to hear you say that because that's exactly what you did with my luggage last year!'

ANIMALS

Abutcher is working when he notices a dog in his shop. He goes to shoo him away when he spots a note in the dog's mouth. The note reads, 'Can I have 12 sausages and a leg of lamb, please?', and wrapped inside the note is a $10 note.

So the butcher takes the money, puts the sausages and lamb in a bag, and places the bag in the dog's mouth. The dog trots happily out of the shop.

Intrigued, the butcher decides to close up shop and follow the dog. It walks down the street and comes to a crossing. The dog puts down the bag, jumps up and presses the crossing button. Then he waits patiently, bag in mouth, for the lights to change. They do, and he walks across the road, with the butcher following.

The dog comes to a bus stop, and looks at the timetable. Then he sits on one of the seats to wait for the bus. The butcher is in awe.

Along comes a bus. The dog walks to the front of the bus, looks at the number, and goes back to his seat.

Another bus comes. Again the dog checks the number and climbs onto bus. The butcher, mouth agape, follows him onto the bus.

The bus travels through town and out to the suburbs. Eventually the dog gets up, moves to the front of the bus and, standing on his hind legs, pushes the button to stop the bus.

The dog gets off, meat still in his mouth and the butcher follows. They walk down the road, and the dog approaches a house. He walks up the path, and drops the package of meat on the step.

Then he walks back down the path, takes a big run, and throws himself against the door. He goes back down the path, takes another run, and throws himself against the door again. There's no answer at the door, so the dog goes to the window and bangs his head against it several times. He sits at the door waiting.

The door swings open. A big bloke looks down at the dog.

'You stupid dog!' he yells.

The butcher is taken aback because, evidently, this dog is not stupid. So he runs up to the bloke and says, 'What the hell are you doing? This dog is a genius. He's so clever, he could be on TV!'

The guy responds, 'Clever? Yeah right. This is the second time this week he's forgotten his key!'

A turtle is walking down an alley in New York when he is mugged by a gang of snails. A police detective comes to investigate and asks the turtle if he could explain what happened.

The turtle turns to the detective with a confused look and replies, 'I don't know officer. It all happened so fast . . .'

Bob was excited about his new rifle and decided to try bear hunting. He travelled up to Alaska, spotted a small brown bear and shot it. Soon after there was a tap on his shoulder, and he turned around to see a big black bear.

The black bear said, 'That was a very bad mistake. That was my cousin. I'm going to give you two choices. Either I maul you to death or we have sex.'

After considering briefly, Bob decided to accept the latter alternative.

So the black bear had his way with Bob.

Even though he felt sore for two weeks, Bob soon recovered and vowed revenge. He headed out on another trip to Alaska where he found the black bear and shot it dead.

Right away, there was another tap on his shoulder. This time a huge grizzly bear stood right next to him.

The grizzly said, 'That was a big mistake, Bob. That was my cousin and you've got two choices: Either I maul you to death or I have sex with you.'

Again, Bob thought it was better to cooperate with the grizzly bear than be mauled to death, so the grizzly had his way with Bob.

Although he survived, it took several months before Bob fully recovered from his run-in with the bear. By then, Bob was completely outraged, so he headed back to Alaska and managed to track down the grizzly bear and shoot it.

He felt the joy of sweet revenge, but then there was a tap on his shoulder. He turned around to find a giant polar bear standing there.

The polar bear looked at him and said, 'Admit it Bob, you don't come here for the hunting, do you?'

Two guys are out hiking. Suddenly, a bear starts chasing them. They climb a tree, but the bear starts climbing up the tree after them.

The first guy gets his sneakers out of his knapsack and starts putting them on.

'What are you doing?' asks the second guy.

'When the bear gets close to us, I thought we'd jump down and make a run for it.'

'Are you crazy? You can't outrun a bear.'

'I don't have to outrun the bear. I only have to outrun you.'

An old farmer's rooster was getting along in years so the farmer decided to get a new rooster for his hens. The old rooster saw the young one strutting around and realised that he was being replaced. He decided to do something about it.

He walked up to the new bird and said, 'So you're the new

stud in town? Well, I'm not ready for the chopping block yet. To prove it, I challenge you to a race around that hen house over there. We'll run around it 10 times and whoever finishes first gets to have all the hens for himself.'

The young rooster was a proud sort, and he thought he was easily a match for the old guy.

'You're on,' he said, 'and since I'm so great, I'll even give you a head start of half a lap. I'll still win easily!'

So the two roosters went over to the henhouse and all the hens gathered to watch.

The race began and the hens started cheering the old rooster on. After the first lap, the old rooster was still in the lead. After the second lap, the old guy's lead had slipped a little, but he was still hanging in there. Unfortunately, the old rooster's lead continued to slip each time around, and by the fifth lap he was just barely in front of the young fella.

By then the farmer had heard the commotion. He thought there was a fox after his chickens so he ran into the house, got his shotgun and ran into the barnyard.

When he got there, he saw the two roosters running around the henhouse, with the old rooster still slightly in the lead.

He immediately took his shotgun, aimed, fired and blew the young rooster away.

As he walked away he said to himself, 'Damn, that's the third gay rooster I've bought this month.'

A police officer came upon a terrible car crash where two people had been killed. As he looked at the wreckage a little monkey came out of the brush and hopped around the crashed car. The officer looked down at the monkey and said, 'I wish you could talk.'

The monkey looked up at the officer and nodded his head.

'You can understand what I'm saying?' asked the officer.

Again, the monkey nodded.

'Well, did you see what happened?'

The monkey nodded. He pretended to have a can in his hand and turned it up to his mouth.

'They were drinking?' asked the officer.

The monkey nodded.

The monkey then pinched his fingers together and held them to his mouth, sucking deeply.

'They were smoking marijuana too?' asked the officer.

The monkey nodded. He made a sexual sign with his fingers.

'So they were playing around as well!?' asked the astounded officer.

Again, the monkey nodded.

'Now wait, you're saying your owners were drinking, smoking and playing around before they wrecked the car?'

The monkey nodded.

'What were you doing during all this?' asked the officer.

The monkey held up his hands on an imaginary steering wheel.

One day an out-of-work mime visits the zoo and attempts to earn some money as a street performer. Unfortunately, as soon as he starts to draw a crowd, a zookeeper grabs him and drags him into his office.

He thinks he is in trouble, but in fact, the zookeeper explains to the mime that the zoo's most popular attraction, a gorilla, has died suddenly and the keeper fears that attendance at the zoo will fall off. He offers the mime a job to dress up as the gorilla and play the role until they can get another one.

The mime accepts and the next morning he puts on a gorilla suit and enters the cage before the crowd arrives.

He discovers that it's a great job. He can sleep all he wants, play and make fun of people, and he draws bigger crowds than he ever did as a mime.

However, eventually the crowds get bored with him and he tires of just swinging around on tyres. He begins to notice that the people are paying more attention to the lion in the cage next to his. Not wanting to lose the attention of his audience, he climbs to the top of his cage, crawls across a partition, and dangles from the top to the lion's cage. Of course, this makes the lion furious, but the crowd loves it.

At the end of the day the zookeeper comes and gives the mime a raise for being such a good attraction. This goes on for some time. The mime keeps taunting the lion, the crowds grow larger, and his salary keeps going up.

Then one terrible day when he is dangling over the furious lion he slips and falls. The mime is terrified. The lion gathers itself and prepares to pounce. The mime is so scared that he begins to run round and round the cage with the lion close behind.

Finally, the mime starts screaming and yelling, 'Help, Help me!', but the lion is quick and pounces. The mime soon finds himself flat on his back looking up at the angry lion and the lion says, 'Shut up you idiot! Do you want to get us both fired?'

DOGS VS CATS

What Is a Dog?

1. Dogs lie around all day, sprawled on the most comfortable piece of furniture.
2. They can hear a package of food opening half a block away, but don't hear you when you're in the same room.
3. They can look dumb and lovable all at the same time.
4. When you want to play, they want to play.
5. When you want to be alone, they want to play.
6. They are great at begging.
7. They do disgusting things with their mouths and then try to give you a kiss.

Conclusion: Dogs are tiny men in little fur coats.

What Is a Cat?
1. Cats do what they want, and they rarely listen to you.
2. They're totally unpredictable and moody.
3. They whine when they are not happy.
4. When you want to play, they want to be alone.
5. When you want to be alone, they want to play.
6. They expect you to cater to their every whim.
7. They drive you nuts and cost an arm and a leg.

Conclusion: Cats are tiny women in little fur coats.

One night a man breaks into a house and is in the middle of stealing the home entertainment centre, when out of nowhere he hears, 'Jesus is watching.'

This totally spooks him so he searches around with his torch. Up in the corner he finds a birdcage with a parrot inside.

Relieved, he says, 'pretty Polly,' to which the parrot replies, 'Jesus is watching.'

The thief asks the bird what his name is and the bird says 'Moses.'

The thief says, 'What a silly name for a bird.'

The bird replies, 'You think that's funny, the Rottweiler's name is Jesus.'

A local business is looking for office help. They put a sign in the window saying: 'Help Wanted. Must be able to type, must be good with a computer and must be bilingual. We are an Equal Opportunity Employer.'

A short time afterwards, a dog trots up to the window, sees the sign and goes inside. He looks at the receptionist and wags his tail, then walks over to the sign, looks at it and whines. Getting the idea, the receptionist gets the office manager. The office manager looks at the dog and is surprised, to say the least.

However, the dog looks determined, so he leads him into the office. Inside, the dog jumps up on the chair and stares at the manager.

The manager says, 'I can't hire you. The sign says you have to be able to type.'

The dog jumps down, goes to the typewriter and types out a perfect letter. He takes out the page and trots over to the manager, gives it to him, then jumps back on the chair.

The manager is stunned, but then tells the dog, 'The sign says you have to be good with a computer.'

The dog jumps down again and goes to the computer. He demonstrates his expertise with various programs, produces a sample spreadsheet and database and presents them to the manager.

By this time the manager is totally dumbfounded! He looks at the dog and says, 'I realise that you are a very intelligent dog and have some interesting abilities. However, I still can't give you the job.'

The dog jumps down and goes to the sign and puts his paw on the part about being an Equal Opportunity Employer.

The manager says, 'Yes, but the sign also says that you have to be bilingual.'

The dog looks him straight in the face and says, 'Meow.'

A man brings a very limp dog into the veterinary clinic. As he lays the dog on the table, the doctor pulls out his stethoscope and places the receptor on the dog's chest.

After a moment or two, the vet shakes his head sadly and says, 'I'm sorry, but your dog has passed away.'

'What?' screams the man. 'How can you tell? You haven't done any testing on him or anything. I want another opinion.'

With that, the vet turns and leaves the room. In a few moments, he returns with a Labrador Retriever. The Retriever goes right to work, checking the poor dead dog out thoroughly with his nose. After a considerable amount of sniffing, the Retriever sadly shakes his head and says, 'Bark'.

The veterinarian then takes the Labrador out and returns in a few moments with a cat, who also carefully sniffs out the poor dog on the table. As had his predecessors, the cat sadly shakes his head and says, 'Meow'.

He then jumps off the table and runs out of the room. The veterinarian hands the man a bill for $600. The dog's owner goes berserk.

'What, $600! Just to tell me my dog is dead? This is outrageous!'

The vet shakes his head sadly and says, 'If you had taken my word for it, the charge would have been $50, but with the lab work and the cat scan . . .'

There are three dogs all in the pound. The first dog turns to the second dog and asks, 'What are you in for?'

The dog replies, 'Well my master said that if I keep chewing up his newspapers he will put me to sleep. I kept chewing them and today I'm getting put to sleep.'

The other dogs start to comfort him. The second dog turns to the third dog and asks him the same question.

The dog replies, 'Well my master said that if I kept drinking out of the toilet I would get put to sleep. And here I am about to get put to sleep.'

The other dogs start to comfort him too. Then the second and third dog turn to the first dog and ask him the same question.

The dog says, 'When my mistress got out of the shower her towel fell off of her, and when she bent over I just couldn't help myself and started to screw her up the arse.'

The dogs say, 'Oh, we understand why you're getting put to sleep.'

The first dog turns around and says, 'I'm not here to get put to sleep, I'm here to get my nails trimmed.'

A duck walks into a convenience store and asks the clerk, 'Do you have any grapes?'

The clerk says no, and the duck leaves. The next day, the duck returns and asks, 'Do you have any grapes?'

The clerk again says no, and the duck leaves. The day after that, the duck walks in the store again and asks, 'Do you have any grapes?'

The clerk screams at the duck, 'You've come in here twice before and asked if we had any grapes. I tell you no every time! I swear if you come back in here again, and ask for grapes, I'll nail your webbed feet to the floor.'

The duck leaves, and returns the next day.

This time he asks, 'Do you have any nails?'

The clerk replies, 'No.'

The duck says, 'Good! Got any grapes?'

A man takes his Rottweiler to the vet and says to him, 'My dog's cross-eyed. Is there anything you can do for it?'

'Well,' says the vet, 'let's have a look at him.'

So he picks the dog up by the ears and has a good look at its eyes.

'I'm going to have to put him down,' says the vet.

'Just because he's cross-eyed?' says the man.

'No, because he's heavy,' says the vet.

A vampire bat comes flapping in from the night, covered in fresh blood, and parks himself on the roof of the cave to get some sleep. Pretty soon all the other bats smell the blood and begin hassling him about where he got it. He tells them to go away and let him get some sleep, but they persist until finally he gives in.

'OK, follow me,' he says.

He flies out of the cave with hundreds of bats behind him. Down through a valley they go, across a river and into a forest full of trees. Finally he slows down and all the other bats excitedly mill around him.

'Now, do you see that tree over there?' he asks.

'Yes, yes, yes!' the bats all scream in a frenzy.

'Good,' says the first bat, 'because I didn't!'

A male whale and a female whale are swimming off the coast of Japan, when they notice a whaling ship. The male whale recognises it as the same ship that had harpooned his father many years earlier.

He says to the female whale, 'Let's both swim under the ship and blow out of our air holes at the same time and it should cause the ship to turn over and sink.'

They try it and sure enough, the ship turns over and quickly sinks.

Soon however, the whales realise that the sailors have jumped overboard and are swimming to the safety of the shore. The male is enraged that they are going to get away and says to the female, 'Let's swim after them and gobble them up before they reach the shore.'

But the female is reluctant to follow him.

'Look,' she says, 'I went along with the blow job, but I absolutely refuse to swallow the seamen.'

Deep within a forest a little turtle begins to climb a tree. After hours of effort he reaches the top, jumps into the air waving his front legs and crashes to the ground. After recovering, he slowly climbs the tree again, jumps, and falls to the ground.

The turtle tries again and again while a couple of birds sitting on a branch watch his sad efforts. Finally, the female bird turns to her mate.

'Dear,' she chirps, 'I think it's time to tell him he's adopted.'

A certain zoo has acquired a female of a very rare species of gorilla. Within a few weeks, the gorilla becomes very difficult to handle. Upon examination, the zoo veterinarian determines the problem. The gorilla is on heat. To make matters worse, there are no male gorillas available. While reflecting on their problem, the zoo administrators notice Paul, an employee responsible for cleaning the animals' cages. Paul, it is rumoured, possesses ample ability to satisfy any female, but he isn't very bright. So, the zoo administrators think they might have a solution. Paul is approached with a proposition. Would he be willing to screw the gorilla for $500? Paul shows some interest, but says he will have to think the matter over carefully. The following day, Paul announces that he will accept their offer, but only on three conditions.

'First,' he says, 'I don't want to kiss her. Secondly, I want nothing to do with any offspring that may result from this union.'

The zoo administration quickly agrees to these conditions, so they ask for his third condition.

'Well,' says Paul, 'you've gotta give me another week to come up with the $500.'

A very lonely woman buys a parrot from a pet store, complete with cage. Before purchasing it she gets a guarantee that the parrot will talk and then she takes the parrot home. In a week and a half she returns to the store very disappointed.

'The parrot doesn't talk.'

'Did you buy a mirror?'

'No.'

'Every parrot needs a mirror.'

So she buys a mirror and installs it in the parrot's cage. Another week and a half goes by and she returns.

'The parrot still doesn't talk.'

'Did you buy a ladder?'

'No.'

'Every parrot needs a ladder.'

So she buys a ladder and installs it in the cage. Another week and a half pass and she returns.

'The parrot still doesn't talk.'

'Did you buy a swing?'

'No.'

'Every parrot needs a swing.'

So she buys a swing and installs it in the cage. A week and a half later she returns. She is furious.

The store owner asks, 'Did the parrot talk?'

'No. He died.'

'Oh, that's terrible. Did he say anything before he died?'

'Yes.'

'What?'

'He gasped "Don't they have any food down at that store?"'

BLONDES

Why pick on blondes? Because it's fun, that's why!

A bartender is sitting behind the bar on a typical day when the door bursts open and in come four exuberant blondes. They come up to the bar, order five bottles of champagne and ten glasses, take their order and sit down at a large table.

The corks are popped, the glasses are filled and they begin toasting and chanting, 'Fifty-one days, fifty-one days, fifty-one days!'

Soon, three more blondes arrive, take up their drinks and the chanting grows.

'Fifty-one days, fifty-one days, fifty-one days!'

Two more blondes show up and soon their voices are joined in raising the roof.

'Fifty-one days, fifty-one days, fifty-one days!'

Finally, the tenth blonde comes in with a picture under her arm. She walks over to the table, sets the picture in the middle and the table erupts.

Up jump the others, they begin dancing around the table, exchanging high-fives, all the while chanting, 'Fifty-one days, fifty-one days, fifty-one days!'

The bartender can't contain his curiosity any longer, so he walks over to the table. There in the centre is a beautifully framed child's puzzle of the Cookie Monster.

When the frenzy dies down a little bit, the bartender asks one of the blondes, 'What's all the chanting and celebration about?'

The blonde who brought in the picture pipes up, 'Everyone thinks that blondes are dumb and they make fun of us, so, we decided to set the record straight. Ten of us got together, bought that puzzle and put it together. The side of the box said "two to four years", but we put it together in fifty-one days!'

A ventriloquist is touring the clubs and stops to entertain at a bar in a small town. He's going through his usual run of silly blonde jokes when a big blonde woman in the fourth row stands on her chair and says, 'OK jerk, I've heard just about enough of your denigrating blonde jokes. What makes you think you can stereotype women that way? What do a person's physical attributes have to do with their worth as a human being? It's guys like you who keep women like me from being respected at work and in my community, from reaching my full potential as a person, because you and your kind continue to perpetuate discrimination against not only blondes but women at large, all in the name of humour.'

Flustered, the ventriloquist begins to apologise, when the blonde pipes up, 'You stay out of this mister, I'm talking to that little bastard on your knee!'

A blonde decides one day that she is sick and tired of all these blonde jokes and how all blondes are perceived as stupid, so she decides to show her husband that blondes really are smart. While her husband is off at work, she decides that she is going to paint a couple of rooms in the house. The next day, straight after her husband leaves for work, she gets down to the task at hand. Her husband arrives home at 5.30 p.m. and smells the distinctive smell of paint. He walks into the living room and finds his wife lying on the floor in a pool of sweat. He notices that she is wearing a ski jacket and a fur coat at the same time.

'Honey, are you OK?' he asks her.

'Yes,' she replies.

'Then what are you doing?' he asks.

'I wanted to prove to you that not all blonde women are dumb and I wanted to do it by painting the house,' she replies.

'Then why are you wearing a ski jacket over a fur coat?' he asks.

'Well,' she replies, 'I was reading the directions on the paint can and it says: "For best results, put on two coats".'

A business man gets on an elevator. When he enters, there's a blonde already inside and she greets him by saying, 'T-G-I-F.'

He smiles at her and replies, 'S-H-I-T.'

She looks at him, puzzled, and again says, 'T-G-I-F.'

He acknowledges her remark again by answering, 'S-H-I-T.'

The blonde is trying to be friendly, so she smiles her biggest smile and says as sweetly as possible, 'T-G-I-F.'

The man smiles back to her and once again replies with a quizzical expression, 'S-H-I-T.'

The blonde finally decides to explain things, and this time she says, 'T-G-I-F, Thank Goodness It's Friday, get it?'

The man answers, 'Sorry, Honey, it's Thursday.'

A blonde is overweight, so her doctor puts her on a diet. 'I want you to eat regularly for two days, then skip a day, and repeat this procedure for two weeks. The next time I see you, you'll have lost at least two kilos.'

When the blonde returns, she's lost nearly eight kilos.

'Why, that's amazing!' the doctor says. 'Did you follow my instructions?'

The blonde nods. 'I'll tell you, though, I thought I was going to drop dead that third day.'

'From hunger, you mean?' asks the doctor.

'No, from all that skipping.'

A highway patrolman pulls alongside a speeding car on the freeway. Glancing at the car, he is astounded to see that the blonde behind the wheel is knitting! Realising that she was oblivious to his flashing lights and siren, the cop cranks down his window, turns on his bullhorn and yells, 'Pull over!'

'No,' the blonde yells back. 'It's a scarf.'

A blonde is playing *Trivial Pursuit* one night. It's her turn. She rolls the dice and she lands on 'Science and Nature'. Her question is: 'If you are in a vacuum and someone calls your name, can you hear it?'

She thinks for a while and then asks, 'Is it on or off?'

A blonde arrives for her university final examination, which consists of questions requiring yes or no answers. She takes her seat in the examination hall and stares hopelessly at the exam paper for five minutes. Then in a fit of inspiration, she takes her purse out, removes a coin and starts tossing the coin and marking the answer sheet 'yes' for heads and 'no' for tails. Within half an hour she is finished, while the rest of the class is still writing madly. During the last few minutes, she is seen desperately throwing the coin, muttering and sweating. The moderator, alarmed, approaches her and asks what is going on.

'I finished the exam in half an hour,' she tells him, 'but I'm rechecking my answers.'

What do a blonde and a turtle have in common? Once they're on their back, they're screwed.

What's the mating call of a blonde? 'I'm sooooo drunk!'

What do a bleach blonde and an aeroplane have in common? They both have black boxes.

A university lecturer in an anatomy class asks his students to sketch a naked man. As the lecturer walks around the class checking the sketches he notices that a sexy, young, blonde student has sketched the man with an erect penis.

The lecturer comments, 'Oh, no, I wanted it the other way.'

She replies, 'What other way?'

What do you do if a blonde throws a pin at you? Run, she's got a grenade in her mouth!

Three seventeen-year-old girls – a blonde, a brunette and a redhead – are drinking in a bar. Suddenly, a cop walks in and the three run outside. He notices and follows them into an alley where there are three garbage bags but no sign of the girls. The police officer walks over to the first garbage bag and gives it a small kick.

The brunette, hiding inside, says, 'Meow.'

The officer says, 'Oh it's just a bunch of cats.'

He then kicks the next bag where the redhead is hiding.

She says, 'Woof, woof.'

The officer says, 'It's only a bunch of dogs.'

Finally, he kicks the last bag where the blonde is hiding.

She says, 'Potatoes, potatoes.'

What did the dumb blonde say when she found out she was pregnant?

'Gee, I hope it's mine.'

A blonde is driving down an old country road when she spots another blonde in a wheat field rowing a boat. She pulls over to the side of the road and stops the car. Staring in disbelief she stands at the side of the road to watch the woman for a while.

When she can't stand it any more she calls out to the blonde in the field, 'Why are you rowing a boat in the middle of the field?'

The blonde in the field stops rowing and responds, 'Because it's an ocean of wheat.'

The blonde standing on the side of the road is furious.

She yells at the blonde in the field, 'It's blondes like you that give the rest of us a bad name.'

The blonde in the field just shrugs her shoulders and begins rowing again.

The blonde on the side of the road is beside herself and shakes her fist at the blonde in the field, then yells, 'If I could swim I would come out there and kick your arse.'

A blonde, a redhead and a brunette are competing in the English Channel Breast Stroke Competition. The redhead wins and the brunette comes second. However, there is no sign of the final contestant. Hours and hours go by, causing grave concern and worry. Just as everyone is losing hope, the blonde finally arrives. The crowd is extremely happy and relieved to see her. They embrace the young woman as she comes ashore.

After all of the excitement dies down, the blonde leans over to the judge and whispers, 'I hate to be a bad loser, but I think those other girls used their arms.'

Two tourists are driving through Louisiana. As they approach Natchitoches, they start arguing about the pronunciation of the town. They argue back and forth until they stop for lunch.

As they stand at the counter, one tourist asks the blonde employee, 'Before we order, could you please settle an argument for us? Would you pronounce the name of this place . . . very slowly?'

The blonde girl leans over the counter and says, 'Burrrrrrrr, gerrrrrrr, Kiiiiing.'

A blonde gets a dent in her car and takes it to the repair shop. The panel-beater, noticing that the woman is blonde, decides to have a wee bit of fun. So he tells her all she has to do is take her car home and blow in the exhaust pipe until the dent pops itself out.

So the blonde goes home and gives it a try. After fifteen minutes of this the blonde's friend, who is also blonde, comes over and asks what she is doing.

'I'm trying to pop out this dent, but it's not really working.'

'Duh. You have to roll up the windows first!'

A blonde has a sharp pain in her side. The doctor examines her and says, 'You have acute appendicitis.'

The blonde yells at the doctor, 'I came here to get medical help, not a stupid compliment!'

A blonde goes for a job interview in an office. The interviewer starts with the basics.

'So, Miss, can you tell us your age, please?'

The blonde counts carefully on her fingers for half a minute before replying, 'Ehhhh . . . twenty-two!'

The interviewer tries another straightforward one to break the ice.

'And can you tell us your height, please?'

The young woman stands up and produces a measuring tape from her handbag. She then traps one end under her foot and extends the tape to the top of her head.

She checks the measurement and announces 'Five foot two!'

This isn't looking good so the interviewer goes for the real basics; something the interviewee won't have to count, measure, or lookup.

'Just to confirm for our records, your name please?'

The blonde bobs her head from side to side for about ten

seconds, mouthing something silently to herself, before replying, 'Mandy!'

The interviewer is completely baffled at this stage, so he asks, 'What in the world were you doing when I asked you your name?'

'Ohhhh, that!' replies the blonde. 'I was just running through that song, "Happy birthday to you, happy birthday to you, happy birthday dear . . ."'

A blonde sits down in a bar next to a redhead. Both of them are having a good time when the news comes on the TV.

The woman reporter shouts out, 'This just in! A man is at the edge of a cliff attempting to jump.'

The redhead leans over to the blonde and whispers, 'I bet you $50 that the man's gonna jump.'

The blonde responds, 'You're on.'

So, both of the women stare at the news waiting to find out what happens next. Finally, the man jumps. The blonde turns to the redhead and hands her the $50.

The redhead, feeling guilty, says, 'I can't take that money. I saw the news earlier this morning. I knew he was going to jump off the cliff.'

The blonde says, 'Well, I saw it too. But I never would have thought that he'd do it again.'

What do you call a couple of blondes in the front seat of a car?
Air bags.

Did you hear about the blonde who bought a pair of water-skis?
She's still looking for a lake with a slope.

What's the difference between a blonde guy and a blonde girl?
The blonde girl's sperm count is higher.

How do blondes' brain cells die?
Alone.

A blonde is visiting interstate for the first time. She wants to
see the art gallery but doesn't know how to get there.
Fortunately, a police officer walks past.

'Excuse me, officer,' asks the blonde. 'How do I get to the art
gallery?'

The officer replies, 'Wait at this bus stop for the No. 54 bus.
It'll take you straight there.'

She thanks the officer and he walks off. Three hours later the
police officer returns to the same area and, sure enough, the
blonde is still waiting at the same bus stop.

The officer says, 'Excuse me, but to get to the art gallery, I said
to wait here for the No. 54 bus and that was three hours ago!
Why are you still waiting?'

The blonde replies, 'Don't worry, officer, it won't be long
now. The forty-fifth bus just went by!'

What do blondes and cow pies have in common?
The older they get, the easier they are to pick up.

SHE WAS SO BLONDE . . .

. . . she asked for a price check at the $2 Shop.

. . . when she saw a sign that said Under 17 Not Admitted, she
went home and got sixteen friends.

. . . when she heard that 90% of all crimes occur around the
home, she moved.

A blonde walks into a pharmacy and asks the pharmacist for a
bottom deodorant.

'Sorry, we don't sell bottom deodorant,' the pharmacist replies, struggling to keep from laughing.

'But I always buy it here,' the blonde says. 'I bought one last month.'

Thinking quickly, the pharmacist suggests, 'I don't know what you bought before, maybe you can bring in the empty container next time.'

'Sure,' the blonde replies. 'I'll bring it with me tomorrow.'

The next day, the blonde walks into the shop again and hands the pharmacist an almost-empty deodorant stick.

'This is just a normal deodorant,' the pharmacist tells her. 'You use it under your arms.'

'No, it is not,' the blonde answers. 'It says so here – "To apply, push up bottom".'

A blonde received a certificate for helicopter flying lessons for her birthday. One day she was bored and decided to give it a try.

When she arrived at the helipad, the instructor said, 'Well, there's only one helicopter here, and it only has one seat. If I show you how to do it, do you mind going up solo?'

'No problem, I can handle it,' replied the blonde.

He showed her the inner workings of the helicopter and sent her on her way, only asking that she radio in every 400ft, just to make sure everything was going smoothly.

At 400ft, she radioed in saying 'Wow! This is so much fun!'

At 800 ft she radioed in again saying, 'This is pretty easy, I could do this all day!'

The instructor waited and waited for her to radio in at 1200 ft, but he didn't hear from the blonde. Soon he heard a crash in the field next to the station. He ran out to find that the blonde crashed! Luckily she survived.

'What happened?' he exclaimed.

'Well, I was doing fine, but, I started to get cold, so I just turned off the big fan.'

Q: Why do blondes take the pill?
A: So they know which day of the week it is.

TOP 10 BLONDE INVENTIONS

1. Waterproof towel.
2. Solar-powered torch.
3. Submarine screen door.
4. A book on how to read.
5. Inflatable dart board.
6. Dictionary index.
7. Ejector seat in a helicopter.
8. Powdered water.
9. Pedal-powered wheel chair.
10. Waterproof tea bags.

Q: How can you tell if a blonde has been using the computer?
A: The joystick is wet.

Q: What is the quickest way to get into a blonde's pants?
A: Pick them up off the floor.

Q: Why don't blondes play Frisbee?
A: It hurts their teeth.

A blonde walks into an electronics store and says, 'I'd like to buy that television please.'

The salesperson replies, 'I'm sorry. We don't sell to blondes here.'

The blonde goes home and dyes her hair brown. She returns to the store a few days later and again asks to buy the TV.

'I told you, we don't sell to blondes. Please go home!' the salesperson tells her.

The blonde goes home, shaves her head and puts on a baseball cap. She waits a few days once again goes to the shop to buy the television.

'We just don't sell to blondes here. It's store policy. Please, give up. Go home!' the salesperson exclaims.

'Look I dyed my hair, and you still knew I was blonde. I shaved my head and wore a hat, but you still knew I was blonde! How do you do it?' she asks exasperated.

The salesperson points to the item she wants to buy. 'Well, first of all, that's a microwave.'

Three blondes are attempting to change a light bulb. Finally, one of them decides to call 000.

'Help!' she says. 'We need help. We are three blondes changing a light bulb.'

'Hm!' replies the operator. 'You put in a fresh bulb?'

'Yes.'

'The power in the house is on?'

'Of course.'

'And the switch is on?'

'Yes, yes.'

'And the bulb still won't light up?'

'No, it's working fine.'

'Then what's the problem?' asks the operator.

'We got dizzy spinning the ladder around and we all fell and hurt ourselves.'

Q: What's the difference between a blonde and a 747?
A: Not everyone has been in a 747.

A cop was driving down a country road when he saw a car in a ditch. He pulled over to see if anyone was in the car.

A blonde popped her head out the window and said, 'Oh officer, thank god. I was in an accident!'

ULTIMATE ADULT ONLY JOKE BOOK

'Well I can see that! Are you OK?' replied the officer.

The blonde nodded.

'What happened?'

'It was so strange. I was driving down the road and from nowhere a tree jumped in front of me, so I swerved to the other side and there was another tree, so I swerved again, but another one was there, so one last time I swerved to the other side but the damn tree got me and sent me into this ditch!'

The officer started laughing hard.

'What's so funny?' the blonde asked.

'Miss, there are no trees on this road for miles. That was your car air freshener swinging back and forth!'

A blonde with two very red ears went to see her doctor. The doctor asked her what had happened.

'I was ironing a shirt and the phone rang,' she said. 'But instead of picking up the phone, I accidentally picked up the iron and stuck it to my ear.'

'Jeezus!' the doctor exclaimed in disbelief. 'So, what happened to your other ear?'

'My friend rang back.'

A young blonde was on holiday in north Queensland. She was desperate for a pair of genuine crocodile shoes but was reluctant to pay the high prices the local vendors were asking.

After becoming very frustrated with the 'no haggle' attitude of one of the shopkeepers, the blonde shouted, 'Maybe I'll just go out and catch my own crocodile so I can get a pair of shoes at a reasonable price!'

'By all means, be my guest. Maybe you'll be lucky and catch yourself a big one!' said the shopkeeper.

Determined, the blonde turned and headed for the mangroves, set on catching herself a crocodile.

Later in the day, the shopkeeper was driving home, when he spotted the young woman standing waist deep in the water, shotgun in hand. Just then, he saw a huge 4m croc swimming quickly toward her.

She took aim, killed the creature, and with a great deal of effort hauled it on to the bank. Lying nearby were several more of the dead creatures. The shopkeeper watched in amazement as the blonde flipped the crocodile on its back.

'Damn it, this one isn't wearing any shoes either!' she shouted in frustration.

Q: How can you tell if a blonde is having a bad day?
A: Her tampon is behind her ear and she can't find her pen!

Eleven people were clinging precariously to a wildly swinging rope suspended from a crumbling outcrop on Mount Everest. Ten were blonde, one was brunette.

For the group to survive one of them would have to sacrifice their life and let go of the rope. If that didn't happen the rope would break and everyone would perish.

For an agonising few moments no one volunteered. Finally the brunette gave a truly touching speech saying she would sacrifice herself to save the lives of the others.

And all the blondes applauded.

A blonde arrived for her first golf lesson and the pro asked her to take a swing at a ball to see how well she'd do.

The blonde did so and completely stuffed the shot.

The pro said, 'Your swing is good but you're gripping the club too hard. Grip the club gently as you would your husband's penis.'

The blonde took another shot and nailed the ball 350 metres straight down the fairway.

The pro said, 'That was excellent!! Let's try it again, only this time take the club out of your mouth.'

Three girls are walking in a magical forest. Suddenly, a witch comes out of the woods.

'Each of you has to say one good thing about herself,' says the witch. 'If you lie, I will make you disappear!'

The first girl, a brunette, says, 'I think I am a very kind and thoughtful person'.

'Poof!' and she disappears.

The second girl, a redhead, says, 'I think I am very sexy'.

'Poof!' she also disappears.

The third girl, a blonde, says, 'Well, I think –'

'Poof!' and she is gone.

A blonde goes into a drug store to buy some condoms because her friend told her that she should learn about safe sex. She walks up to the pharmacist and asks: 'How much for a box of rubbers?'

'They're $6 for a box of three,' he replies. 'Plus 60c for the tax.'

'Oh,' replies the blonde, 'I always wondered how they kept them on.'

It was a really hot day and a blonde decided she would buy a drink. She went to a vending machine and when she put her money in, a can of drink came out. So she kept putting money in.

She was there for so long that a line formed behind her. Finally, a guy in line said, 'Will you hurry up? We're all hot and thirsty!'

'No way,' replied the blonde. 'I'm still winning!'

While out one morning in the park, a jogger found a brand new tennis ball, and, seeing no-one around that it might belong to, he slipped it into the pocket of his shorts.

Later, on his way home, he stopped at the pedestrian

crossing, waiting for the lights to change. A blonde girl standing next to him eyed the large bulge in his shorts.

'What's that?' she asked, her eyes gleaming with lust.

'Tennis ball,' came the breathless reply.

'Oh,' said the blonde girl sympathetically, 'that must be painful. I had tennis elbow once.'

Three women are about to be executed – a redhead, a brunette, and a blonde. The guard brings the redhead forward and the executioner asks if she has any last requests. She says no, and the executioner shouts, 'Ready! Aim –'

Suddenly the redhead yells, 'Earthquake!'

Everyone is startled and they all throw themselves on the ground for safety. When they look up the redhead has escaped.

The guard brings the brunette forward and the executioner asks if she has any last requests. She says no, and the executioner shouts, 'Ready! Aim –'

Suddenly the brunette yells, 'Tornado!'

Again, everyone is startled and dives for cover. When they look up, the brunette has escaped.

By now the blonde has it all worked out. The guard brings her forward and the executioner asks if she has any last requests. She says no, and the executioner shouts, 'Ready! Aim –'

And the blonde yells, 'Fire!'

A blonde had two horses. She couldn't tell her two horses apart so she decided to ask her neighbour for some advice.

'Maybe you should nick the ears of one horse,' said her neighbour, 'and then you could tell them apart.'

So the blonde went home and did that. The next day the blonde went to check up on her horses. However she still could not tell them apart, because the other horse also had a nicked ear. She went back over to her neighbour's.

'My other horse has a nicked ear, too.' she said, 'Do you have any other ideas as to how to tell them apart? They are both girls.'

'Hmmmm.' said her neighbour, 'cut one's tail shorter than the other.'

So the blonde went home and did that. The next day, though, when she looked at them, both horses had the same length of tail.

As a last resort the neighbour suggested that she should consider measuring the horses. Maybe one stood taller than the other one.

The blonde did this and excitedly rushed home and phoned her neighbour. 'You were right!' she said. 'The black horse is bigger than the white one!'

Derek drove his brand new Mercedes to his favourite bar, and put it in the car park at the back. He went inside, where the bar was being looked after by Beverley, the regular waitress.

Beverley was a pretty blonde, and as Derek walked into the bar, she greeted him happily. He bought a drink, and went and sat at a table.

A few minutes later, Beverley ran up to him yelling, 'Derek! Derek! I was putting the rubbish out the back and I just saw someone driving off with your new Mercedes!'

'Dear God! Did you try to stop him?'

'No,' she said, 'I did better than that! I got the licence plate number!'

A young blonde woman is distraught because she fears her husband is having an affair, so she goes to a gun shop and buys a handgun. The next day she comes home to find her husband in bed with a beautiful redhead.

She grabs the gun and holds it to her own head. The husband

jumps out of bed, begging and pleading with her not to shoot herself.

Hysterically the blonde responds to the husband, 'Shut up. You're next!'

On a plane bound for New York, the flight attendant approached a blonde sitting in the first-class section and requested that she move to economy since she did not have a first-class ticket.

The blonde replied, 'I'm blonde, I'm beautiful, I'm going to New York and I'm not moving.'

Not wanting to argue with a customer, the flight attendant asked the co-pilot to speak with her. He went to talk with the woman, asking her to please move out of the first-class section.

Again, the blonde replied, 'I'm blonde, I'm beautiful, I'm going to New York and I'm not moving.'

The co-pilot returned to the cockpit and asked the captain what to do. The captain said, 'I'm married to a blonde. I know how to handle this.'

He went to the first-class section and whispered in the blonde's ear. She immediately jumped up and ran to the economy section mumbling, 'Why didn't anyone just say so?'

Surprised, the flight attendant and the co-pilot asked what he said to her that finally convinced her to move from her seat.

He said, 'I told her the first-class section wasn't going to New York.'

Then there was the blonde working at reception. A fellow worker came up and said, 'Would you like to buy a raffle ticket? Janice in production died suddenly last week. It's for her husband and four children.'

'No thanks,' said the blonde. 'I've already got a husband and two kids of my own.'

BATTLE OF THE SEXES

As someone much wiser than me once said, 'Men are from Earth. Women are from Earth. Deal with it.'

When a woman says, 'C'mon, This place is a mess! You and I need to clean. Your pants are on the floor and you'll have no clothes if we don't do laundry now!'

A man hears, 'C'mon . . . blah, blah, blah . . . You and I . . . blah, blah, blah, blah, blah . . . on the floor . . . blah, blah, blah . . . no clothes . . . blah, blah, blah, blah . . . now!'

HOW TO SATISFY A WOMAN EVERY TIME

Caress, praise, pamper, relish, savour, massage, make plans, fix, empathise, serenade, compliment, support, feed, tantalise, bathe, humour, placate, stimulate, stroke, console, purr, hug, coddle, excite, pacify, protect, phone, correspond, anticipate, nuzzle, smooch, toast, minister to, forgive, sacrifice for, ply, accessorise, leave, return, beseech, sublimate, entertain, charm, lug, drag, crawl, treat equally, spackle, oblige, fascinate, attend, implore, bawl, shower, shave, trust, grovel, ignore, defend, coax, clothe, brag about, acquiesce, fuse, fizz, rationalise, detoxify, sanctify, help, acknowledge, polish, upgrade, spoil, embrace, accept, butter-up, hear, understand, jitterbug, locomote, beg, plead, borrow, steal, climb, swim, nurse, resuscitate, repair, patch, super-glue, respect, entertain, calm, allay, kill for, die for, dream of, promise, deliver, tease, flirt, commit, enlist, pine, cajole, murmur, snuggle, snoozle, snurfle, elevate, enervate, alleviate, spot-weld, serve, rub, rib, salve, bite, taste, nibble, gratify, take her places, scuttle like a crab on the ocean floor of her existence, diddle, doodle, hokey-pokey, hanky-panky, crystal blue persuade, flip, flop, fly, don't care if I die, swing, slip, slide, slather, mollycoddle, squeeze, moisturise, humidify, lather, tingle, slam-dunk, keep on rockin' in the free world, wet, slicken, undulate, gelatinise, brush, tingle, dribble, drip, dry, knead, fluff, fold, ingratiate, indulge, wow, dazzle, amaze, flabbergast, enchant, idolise and worship, and then go back, Jack, and do it again.

HOW TO SATISFY A MAN EVERY TIME

Show up naked . . . with beer.

Why do men become smarter during sex?
Because they are plugged into a genius.

Why don't women blink during foreplay?
They don't have time.

Why does it take one million sperm to fertilise one egg?
They won't stop for directions.

Why did God put men on earth?
Because a vibrator can't mow the lawn.

What do electric trains and breasts have in common?
They're intended for children, but it's the men who usually end up playing with them.

Why were men given larger brains than dogs?
So they won't hump women's legs at cocktail parties.

Why is a man's pee yellow and his sperm white?
So he can tell if he is coming or going.

How are men like parking spots?
The good ones are always taken and the only ones left are disabled.

THE BENEFITS OF BEING A WOMAN

• Our boyfriends' clothes make us look elfin and gorgeous. Guys look like complete idiots in ours.

• We can be groupies. Male groupies are stalkers.

• We can cry and get off speeding fines.

• Men die earlier, so we get to cash in on the life insurance.

• We don't look like a frog in a blender when dancing.

• Free drinks, free dinners.

• We can hug our friends without wondering if they're gay.

• We can hug our friends without wondering if *we're* gay.

• It's possible to live our whole lives without ever taking a group shower.

• We don't have to fart to amuse ourselves.

- If we forget to shave, no-one has to know.

- We can congratulate our team-mate without ever touching her bum.

- If we have a zit, we know how to conceal it.

- We don't have to reach down every so often to make sure our privates are still there.

- If we're dumb, some people will find it cute.

- We don't have to memorise *Caddyshack* or *Fletch* to fit in.

- If we marry someone twenty years younger, we're aware that we look like an idiot.

- We know that there are times when chocolate really can solve all your problems.

- We can fully assess a person just by looking at their shoes.

MEN ARE LIKE . . .

. . . bananas – they older they get, the less firm they are.

. . . bank accounts – without a lot of money, they don't generate much interest.

. . . bike helmets – handy in an emergency, but otherwise they just look silly.

. . . blenders – you need one, but you're not quite sure why.

. . . coolers – load them with beer and you can take them anywhere.

. . . copiers – you need them for reproduction, but that's about it.

. . . chocolate bars – sweet, smooth and they usually head right for your hips.

. . . lava lamps – fun to look at, but not all that bright.

. . . plungers – they spend most of their lives in a hardware store or the bathroom.

A man is talking to God and asks, 'God, why did you make women so beautiful?'

'So that you would find them attractive,' God replies.

Then the man asks, 'But why did you have to make them so dumb?'

'So that they would find you attractive!'

A passenger plane runs into a terrible storm. The plane gets pounded by rain, hail, wind, and lightening. The passengers are screaming. They are sure the plane is going to crash and they are all going to die.

At the height of the storm, a young woman jumps up and exclaims, 'I can't take this anymore! I can't just sit here and die like an animal, strapped into a chair. If I am going to die, let me die feeling like a woman. Is there anyone here man enough to make me feel like a woman?'

She sees a raised hand in the back and a muscular man starts to walk up to her seat. As he approaches her, he takes off his shirt. She can see the man's muscles even in the poor lighting of the plane.

He stands in front of her, shirt in hand and says to her, 'I can make you feel like a woman before you die. Are you interested?'

She nods her head yes.

The man hands her his shirt and says, 'Here. Iron this.'

How many men does it take to open a beer?
None. It should be opened by the time she brings it.

Why do women have smaller feet then men?
So they can stand closer to the kitchen sink.

How do you fix a woman's watch?
You don't. There's a clock on the oven.

Why do men pass more gas than women do?
Because women don't shut up long enough to build up pressure.

What do you call a woman with two brain cells?
Pregnant.

A woman walks into a supermarket and loads up her trolley with the following items:
- 1 bar of soap
- 1 toothbrush
- 1 tube of toothpaste
- 1 loaf of bread
- 1 pint of milk
- 1 single serving of cereal
- 1 single-serve frozen dinner
- 1 can of Soup For One
- 1 can of light beer

The guy at the check-out looks at her and says, 'Single, are you?'

The woman smiles sweetly and replies, 'How did you guess?'

'Because you're ugly.'

Three guys are having a relaxing day fishing. Out of the blue, they catch a mermaid who begs to be set free, in return for granting each of them a wish.

One of the guys just doesn't believe it, and says, 'OK, if you can really grant wishes, then double my IQ.'

The mermaid says, 'Done!'

Suddenly, the guy starts reciting Shakespeare flawlessly and analysing it with extreme insight.

The second guy is so amazed he says to the mermaid, 'Triple my IQ.'

The mermaid says, 'Done!'

The guy starts to spout out all the mathematical solutions to problems that have been stumping scientists and mathematicians for years.

The last guy is so enthralled with the changes in his friends that he says to the mermaid, 'Quintuple my IQ.'

The mermaid looks at him and says, 'You know, I normally don't try to change people's minds when they make a wish, but I really wish you'd reconsider.'

The guy says, 'Nope, I want you to increase my IQ times five, and if you don't do it, I won't set you free.'

'Please,' says the mermaid, 'You don't know what you're asking. It'll change your entire view on the universe, won't you ask for something else? A million dollars, anything?'

But no matter what the mermaid says, the guy insists on having his IQ increased by five times its usual power.

So the mermaid sighs and says, 'Done.'

And he becomes a woman.

A woman and a man are involved in a car accident; it's a bad one. Both of their cars are totally demolished but amazingly neither of them is hurt.

After they crawl out of their cars, the woman says, 'Wow, just look at our cars! There's nothing left, but fortunately we are unhurt. This must be a sign from God that we should meet and be friends and live together in peace for the rest of our days.'

The man replies, 'I agree with you completely. This must be a sign from God!'

The woman continues, 'And look at this, here's another miracle. My car is completely demolished but this bottle of wine didn't break. Surely God wants us to drink this wine and celebrate our good fortune.'

Then she hands the bottle to the man. The man nods his head in agreement, opens it, drinks half the bottle, and extends it back to the woman. Politely, the woman refuses to accept the bottle.

The man asks, 'Aren't you having any?'

The woman replies, 'No. I think I'll just wait for the police . . .'

THE FIVE SECRETS TO A GREAT RELATIONSHIP (FEMALE VERSION)

1. It is important to find a man who works around the house, occasionally cooks and cleans and who has a job.
2. It is important to find a man who makes you laugh.
3. It is important to find a man who is dependable, respectful and doesn't lie.
4. It is important to find a man who's good in bed and who loves to have sex with you.
5. It is important that these four men never meet.

If you love something, set it free. If it comes back, it was, and always will be yours. If it never returns, it was never yours to begin with.

If it just sits in your house, messes up your stuff, eats your food, uses your phone, takes your money, and never behaves as if you actually set it free in the first place, you either married it or gave birth to it.

PICK-UP LINES & THEIR COMEBACKS

Man: Haven't we met before?
Woman: Perhaps. I'm the receptionist at the VD Clinic.

Man: Is that seat empty?
Woman: Yes, and this one will be too if you sit down.

Nan: Your place or mine?
Woman: Both. You go to yours and I'll go to mine.

Man: So what do you do for a living?
Woman: I'm a female impersonator.

Man: Hey, baby, what's your sign?
Woman: Do not enter.

Man: How do you like your eggs in the morning?
Woman: Unfertilised.

Nan: Hey, come on, we're both here at this bar for the
              same reason.
Woman: Yeah. Let's pick up some chicks.

Man: I would go to the end of the world for you.
Woman: Yes, but would you stay there?

Mrs Brown, who was a little on the chubby side, was at her weight-watchers meeting.

'My husband insists I come to these meetings because he would rather screw a woman with a trim figure,' she lamented to the woman next to her.

'Well,' the woman replied, 'what's wrong with that?'

'He likes to do it while I'm at these damn meetings.'

HE SAYS; SHE SAYS

He says: I don't know why you wear a bra; you've got nothing to put in it.
She says: You wear briefs, don't you?

He says: Do you love me just because my father left me a fortune?
She says: Not at all honey, I would love you no matter who left you the money.

He says: This coffee isn't fit for a pig!
She says: No problem, I'll get you some that is.

She says: What do you mean by coming home half drunk?
He says: It's not my fault. I ran out of money.

He says: Since I first laid eyes on you, I've wanted to make love to you in the worst way.
She says: Well, you succeeded.

He says: Why do you women always try to impress us with your looks, not with your brains?
She says: Because there is a bigger chance that a man is a moron than he is blind.

He says: What have you been doing with all the grocery money I gave you?
She says: Turn sideways and look in the mirror.

He says: Let's go out and have some fun tonight.
She says: OK, but if you get home before I do, leave the hall light on.

And God created Woman, and gave her three breasts. God spoke, saying to her, 'I have created thee as I see fit. Is there anything about thee that thou would prefer differently?'

And Woman spoke, saying, 'Lord, I am not made to birth whole litters. I need but two breasts.'

'Thou speakest wisely, as I have created thee with wisdom.'

There was a crack of lightning and a lingering odour of ozone, and it was done, and God stood holding the surplus breast in his hands.

'What are you going to do with that useless boob?' Woman asked.

And so it was, God created Man.

PICK-UP LINES NEVER TO REPEAT

- The word of the day is 'legs'. Let's go back to my place and spread the word.
- That outfit would look great in a crumpled heap on my bedroom floor tomorrow morning.
- I like every bone in your body, especially mine.
- How about you sit on my lap and we'll see what pops up?
- Is that a mirror in your pants, because I can see myself in them?
- I want to kiss you passionately on the lips, and then move up to your belly-button.
- Baby, I'd run a mile for your vertical smile.
- I've got the F, the C and the K. All I need is U.
- Hey baby, can I tickle your belly-button from the inside?
- So do ya wanna see something really swell?
- I may not be Fred Flintstone, but I sure can make your bed rock.
- You have nice legs. What time do they open?
- Hey that dress looks nice. Can I talk you out of it?

Q: How can you tell when a man is well hung?
A: When you can just barely slip your finger in between his neck and the noose.

Q: How do men exercise on the beach?
A: By sucking in their stomachs every time they see a bikini.

Q: How do you get a man to stop biting his nails?
A: Make him wear shoes.

Q: How do you keep your husband from reading your email?
A: Rename the mail folder 'Instruction Manuals.'

Q: What do most men consider a gourmet restaurant?
A: Any place without a drive-thru window.

Q: What do you call the useless piece of skin on the end of a man's penis?
A: His body.

Q: What makes a man think about a candlelight dinner?
A: A power failure.

Q: What should you give a man who has everything?
A: A woman to show him how to work it.

Q: What do men and mascara have in common?
A: They both run at the first sign of emotion.

Q: What do you instantly know about a well-dressed man?
A: His wife is good at picking out clothes.

Q: What's a man's definition of a romantic evening?
A: Sex.

Q: What's a man's idea of honestly in a relationship?
A: Telling you his real name.

Q: Why can't men get mad cow disease?
A: Because they're all pigs.

Q: Why do men name their penises?
A: Because they don't like the idea of having a stranger make 90% of their decisions.

Q: Why do men whistle when they're sitting on the toilet?
A: Because it helps them remember which end they need to wipe.

Q: What do you call a woman who knows where her husband is every night?
A: A widow.

Q: When do you care for a man's company?
A: When he owns it.

A couple is in bed sleeping when there's a rat-a-tat-tat on the door. The husband rolls over and looks at the clock, it's 3.30am.

'I'm not getting out of bed at this time,' he thinks, and rolls over.

There's a louder knock. So he drags himself out of bed, goes downstairs, opens the door, and a man is standing on the doorstep. It doesn't take the homeowner long to realise the man is drunk.

'Hi there,' slurs the stranger, 'Can you give me a push?'

'No, get lost. It's 3.30am and I was in bed.'

The man slams the door and goes back up to bed.

He tells his wife what happened and she says, 'That wasn't very nice of you. Remember that night we broke down in the pouring rain on the way to pick the kids up from the babysitter and you had to knock on that man's house to get us started again? What would have happened if he'd told us to get lost?'

'But the guy was drunk,' says the husband.

'It doesn't matter. He needs our help and it would be the Christian thing to help him.'

So the husband gets out of bed again, gets dressed, and goes downstairs. He opens the door, and not being able to see the stranger anywhere, he shouts, 'Hey, do you still want a push?'

And he hears a voice cry out, 'Yes please.'

'Where are you?'

'Over here, on the swing.'

DEFINITIONS BY GENDER

Butt (*but*) n.
Female: The part of the body that every item of clothing manufactured makes look bigger.
Male: What you slap when someone's scored a goal. Also useful for mooning.

Commitment (*ko-mit-ment*) n.
Female: A desire to get married and raise a family.
Male: Not trying to pick up other women while out with one's girlfriend.

Communication (*ko-myoo-ni-kay-shon*) n.
Female: The open sharing of thoughts and feelings with one's partner.
Male: Scratching out a note before suddenly taking off for a weekend with the boys.

Entertainment (*en-ter-tayn-ment*) n.
Female: A good movie, concert, play or book.
Male: Anything that can be done while drinking.

Flatulence (*flach-u-lens*) n.
Female: An embarrassing by-product of digestion.
Male: An endless source of entertainment, self-expression and male bonding.

Making love (*may-king luv*) n.
Female: The greatest expression of intimacy a couple can achieve.
Male: Call it whatever you want just as long as we end up in bed.

Thingy (*thing-ee*) n.
Female: Any part under a car's hood.
Male: The strap fastener on a woman's bra.

Vulnerable (*vul-ne-ra-bel*) adj.
Female: Fully opening up emotionally to another.
Male: Riding a motorbike without a helmet.

10 FACTS THAT EVERY MAN SHOULD KNOW ABOUT WOMEN

1. 'Oh, nothing,' has an entirely different meaning in woman-language than it does in man-language.
2. Only women understand the reason for 'guest towels' and the 'good china'.
3. Women do not want an honest answer to the question, 'How do I look?'
4. PMS really stands for: Permissible Man-Slaughter, Preposterous Mood Swings or Punish My Spouse.

5. Men can never catch women checking out other men; but women will always catch men checking out other women.

6. Women love to talk on the phone. A woman can visit her girlfriend for two weeks, and upon returning home, she will call the same friend and they will talk for three hours.

7. Women can't use a map without turning the map to correspond to the direction that they are heading.

8. All women seek equality with men until it comes to sharing the closet, taking out the rubbish, and picking up the cheque.

9. Women never check to see if the seat of the toilet is down. They seem to prefer taking a flying butt leap towards the bowl, and then becoming enraged because 'you left the seat up' instead of taking two seconds and lowering it themselves.

10. Women don't really care about a sense of humour in a guy, despite claims to the contrary. You don't see women trampling over Brad Pitt to get to Danny DeVito, do you?

GREAT REASONS TO BE A GUY

- Your ass is never a factor in a job interview.
- Your orgasms are real. Always.
- Your last name stays put.
- Wedding plans take care of themselves.
- You don't have to curl up next to a hairy bottom every night.
- Chocolate is just another snack.
- Foreplay is optional.
- Car mechanics tell you the truth.
- You don't give a rat's ass if someone notices your new haircut.
- The world is your urinal.
- Hot wax never comes near your pubic area.
- Same work . . . more pay.
- Wrinkles add character.

- You don't have to leave the room to make emergency crotch adjustments.
- Wedding Dress $2000; Tux rental $100. Nuff said.
- People never glance at your chest when you're talking to them.
- Princess Di's death was just another obituary.
- New shoes don't cut, blister, or irreparably damage your feet.
- Porn movies are designed with you in mind.
- Your pals can be trusted never to trap you with, 'So, notice anything different?'

10 THINGS NOT TO SAY TO YOUR PREGNANT WIFE

1. 'Not to imply anything, but I don't think the kid weighs 10kg.'
2. 'Y'know, looking at her, you'd never guess that Elle McPherson has had a baby.'
3. 'Well, couldn't they induce labour? The 25th is the grand final.'
4. 'Fred at the office passed a stone the size of a pea. Boy, that's gotta hurt.'
5. 'I'm jealous. Why can't men experience the joy of childbirth?'
6. 'Are your ankles supposed to look like that?'
7. 'Get your own ice cream.'
8. 'Geez, you're looking awfully puffy today.'
9. 'Got milk?'
10. 'Man! That rose tattoo on your hip is the size of Madagascar!'

Harold's wife bought a new line of expensive cosmetics guaranteed to make her look years younger.

After applying her 'miracle' products, she asked, 'Darling, honestly, what age would you say I am?'

Looking over her carefully, Harold replied, 'Judging from your skin, 20; your hair, 18; and your figure, 25.'

'Oh, you flatter me!'

'Hey, wait a minute! I haven't added them up yet.'

Women will never be equal to men until they can walk down the street bald and still think they are beautiful.

A couple was told to individually write a sentence using the words 'sex' and 'love'.

The woman wrote, 'When two people love each other very much, like Bob and I do, it is morally acceptable for them to engage in sex.'

Bob wrote, 'I love sex.'

FIVE QUOTES FOR MARRIED MEN

1. I married Miss Right. I just didn't know her first name was Always.
2. It's not true that married men live longer than single men. It only seems longer.
3. Losing a wife can be hard. In my case, it was almost impossible.
4. A man is incomplete until he is married. After that, he is finished.
5. I haven't spoken to my wife for 18 months – I don't like to interrupt her.

Q: What do you do if a bird shits on your car?

A: You never take her out again.

A man is dating three women and wants to decide which to marry. He decides to give them a test. He gives each woman a present of $5000 and watches to see what they do with the money.

The first does a total make over. She goes to a fancy beauty salon, gets her hair done, gets new make up, and buys several new outfits to dress up very nicely for the man. She tells him that she has done this to be more attractive for him because she loves him. The man is impressed.

The second goes shopping to buy the man gifts. She gets him a new set of golf clubs, some new gizmos for his computer, and some expensive clothes. As she presents these gifts, she tells him that she has spent all the money on him because she loves him so much. Again, the man is impressed.

The third invests the money in the stock market. She earns several times the $5,000. She gives him back his $5000 and reinvests the remainder in a joint account. She tells him that she wants to save for their future because she loves him. Obviously, the man is impressed.

He thinks for a long time about what each woman has done with the money he's given her. Then, he marries the one with the biggest boobs.

Peter wakes up at home with a huge hangover. He forces himself to open his eyes and the first thing he sees is a couple of Panadol and a glass of water on the side table. He sits down and sees his clothing in front of him, all clean and pressed. Peter looks around the room and sees that it is in perfect order, spotlessly clean. So is the rest of the house.

He takes the Panadol and notices a note on the table 'Honey, breakfast is on the stove, I left early to go shopping. Love you.'

So he goes to the kitchen and sure enough there is a hot breakfast and the morning newspaper. His daughter is also at the table, eating.

Peter asks, 'Victoria, what happened last night?'

'Well, you came home after 3am, drunk and delirious. Broke some furniture, puked in the hallway, and gave yourself a black eye when you stumbled into the door.'

'So, why is everything so clean, and why is breakfast on the table waiting for me?'

'Oh that! Well, Mum dragged you to the bedroom, and when she tried to take your pants off, you said, "Lady, leave me alone, I'm married."'

10 THINGS THAT ONLY WOMEN UNDERSTAND

1. Cats' facial expressions.
2. The need for the same style of shoes in different colours.
3. Why bean sprouts aren't just weeds.
4. Fat clothes.
5. Taking a car trip without trying to beat your best time.
6. The difference between beige, off-white, and eggshell.
7. Cutting your hair to make it grow faster.
8. Eyelash curlers.
9. The inaccuracy of every bathroom scale ever made.
10. That a cuddle does not necessarily need to turn into full-blown sex.

Three married couples, aged 20, 30 and 40 years old, wish to join the Orthodox Church of Sexual Repression. Near the end of the interview, the priest informs them that before they can be accepted they will have to pass one small test. They will have to abstain from all sex for a month. They agree to try.

A month later, they are having their final interview with the cleric. He asks the 40-year-old couple how they went.

'Well, it wasn't too hard. I spent a lot of time in the workshop and my partner has a garden, so we had plenty of other things to do. We did OK,' the husband says.

'Very good, my children,' says the priest. 'You are welcome in the Church.'

'And how well did you manage?' he asks the 30-year-old couple.

'It was pretty difficult,' the husband answers. 'We thought

about it all the time. We had to sleep in different beds and we prayed a lot. But we were celibate for the entire month.'

'Very good, my children, you also are welcome in the Church.'

'And how about you?' he asks the 20-year-old couple.

'Not too good, I'm afraid, Father. We did OK for the first week,' the man says sheepishly. 'By the second week we were going crazy with lust. Then one day during the third week my wife dropped a head of lettuce, and when she bent over to pick it up, I weakened and took her right there.'

'I'm sorry my son, you are not welcome in the Church'

'Yeah, and we're not too welcome in the Safeway supermarket anymore, either.'

For sale by owner: Complete set of Encyclopaedia Britannica, 45 volumes. Excellent condition. $1000 or best offer. No longer needed. Got married last weekend. Wife knows f#*#ing everything.

A new study has just been released mapping women's thoughts on marriage. The results were somewhat surprising:

85% of women think their ass has grown too big since getting married.

10% of women think their ass is just as big as it was when they got married.

The other 5% say that they don't care, they love him and would have married him anyway.

My wife suggested a book for me to read to enhance our relationship. It's called Women are from Venus, Men are Wrong.

A boy and his date were parked on a back road some distance from town, doing what boys and girls do on back roads some distance from town. The girl stopped the boy.

'I really should have mentioned this earlier, but I'm actually a hooker and I charge $20 for sex,' she said.

The boy reluctantly paid her, and they did their thing.

After a cigarette, the boy just sat in the driver's seat looking out the window.

'Why aren't we going anywhere?' asked the girl.

'Well, I should have mentioned this before, but I'm actually a taxi driver, and the fare back to town is $25.'

Women want a relationship without the complication of unnecessary sex. Men want sex without the complication of an unnecessary relationship.

REJECTED DR SEUSS BOOKS

Are You My Proctologist?

Aunts in My Pants!

Fox in Detox!

Herbert the Pervert Likes Sherbet!

Horton Fakes an Orgasm!

Horton Hires a Ho!

My Pocket Rocket Needs a Socket!

Oh, the Places You'll Scratch and Sniff!

One Bitch, Two Bitch, Dead Bitch, Blue Bitch!

The Cat in the Blender!

The Flesh-Eating Lorax!

The Grinch's Ten Inches!

Who Shat in the Hat?

Yentl the Lentil!

Your Colon Can Moo – Can You?

Zippy the Rabid Gerbil!

THE SANCTITY OF MARRIAGE

There's no institution more worthy, more satisfying or more important than marriage – so my wife tells me!

A man spends six hours in a bar before rolling home to his wife blind drunk.

'Where have you been?' she demands.

'I've been to this amazing bar,' he slurs, rocking on his feet. 'It's called the Golden Saloon and everything there is golden. At the front there are two huge golden doors, the floors are golden and even the urinals are golden.'

'What rubbish,' snaps the wife. 'I don't believe a word of it.'

'Here,' said the husband, rummaging in his pocket for a piece of paper. 'Ring this number if you don't believe me.'

So the following day she phones the number on the slip of paper.

'Is this the Golden Saloon?' she asks.

'It is,' replies the bartender.

'Tell me,' says the wife, 'do you have two huge golden doors at the front of the building?'

'Sure do,' says the bartender.

'And do you have golden floors?'

'Yup.'

'What about golden urinals?'

There's a long pause and then the wife hears the bartender yell, 'Hey, Duke, I think I got a lead on the guy that pissed in your saxophone last night.'

A rich man and a poor man are Christmas shopping for their wives. The poor man asks the rich man what he is getting for his wife.

'I'm getting her a mink coat and a Porsche. I reckon if she doesn't like the mink coat, she'll like the Porsche. What about you?'

The poor man replies, 'I'm getting her a pair of slippers and a dildo. I reckon if she doesn't like the slippers she can go screw herself.'

A man and a woman are married. One day the husband, thinking he's being funny, grabs his wife's boobs as she's getting into the shower and says to her, 'You know, if these were firm, you wouldn't need a bra!'

His wife is really angry; it was a rude thing to say. The next day, as she's getting out of the shower, he grabs her arse and says, 'You know, if this was firm, you wouldn't need a girdle!'

Now the wife is really pissed off and she's plotting her revenge. So the next day, as her husband is getting out of the shower, she grabs his dick and says, 'You know, if this was firm I wouldn't need your brother!'

A newly-married couple move into a house and the wife notices a mirror hanging on the wall.

She goes up to it and says, 'Mirror Mirror on the wall, what part of my body does my husband like most of all?'

And the mirror replies, 'Your tits.'

She then says, 'Mirror Mirror on the wall, give me size forty-four.'

And hey presto, she gets really big tits. Excitedly she rushes downstairs to show her husband, who is amazed upon seeing her. He asks her what happened and she tells him about the mirror.

The husband rushes upstairs to the mirror and says, 'Mirror Mirror on the wall, what part of my body does my wife like most of all?'

'Your dick.'

'Mirror Mirror on the wall, make my dick touch the floor.'

So his legs fall off.

A wife wakes in the middle of the night to find her husband missing from bed. She gets out of bed and checks around the house. She hears sobbing from the cellar. After turning on the light and descending the stairs, she finds her husband curled up into a little ball, sobbing.

'Honey, what's wrong?' she asks, worried about what could hurt him so much.

'Remember, twenty years ago, I got you pregnant? And your father said I had to marry you or go to jail?'

'Yes, of course,' she replies.

'Well, today I would have been a free man.'

A businessman is on an overnight train trip with his secretary. They both retire to their respective rooms but a while later the secretary comes into the man's room and says, 'Excuse me Mr Johnston, but could you please pass me a blanket?'

Mr Johnston asks, 'Do you want to be Mrs Johnston for the night?'

The secretary thinks for a moment then says, 'That would be nice.'

To this Mr Johnston says, 'Good. Get your own bloody blanket.'

A man has six children and is very proud of his achievement. He is so proud of himself that he starts calling his wife Mother of Six, in spite of her objections.

One night they go to a party. The man decides that it's time to go home, and wants to find out if his wife is ready to leave as well. He shouts at the top of his voice, 'Shall we go home Mother of Six?'

His wife, irritated by her husband's lack of discretion shouts back, 'Anytime you're ready, Father of Four!'

A man is drunk and in no shape to drive, so he wisely leaves his car parked and walks home. As he is walking unsteadily along, he is stopped by a policeman.

'What are you doing out here at 2 a.m.?' asks the officer.

'I'm going to a lecture,' the man says.

'And who is going to give a lecture at this hour?' the cop asks.

'My wife,' says the man.

This man is sitting quietly reading his paper one morning, peacefully enjoying himself, when his wife sneaks up behind him and whacks him on the back of his head with a huge black frying pan.

'What was that for?' asks the man

'What was that piece of paper in your pants pocket with the name Marylou written on it?'

'Oh honey. Don't you remember two weeks ago when I went to the horse races? Marylou was the name of one of the horses I bet on.'

The wife seems satisfied and goes off to work, feeling a bit sheepish.

Three days later the man is once again sitting in his chair reading and his wife repeats the frying-pan swatting.

'What's that for this time?' he asks.

'Your horse rang,' says his wife.

A husband is sent out by his wife to buy some fruit and vegetables. But they have to be organic. He goes to the market and has a good look around but can't find any.

So he grabs an old, tired-looking employee and says, 'These vegetables are for my wife. Have they been sprayed with any poisonous chemicals?'

The produce guy looks at him and says, 'No. You'll have to do that yourself.'

A man goes to the police station wanting to speak to the burglar who broke into his house the night before.

'You'll get your chance in court,' says the desk sergeant.

'No, no, no!' says the man. 'I want to know how he got into the house without waking my wife. I've been trying to do that for years!'

A woman goes into a store to buy her husband a pet for his birthday. After looking around, she finds that all the pets are very expensive. She tells the clerk she wants to buy a pet, but she doesn't want to spend a fortune.

'Well,' says the clerk. 'I have a very large bullfrog. They say it's been trained to give blowjobs.'

'Blowjobs!'

'It hasn't been proven, but we've sold thirty of them this month,' he says.

The woman thinks it will make a great gag gift, and what if it's true . . . no more blowjobs for her. So she buys the frog and gives it to her husband. When she explains froggy's ability to him, he is extremely sceptical and laughs it off.

The woman goes to bed happy, thinking she may never need to perform this less than riveting act again. In the middle of the night, she is awakened by the noise of pots and pans flying everywhere. She runs downstairs to the kitchen, only to find her husband and the frog reading cookbooks.

'What are you two doing at this hour?' she asks.

The husband replies, 'If I can teach this frog to cook, you're out of here.'

A young couple, just married, are in the honeymoon suite on their wedding night. As they undress for bed, the husband, who is a big burly man, tosses his pants to his bride and says, 'Here put these on.'

She puts them on and the waist is twice the size of her body.

'I can't wear your pants,' she says.

'That's right,' says the husband, 'and don't you forget it. I'm the one who wears the pants in this family!'

With that she flips him her panties and says, 'Try these on.'

He tries them on and finds he can only get them on as far as his kneecap.

He says, 'I can't get into your panties.'

She says, 'That's right, and that's the way it's going to be until your attitude changes.'

Did you hear about the new edition of Playboy for married men? It has the same centrefold every month.

DATING VS MARRIAGE

When you are dating . . . He takes you out to have a good time.
When you are married . . . He brings home a six pack and says, 'What are you going to drink?'

When you are dating . . . You are turned on at the sight of him naked.
When you are married . . . You think to yourself, 'Was he *always* this hairy?'

When you are dating . . . You enjoy foreplay.
When you are married . . . You tell him, 'If we have sex, will you leave me alone?'

When you are dating . . . You picture the two of you together, growing old together.
When you are married . . . You wonder who will die first.

When you are dating . . . He understands if you aren't in the mood.
When you are married . . . He says, 'It's your job.'

When you are dating . . . He understands that you have male friends.
When you are married . . . He thinks they are all out to steal you away.

When you are dating . . . He likes to discuss things.
When you are married . . . He develops a blank stare.

When you are dating . . . He calls you by name.
When you are married . . . He calls you 'Hey' and refers to you when speaking to others as 'She'.

CULTURAL DIVERSITY

*Cultural diversity is the politically correct term
for taking the piss out of people from particular
backgrounds. Hey, it might not be the right
thing to do, but it's fun, isn't it?*

A Japanese man walks into a currency exchange in America with ¥2000 and walks out with $72. The next week he walks in with ¥2000, but only gets $66. He asks the lady why he got less money this week than last week.

The lady says, 'Fluctuations.'

The man says, 'Fluck you clazy Amelicans too!'

A Swiss guy, looking for directions, pulls up at a bus stop where two Englishmen are waiting.

'*Entschuldigung, koennen Sie Deutsch sprechen?*' he says.

The two Englishmen just stare at him.

'*Excusez-moi, parlez vous Français?*'

The two continue to stare.

'*Parlare Italiano?*'

No response, '*¿Hablan ustedes Espanol?*'

Still nothing. The Swiss guy drives off, extremely disgusted. The first Englishman turns to the second and says, 'Y'know, maybe we should learn a foreign language.'

'Why?' asks the other, 'That bloke knew four languages, and it didn't do him any good.'

Two Swedes, Sven and Ole, work together and are laid off together. They go to the unemployment office. Asked his occupation, Ole says, 'Panty stitcher. I sew the elastic onto cotton panties.'

The clerk looks up panty stitcher. Finding it classed as unskilled labour, she gives him $300 per week unemployment pay. Sven is then asked his occupation.

'Diesel fitter,' he replies.

Since diesel fitter is a skilled job, the clerk gives Sven $600 per week. When Ole finds out he is furious. He storms back to the office to find out why his friend and co-worker is collecting double his pay.

The clerk explains, 'Panty stitchers are unskilled and diesel fitters are skilled labourers.'

'What skill?' yells Ole. 'I sew the elastic on the panties, Sven pulls them down on his head and says, "Yah, diesel fitter."'

Three guys are on a trip to Saudi Arabia. One day, they stumble into a harem tent filled with over 100 beautiful women. They start getting friendly with all the women, when suddenly the sheik comes in.

'I am the master of all these women. No-one else can touch them except me. You three men must pay for what you have done today. You will be punished in a way corresponding to your profession.'

The sheik turns to the first man and asks him what he does for a living.

'I'm a cop,' says the first man.

'Then we will shoot your penis off,' says the sheik. He then turns to the second man and asks him what he does for a living.

'I'm a fireman,' says the second man.

'Then we will burn your penis off,' says the sheik.

Finally, he asks the last man, 'And you, what do you do for a living?'

The third man answers, with a sly grin, 'I'm a lollipop salesman!'

An Englishman, a Frenchman and a Russian are viewing a painting of Adam and Eve frolicking in the Garden of Eden.

'Look at their reserve, their calm,' muses the Englishman. 'They must be English.'

'Nonsense,' the Frenchman disagrees. 'They're naked, and so beautiful. Clearly, they are French.'

'No clothes, no shelter,' the Russian points out, 'they have only an apple to eat, and they're being told this is paradise. They must be Russian.'

An Englishman, an Irishman and a Scotsman have been working as jackaroos out west for many months, and are feeling the need of a woman. They therefore get together and acquire, by mail order from Canberra, an inflatable sex doll. They draw lots, and the Englishman gets the first shot. Half an hour or so later, he comes out of the spare room with a smile on his face.

'Bloody great is that! Better than the wife any day!'

Encouraged, the Scotsman goes in, and emerges after a few minutes with a grin. 'Yer nae bloody wrong, Jimmy. It was worth the cost o' a pint.'

The Irishman takes his turn, and emerges after only a short while with a puzzled and frustrated frown. 'Oi don't know what youse was raving on about. It's bloody useless! All oi did was give her a little love bite, and she lets out a bloody great fart and flies out the window.'

A cowboy is caught by some Indians and is about to be executed when they ask him if he has a last request. The cowboy says yes, walks over to his horse and whispers something in its ear. The horse takes off like a mad thing over the hills and returns after a short while with a beautiful, naked blonde on its back. The cowboy takes the blonde to a teepee and has sex with her. Then he comes back out and requests another talk with his horse. The Indians, amazed, agree. So the cowboy walks over to the horse and whispers in his ear again. The horse takes off and return with a beautiful, naked redhead. The cowboy takes her into another teepee and has sex with her. He comes out and once more asks to talk to his horse. The Indians once more agree. So he walks over to the horse and whispers something else into its ear. The horse takes off and returns with a beautiful, naked brunette on its back. The cowboy takes the brunette to a teepee and has sex with her. Then he comes back out and requests another talk with his horse. The Indians, totally amazed by this point, agree again.

So the cowboy walks over to his horse and says, 'I'm only going to do this once more, now read my lips, "posse".'

A Texan lands in Sydney, and is picked up by a taxi. After requesting a tour of the city, he starts into a tirade about the small-town airport and how in Texas they have larger runways on their ranches.

They are soon crossing the Sydney Harbour Bridge, and the Texan is further unimpressed, 'I have a duck pond bigger than that harbour, and an ornamental bridge to span it that makes this look like a toy.'

The Sydney-Newcastle Expressway also gets his scorn.

'Is this a road, or a track?' he shouts with contempt.

So when a kangaroo jumps out in front of the cab, causing the sudden and severe application of the brakes, the driver can't help himself.

'Bloody grasshoppers!' he says.

P addy is sitting at a bar when a very well-dressed gentleman comes and sits down next to him. After a while they start a conversation. Paddy asks the gentleman what he does for a living.

The gentleman replies, 'I'm Professor of Logic at Dublin University.'

'Oh,' says Paddy, 'What's this here logic?'

'Well,' says the Professor, 'logic is when things or events follow each other. To give you a demonstration, I've noticed that you have very rough hands. This tells me that you are a manual labourer.'

'Dat's roight,' says Paddy, 'Oi works digging trenches.'

'And to carry this one point further, being a manual worker, you would have a big garden shed,' says the Professor.

'Dat's roight,' says Paddy, 'Oi has a big garden shed.'

'Well there you are,' says the Professor. 'Logic . . . one thing follows another in a logical sequence. And to take it one step further, if you have a big garden shed, then you would have a big garden.'

'Yes, Oi have half an acre at home, vegies for all the family,' says Paddy.

'See . . . logical progression. One thing follows another. And, to take it one step further, if you have a big garden, you would have a big family,' says the Professor.

'Ah, yes, dere is nine in the family,' says Paddy.

'There, logical progression,' says the Professor. 'And, to take it even one step further, if you have a big family, you would be having sex regularly.'

'Certainly,' Paddy emphasises. 'Six nights a week and twice on Sunday.'

'Ah, and if you were having sex that regularly, you would not have to masturbate,' says the Professor.

'Oh, never, never, not for many, many years,' says Paddy.

'Well,' says the Professor. 'There you are, logical progression. One thing follows another.'

With that the Professor bids farewell to Paddy and leaves the pub.

Patrick, sitting at the bar, then sidles up to Paddy and asks, 'Who was that, Paddy?'

'Oh,' says Paddy, 'That was a very educated gentleman. He's a Professor of Logic at Dublin University.'

'Logic?' says Patrick, 'What's logic?'

'I'll tell you all about it,' says Paddy. 'Tell me, Patrick, have you got a big garden shed?'

'Why no,' says Patrick.

'Well,' says Paddy, 'I always thought you were a wanker!'

An American tourist gets the shock of his life when a Mexican with a six-shooter jumps out from behind a cactus.

'Take my money, my car but don't kill me,' says the tourist.

'I no kill you if you do what I say,' says the Mexican. 'Just unzip your pants and start masturbating.'

Although shocked the tourist does what he is told.

'Right, now do it again,' says the Mexican.

The Yank protests, but with the gun against his nose, he manages again.

'And yet again, Gringo, or I shoot you dead.'

With sweat running down his brow, the Yank manages a final effort and falls to the ground, exhausted.

'Good,' says the Mexican. 'Now, you give my sister a ride to the next village.'

A Scotsman and a Jew go to a restaurant. After a hearty meal, the waitress comes by with the inevitable bill. To the amazement of all, the Scot is heard to say, 'I'll pay it.'

And he actually does. The next morning's newspaper carries a news item headed: 'Jewish Ventriloquist Found Murdered in Alley.'

A salesman is driving toward home in Northern Arizona when he sees a Navajo man hitchhiking. Because the trip has been long and quiet, he stops the car and the Navajo man climbs in. During their small talk, the Navajo man glances surreptitiously at a brown bag on the front seat between them.

'If you're wondering what's in the bag,' offers the salesman, 'it's a bottle of wine. I got it for my wife.'

The Navajo man is silent for awhile, nods several times and says, 'Good trade.'

Two cannibals capture an explorer. Both are hungry and they decide to share him. The first cannibal starts at the feet and the second starts on his head. After about five minutes of gnawing away, the first cannibal asks, 'How are you doing?'

The other cannibal replies, 'I'm having a ball!'

The first cannibal screams, 'Slow down. You're going too fast.'

An Englishman, a Scotsman, and an Irishman walk into a pub. They each buy a pint of Guinness. Just as they are about to enjoy their creamy beverages, three flies land in each of their pints and become stuck in the thick heads.

The Englishman pushes his beer away from him in disgust. The Scot fishes the offending fly out of his beer and continues drinking it as if nothing has happened. The Irishman too, picks the fly out of his drink, holds it out over the beer and then starts yelling, 'Spit it out, spit it out, you bastard.'

An Indian boy goes to his mother one day with a puzzled look on his face.

'Say, mum, why is my bigger brother named Mighty Storm?'

She tells him, 'Because he was conceived during a mighty storm.'

Then he asks, 'Why is my sister named Cornflower?'

His mother replies, 'Well, your father and I were in a cornfield when we made her.'

'And why is my other sister called Moonchild?'

The mother says, 'We were watching the moon landing while she was conceived.' She pauses and asks her son, 'Tell me, Torn Rubber, why are you so curious?'

The National Transportation Safety Board recently divulged that they had funded a project with American car-makers over the past five years. In the covert project, car-makers installed black boxes in 4WD pickup trucks in an effort to determine, in fatal accidents, the circumstances in the last fifteen seconds before the crash.

They were surprised to find in forty-nine of the fifty states the last words of drivers in 61.2% of fatal crashes were, 'Oh, Shit!'

Only the state of Texas was different. There, 89.3% of the final words were, 'Hey Y'all, hold my beer and watch this!'

Three third-graders – a Jew, an Italian, and an African American – are on the playground at recess. The Jewish kid suggests that they play a new game.

'Let's see who has the largest dick,' he says.

'OK,' they all agree.

The Jewish kid pulls down his zipper and whips it out.

'That's nothing,' says the Italian kid.

He whips his out. His is a couple of inches longer. Not to be outdone, the African American whips his out. It is by far the biggest, dwarfing the other two in both length and width. The Jewish and Italian kids are stunned and amazed.

'Wow, that thing is huge,' they exclaim.

That night, eating dinner at home, the African American's mother asks him what he did at school today.

'Oh, we worked on a science project, had a maths test and read out loud from a new book . . . and during recess, my friends and I played "Let's see who has the largest dick."'

'What kind of game is that, honey?' asks his mother.

'Well, me, Sidney and Anthony each pulled out our penises, and I had the biggest! The other kids say it's because I'm black. Is that true, Mum?'

His mum replies, 'No, honey. It's because you're twenty-three.'

Mrs Cohen, Mrs Levy, and Mrs Lefkovitz are discussing their sons. Mrs Cohen says, 'Now my Sheldon, what a man! A world-famous lawyer, he is, with big shot clients, a mansion in Beverly Hills, a summer home in Hawaii. He has a beautiful wife, and everything a man could want in the world.'

Mrs Levy says, 'That's nice. Lemmie tell you about my son Jonathan. He is a doctor, a world-famous researcher. He travels across the world on conferences, talks, lectures. He was nominated for a Nobel Prize in Medicine. What a man!'

Mrs Lefkowitz says, 'My Hershel, he's an engineer. Now, he makes maybe $35 000 a year, and he's not famous. But his penis is so long, you can line up ten pigeons in a row on it.'

The ladies sip their tea for a while.

Then, Mrs Cohen says, 'Actually, I got a confession to make. Sheldon's an up-and-coming lawyer in Los Angeles, but he doesn't have a mansion or a summer home. He's a bright young man with a good future.'

Mrs Levy says, 'Well, I got a confession too. Jonathan is a good doctor, and he got his share of scholarships, but a Nobel prize-winner, he isn't.'

They all look expectantly at Mrs Lefkowitz.

'Well, all right, I'll tell the truth too. The last bird gotta stand on one leg.'

WHITE ONE LINERS

What's white and fourteen inches long?
Absolutely nothing!

What do you call 500 000 white guys jumping out of a plane?
Snow.

Why do so many white people get lost skiing?
It's hard to find them in the snow.

What did the white guy do before his blood test?
He studied.

What's the difference between a white man and a snake?
One is an evil, cold-blooded, venomous, slimy creature of Satan, and the other is a snake.

What's the flattest surface to iron your jeans on?
A white girl's arse.

What did the black guy do with his M&M's?
Ate them.

What did the white guy try to do with his?
Put them in alphabetical order.

What did the white guy see when he looked at his family tree?
A straight line.

An Irish guy is walking down the street carrying a brown paper bag. He runs into one of his friends, who asks, 'What do you have in the bag?'

The man tells his friend that he has some fish in the bag.

His friend says, 'Well, I'll make you a bet. If I can guess how many fish you have in the bag, you have to give me one.'

The man says, 'I'll tell you what. If you can guess how many fish I have, you can have them both.'

An Irish guy is hired to paint the lines on the road. On the first day he paints 10km, and his employers are amazed. But, the second day he paints just five, and on the third day, he paints only 1km of the road. Disappointed, his boss asks what the problem is.

The Irish guy replies, 'Well Sir, every day I have to walk farther and farther to get back to the paint bucket.'

A twelve-year-old boy goes up to his Irish neighbour and says, 'I was looking in your bedroom window last night and I saw your wife giving you a blow job. Nyah, nyah, nyah.'

The Irish guy laughs and answers, 'The joke's on you, Johnny. Nyah, nyah, nyah – I wasn't even home last night.'

An Irish guy is travelling on a plane when the pilot makes an announcement.

'Folks, we just had one engine go out, but don't worry, this plane can fly just fine on two engines. All it means is that we'll be about an hour late.'

An hour later, the pilot gets on the intercom again.

'Folks, don't get alarmed, but a second engine just went out, but please don't worry. This plane is designed to fly safely on one engine. However, it's likely that we'll now be about two hours late.'

After that announcement, the Irish guy turns to the person sitting next to him and says, 'Well, I sure hope that third engine doesn't go out. We'll be up here all night.'

SIGNS COLLECTED BY A FLIGHT ATTENDANT ALONG HER TRAVELS

The sign in a Norwegian lounge reads:
LADIES ARE REQUESTED NOT TO HAVE CHILDREN IN THE BAR

A hotel notice in Madrid informs:
IF YOU WISH DISINFECTION ENACTED IN YOUR
PRESENCE, PLEASE CRY OUT FOR THE CHAMBERMAID

In the window of a Swedish furrier the message reads:
FUR COATS MADE FOR LADIES FROM THEIR OWN SKIN

The room service in a Lisbon hotel tells you:
IF YOU WISH FOR BREAKFAST, LIFT THE TELEPHONE AND
ASK FOR ROOM SERVICE. THIS WILL BE ENOUGH FOR YOU TO
BRING YOUR FOOD UP

A Polish hotel informs prospective visitors in a flyer:
AS FOR THE TROUT SERVED YOU AT THE HOTEL
MONOPOL, YOU WILL BE SINGING ITS PRAISE TO YOUR
GRANDCHILDREN AS YOU LIE ON YOUR DEATHBED

A Seville tailor makes clear how he will handle commissions:
ORDER NOW YOUR SUMMER SUIT, BECAUSE IS BIG RUSH
WE WILL EXECUTE CUSTOMERS IN STRICT ROTATION

A dentist's doorway in Istanbul proclaims:
AMERICAN DENTIST, 2TH FLOOR. TEETH EXTRACTED BY
LATEST METHODISTS.

Some German hospitals now display the sign:
NO CHILDREN ALLOWED IN THE MATERNITY WARDS

A Roman doctor proclaims himself a:
SPECIALIST IN WOMEN AND OTHER DISEASES

A sign in a Kowloon hotel warns:
IS FORBIDDEN TO STEAL HOTEL TOWELS. PLEASE IF YOU
ARE NOT PERSON TO DO SUCH IS PLEASE NOT TO READ
NOTICE.

Visitors in a Czechoslovakian tourist agency are invited to:
TAKE ONE OF OUR HORSE-DRIVEN CITY TOURS – WE
GUARANTEE NO MISCARRIAGES

A sign posted in Germany's Black Forest reads:
IT IS STRICTLY FORBIDDEN ON OUR BLACK FOREST
CAMPING SITE THAT PEOPLE OF DIFFERENT SEX, FOR
INSTANCE, MEN AND WOMEN, LIVE TOGETHER IN ONE TENT
UNLESS THEY ARE MARRIED WITH EACH OTHER FOR THAT
PURPOSE

A notice in a Vienna hotel urges:
IN CASE OF FIRE DO YOUR UTMOST TO ALARM THE HALL
PORTER

On a Paris hotel elevator:
PLEASE LEAVE YOUR VALUES AT THE FRONT DESK

In an Athens Hotel:
VISITORS ARE EXPECTED TO COMPLAIN AT THE OFFICE
BETWEEN 9 A.M. AND 11 A.M. DAILY

On a Belgrade (Yugoslavia) elevator:
TO MOVE THE CABIN, PUSH BUTTON FOR WISHING
FLOOR. IF THE CABIN SHOULD ENTER MORE PERSONS, EACH
ONE SHOULD PRESS A NUMBER OF WISHING FLOOR.
DRIVING IS THEN GOING ALPHABETICALLY BY NATIONAL
ORDER.

In a Japanese Hotel:
YOU ARE INVITED TO TAKE ADVANTAGE OF THE
CHAMBERMAID

In a Moscow Hotel:
YOU ARE WELCOME TO VISIT THE CEMETERY
WHERE FAMOUS RUSSIAN AND SOVIET COMPOSERS, ARTISTS
AND WRITERS ARE BURIED DAILY EXCEPT THURSDAY

On a Swiss menu:
OUR WINES LEAVE YOU NOTHING TO HOPE FOR

On a Polish menu:
SALAD A FIRM'S OWN MAKE; LIMPID RED BEET SOUP
WITH CHEESY DUMPLINGS IN THE FORM OF A FINGER
ROASTED DUCK LET LOOSE; BEEF RASHERS BEATEN UP IN
THE COUNTRY PEOPLE'S FASHION.

In a Bangkok dry cleaners:
DROP YOUR TROUSERS HERE FOR BEST RESULTS

In a Paris dress shop:
DRESSES FOR STREET WALKING

In a Soviet newspaper:
THERE WILL BE A MOSCOW EXHIBITION OF ART BY 16 000
SOVIET REPUBLIC PAINTERS AND SCULPTORS. THESE WERE
EXECUTED OVER THE PAST TWO YEARS.

At a Swiss mountain inn:
SPECIAL TODAY – NO ICE CREAM

At a Tokyo car rental firm:
WHEN PASSENGER OF FOOT HAVE IN SIGHT, TOOTLE THE
HORN. TRUMPET HIM MELODIOUSLY AT FIRST, BUT IF HE
STILL OBSTACLES YOUR PASSAGE THEN TOOTLE HIM WITH
VIGOUR.

In a Majorcan shop:
ENGLISH WELL TALKING. HERE SPEECHING AMERICAN.

BUSINESS IS BUSINESS

Given that so many jokes are told around the water cooler in the workplace, it's only right that we feature a section with jokes about those very people who spend their valuable working time telling them.

A man is in a VIP airport lounge en route to Seattle. He is meeting with a very important client who is also flying to Seattle but she is running a bit late. While waiting, he notices Bill Gates sitting in a chair enjoying a cognac. Being a forward type of guy, the man approaches Bill Gates and introduces himself. He explains to Gates that he is conducting some very important business and that he would really appreciate it if Gates could throw a quick 'Hello Paul' at the man while he is with his client. Gates agrees. Ten minutes later, while the man is conversing with his client, he feels a tap on his shoulder. It is Gates. The man turns around and looks up at him.

Bill Gates says, 'Hi Paul, what's happening?'

The man replies, 'Piss off, Bill, I'm in a meeting.'

A small business owner has two employees, Jack and Jill. Business is bad and the business owner has to lay one of them off but is having a hard time deciding which one to let go. He decides that the first one to leave for lunch is the one that he'll lay off.

But both of them stay and eat at their desks.

Then he decides that the first one to leave work at the end of the day will be the one he fires. They both get up and leave at the same time.

He has to let one of them go. Which one? He decides on Jill.

The owner walks out to Jill's car as she is about to get in and says, 'Jill, I am trying to decide whether to lay you or Jack off. What do you think?'

Jill says, 'You'd better just jack off. I'm already late for an appointment.'

Smith goes to see his supervisor in the front office. 'Boss,' he says, 'we're doing some heavy house-cleaning at home tomorrow and my wife needs me to help with the attic and the garage, moving and hauling stuff.'

'We're short-handed, Smith' the boss replies. 'I can't give you the day off.'

'Thanks, boss,' says Smith 'I knew I could count on you!'

Four people are in the final stages of interviewing for a prestigious job. The managing director decides to call them in, one by one, and ask them a question. The first applicant is called in.

The managing director poses the question, 'What is the fastest thing in the world?'

The applicant thinks for a moment, then replies, 'That would have to be a thought.'

'Why do you say that?' asks the managing director.

'Well, a thought takes no time at all . . . it is in your mind in an instant, then gone again.'

'Ahh, very good. Thank you,' replies the director.

Next the same question is posed to the second applicant. 'What is the fastest thing in the world?'

She pauses and replies, 'That would have to be a blink.'

'Why?' asks the managing director.

'Because you don't even think about a blink, it's just a reflex. You do it in an instant.'

The managing director thanks her and calls in the next person. The third applicant is asked what the fastest thing in the world is, and after hesitating for a brief moment, he replies, 'I would have to say electricity.'

'Why?'

'Because a man can flip a switch, and immediately, 10km away a light will go on.'

'I see, very good,' replies the managing director.

Then, the final applicant is called in. He, too, is asked, 'What is the fastest thing in the world?'

'That's easy,' he replies. 'That would have to be diarrhoea!'

Rather stunned, the managing director asks, 'Why do you say that?'

'Well, last night after dinner, I was lying in my bed and I got the worst stomach cramps, and before I could think, blink or turn on the lights . . .'

GRADUATES

A graduate with a science degree asks, 'Why does it work?'

A graduate with an engineering degree asks, 'How does it work?'

A graduate with an accounting degree asks, 'How much will it cost?'

A graduate with a law degree asks, 'Who gave it permission to work?'

A graduate with an arts degree asks, 'Would you like fries with that?'

OLD HANDS

Old doctors never die, they just loose their patience.

Old lawyers never die, they just lose their appeal.

Old professors never die, they just lose their faculties.

Old publishers never die, they just go out of print.

Old soldiers never die. Young ones do.

PROFESSIONALS

An actuary is someone who brings a fake bomb on a plane, because that decreases the chances that there will be another bomb on the plane.

An archaeologist is a person whose career lies in ruins.

A banker is someone who lends you his umbrella when the sun is shining and wants it back the minute it begins to rain.

A diplomat is someone who can tell you to go to hell in such a way that you will look forward to the trip.

A lawyer is a person who writes a 10 000 word document and calls it a brief.

A philosopher is a person who doesn't have a job but at least understands why.

A lecturer is someone who talks in someone else's sleep.

A programmer is someone who solves a problem you didn't know you had in a way you don't understand.

A psychologist is someone who charges a lot of money to ask you questions that your wife asks for free.

A schoolteacher is a disillusioned woman who used to like children.

A sociologist is someone who, when a beautiful woman enters the room, is watching everybody else.

A statistician is someone who is good with numbers but lacks the personality to be an accountant.

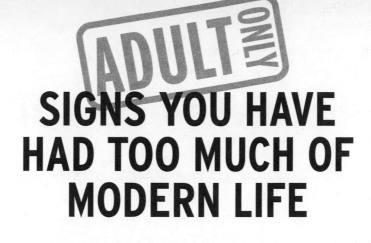

SIGNS YOU HAVE HAD TOO MUCH OF MODERN LIFE

- You buy a computer and a week later it is out of date . . . and now sells for half the price you paid.

- You exchange emails several times a day with a stranger from South Africa, but you haven't spoken to your next door neighbour yet this year.

- You consider second-day air delivery painfully slow.

- You have a list of fifteen phone numbers to reach your family of three.

- You haven't played solitaire with a real deck of cards in years.

- Your reason for not staying in touch with family is that they do not have email addresses.

BELIEVE IT OR NOT

This is the transcript of a radio conversation between a US naval ship and Canadian authorities off the coast of Newfoundland. You decide whether it is real or made up.

Canadians: Please divert your course fifteen degrees to the south to avoid a collision.

Americans: Recommend you divert your course fifteen degrees to the north to avoid a collision.

Canadians: Negative. You will have to divert your course fifteen degrees south to avoid a collision.

Americans: This is the Captain of a US Navy ship. I say again, divert *your* course.

Canadians: No. I say again, you divert *your* course.

Americans: This is the aircraft carrier *U.S.S. Lincoln*, the second-largest ship in the United States' Atlantic fleet. We are accompanied by three destroyers, three cruisers and numerous support vessels. I *demand* that you change your course fifteen degrees north. I say again, that's one five degrees north, or counter-measures will be undertaken to ensure the safety of this ship!

Canadians: This is a lighthouse. You decide.

The following question was supposedly given on a chemistry exam, 'Is hell exothermic (gives off heat) or endothermic (absorbs heat)? Support your answer with proof.'

Most of the students wrote proofs of their beliefs using Boyle's Law (gas cools off when it expands and heats up when it is compressed) or some variant.

One student, however, wrote the following:

'First, we need to know how the mass of hell is changing in time. So, we need to know the rate that souls are moving into hell and the rate they are leaving. I think that we can safely assume that once a soul gets to hell, it will not leave. Therefore, no souls are leaving.

'As for how many souls are entering hell, let's look at the different religions that exist in the world today. Some of these religions state that if you are not a member of their religion, you will go to hell. Since there are more than one of these religions and since people do not belong to more than one religion, we can project that all people and all souls go to hell.

'With birth and death rates as they are, we can expect the number of souls in hell to increase exponentially. Now, we look at the rate of change of the volume in hell because Boyle's Law states that in order for temperature and the pressure in hell to stay the same, the volume of hell has to expand as souls are added. This gives two possibilities:

1. If hell is expanding at a slower rate than the rate at which souls enter hell, then the temperature and pressure in hell will increase until all hell breaks loose.

2. Of course, if hell is expanding at a rate faster than the increase of souls in hell, then the temperature and pressure will drop until hell freezes over.

'So which is it?

'If we accept the postulate given to me by Ms Therese Banyan during my Freshman year, that "it will be a cold night in hell before I sleep with you", and take into account the fact that I still have not succeeded in that area, then (2) cannot be true, and so hell is exothermic.'

This student got the only A.

This is supposedly true. Do you believe it?
On 20 July 1969, as commander of the Apollo 11 Lunar

Module, Neil Armstrong was the first person to set foot on the moon. His first words after stepping on the moon, 'That's one small step for a man, one giant leap for mankind,' were televised to earth and heard by millions.

But just before he re-entered the lander, he made the enigmatic remark, 'Good luck, Mr Gorsky.'

Many people at NASA thought it was a casual remark concerning some rival Soviet Cosmonaut. However, upon checking, there was no Gorsky in either the Russian or American space programs. Over the years many people questioned Armstrong as to what the 'Good luck Mr Gorsky' statement meant, but Armstrong always just smiled. On 5 July 1995, in Tampa Bay, Florida, while answering questions following a speech, a reporter brought up the twenty-six-year-old question to Armstrong. This time he finally responded. Mr Gorsky had died and so Neil Armstrong felt he could answer the question. In 1938 when he was a kid in a small Midwest town, he was playing baseball with a friend in the backyard. His friend hit a fly ball, which landed in his neighbour's yard by the bedroom windows. His neighbours were Mr and Mrs Gorsky. As he leaned down to pick up the ball, young Armstrong heard Mrs Gorsky shouting at Mr Gorsky.

'A blow job! You want a blow job? You'll get a blow job when the kid next door walks on the moon!'

HISTORY AS SEEN BY YOUNG PEOPLE

This is a compilation of answers by American history students.

1. Ancient Egypt was inhabited by mummies and they all wrote in hydraulics. They lived in the Sarah Dessert and travelled by Camelot. The climate of the Sarah is such that the inhabitants have to live elsewhere.

2. Moses led the Hebrew slaves to the Red Sea, where they made unleavened bread which is bread made without any ingredients. Moses went up on Mount Cyanide to get the Ten Commandments. He died before he ever reached Canada.

3. Actually, Homer was not written by Homer but by another man of that name.

4. Socrates was a famous Greek teacher who went around giving people advice. They killed him. Socrates died from an overdose of wedlock. After his death, his career suffered a dramatic decline.

5. Joan of Arc was burnt to a steak and was canonised by Bernard Shaw. Finally Magna Carta provided that no man should be hanged twice for the same offence.

6. In midevil times most people were alliterate. The greatest writer of the futile ages was Chaucer, who wrote many poems and verses and also wrote literature.

7. Another story was William Tell, who shot an arrow through an apple while standing on his son's head.

8. It was an age of great inventions and discoveries. Gutenberg invented removable type and the bible. Another important invention was the circulation of blood. Sir Walter Raleigh is a historical figure because he invented cigarettes and started smoking. And Sir Francis Drake circumcised the world with a 100-foot clipper.

9. The greatest writer of the Renaissance was William Shakespeare. He was born in the year 1564, supposedly on

his birthday. He never made much money and is famous only because of his plays. He wrote tragedies, comedies, and hysterectomies, all in Islamic pentameter. Romeo and Juliet are an example of a heroic couplet.

10. Writing at the same time as Shakespeare was Miguel Cervantes. He wrote Donkey Hote. The next great author was John Milton. Milton wrote Paradise Lost. Then his wife died and he wrote Paradise Regained.

11. During the Renaissance America began. Christopher Columbus was a great navigator who discovered America while cursing about the Atlantic. His ships were called the Nina, the Pinta, and the Santa Fe.

12. Abraham Lincoln became America's greatest Precedent. Lincoln's mother died in infancy, and he was born in a log cabin which he built with his own hands. Abraham Lincoln freed the slaves by signing the Emasculation Proclamation. On the night of 14 April 1865, Lincoln went to the theatre and got shot in his seat by one of the actors in a moving picture show. The believed assassinator was John Wilkes Booth, a supposedly insane actor. This ruined Booth's career.

13. Gravity was invented by Issac Walton. It is chiefly noticeable in the autumn when the apples are falling off the trees.

14. Johann Bach wrote a great many musical compositions and had a large number of children. In between he practised on an old spinster which he kept up in his attic. Bach died from 1750 to the present. Bach was the most famous composer in the world and so was Handel. Handel was half German half Italian and half English. He was very large.

15. Beethoven wrote music even though he was deaf. He was so deaf he wrote loud music. He took long walks in the forest even when everyone was calling for him. Beethoven expired in 1827 and later died for this.

16. The sun never set on the British Empire because the British Empire's in the East and the sun sets in the West.

17. Queen Victoria was the longest queen. She sat on a thorn for sixty-three years. She was a moral woman who practised virtue. Her death was the final event which ended her reign.

18. Louis Pasteur discovered a cure for rabbis. Charles Darwin was a naturalist who wrote the Organ of the Species. Madman Curie discovered radio. And Karl Marx became one of the Marx brothers.

19. The First World War, caused by the assignation of the Arch-Duck by an anarchist, ushered in a new error in the anals of human history.

Excerpt from an article about a bank robbery which supposedly appeared in the *Dublin Times* in May 1999:

'Once inside the bank shortly after midnight, their efforts at disabling the internal security system got underway immediately. The robbers, who expected to find one or two large safes filled with cash and valuables, were surprised to see hundreds of smaller safes scattered throughout the bank. The robbers cracked the first safe's combination, and inside they found only a bowl of vanilla pudding. As recorded on the bank's audio-tape system, one said, 'At least we'll get a bit to eat.'

The robbers opened up a second safe, and it also contained nothing but vanilla pudding. The process continued until all the safes were opened. They found not one pound sterling, a diamond, or an ounce of gold. Instead, all the safes contained covered bowls of pudding. Disappointed, the robbers made a quiet exit, each leaving with nothing more than a queasy, uncomfortably full stomach.

The newspaper headline read:

'Ireland's Largest Sperm Bank Robbed Early This Morning'

EMPLOYEE OF THE MONTH

These individual quotes were reportedly taken from actual employee performance evaluations in a large US Corporation.

- 'Since my last report, this employee has reached rock bottom . . . and has started to dig.'

- 'His men would follow him anywhere . . . but only out of morbid curiosity.'

- 'I would not allow this employee to breed.'

- 'This young lady has delusions of adequacy.'

- 'He certainly takes a long time to make his pointless.'

- 'He's been working with glue too much.'

- 'He brings a lot of joy whenever he leaves the room.'

- 'She has a photographic memory, but with the lens cover glued on.'

- 'Donated his brain to science before he was done using it.'

- 'If he were any more stupid, he'd have to be watered twice a week.'

- 'If you stand close enough to him, you can hear the ocean.'

- 'One neuron short of a synapse.'

- 'Takes him two hours to watch *60 minutes*.'

- 'The wheel is turning, but the hamster is dead.'

TRANSLATION IN ADVERTISEMENTS

The Dairy Association's huge success with the campaign 'Got Milk?' prompted them to expand advertising to Mexico. It was soon brought to their attention that the Spanish translation read 'Are you lactating?'

Coors put its slogan, 'Turn It Loose,' into Spanish, where it was read as 'Suffer from Diarrhoea'.

Scandinavian vacuum manufacturer Electrolux used the following in an American campaign, 'Nothing sucks like an Electrolux'.

Clairol introduced the 'Mist Stick', a curling iron, into Germany only to find out that mist is slang for manure. Not too many people had use for the 'Manure Stick'.

When Gerber started selling baby food in Africa, they used the same packaging as in the US, with the smiling baby on the label. Later they learned that in Africa, companies routinely put pictures on the label of what's inside, since many people can't read.

Colgate introduced a toothpaste in France called Cue, the name of a notorious porno magazine.

An American T-shirt maker in Miami printed shirts for the Spanish market which promoted the Pope's visit. Instead of 'I Saw the Pope' *(el Papa)*, the shirts read 'I Saw the Potato' *(la papa)*.

Pepsi's 'Come Alive with the Pepsi Generation' translated into 'Pepsi Brings Your Ancestors Back from the Grave' in Chinese.

Frank Perdue's chicken slogan, 'It takes a strong man to make a tender chicken' was translated into Spanish as 'It takes an aroused man to make a chicken affectionate.'

When American Airlines wanted to advertise its new leather first class seats in the Mexican market, it translated its 'Fly in Leather' campaign literally, which meant 'Fly Naked' *(vuela en cuero)* in Spanish.

Hunt-Wesson introduced Big John products in French Canada as Gros Jos. Later they found out that in slang this means 'big breasts'.

Bank Caixa Econômica Federal in Brazil offered 'Hot Money' in an advertisement in English, obviously unaware of the fact that hot money means stolen money in normal slang.

The Coca-Cola name in China was first read as *Kekoukela*, meaning 'Bite the Wax Tadpole' or 'Female Horse Stuffed with Wax', depending on the dialect. Coke then researched 40 000 characters to find a phonetic equivalent *kokou kole*, translating into 'happiness in the mouth.'

When Parker Pen marketed a ball-point pen in Mexico, its ads were supposed to have read, 'It won't leak in your pocket and embarrass you.' The company thought that the word *embarazar* (to impregnate) meant to embarrass, so the ad read, 'It won't leak in your pocket and make you pregnant'.

DESERTED ISLANDS

These deserted islands sure have a lot of passing traffic.

A man a dog and a sheep are stranded on an island with no food or water, nothing. Months have passed and there is no hope of them ever getting off this island; they are pretty much going to die there. One night, as they all go to sleep, the man quietly gets up and moves close to the sheep and puts his arm round it. He then carefully flips the sheep onto its stomach, pulls his pants down, and flopps his dick out. Suddenly, the dog gets up and starts barking at the man and scares him away from the sheep. The days and nights pass and the more the man tries to have sex with the sheep, the more the dog scares him off. One morning they all go for a walk along the beach looking for ships and boats. Suddenly, the man hears screaming coming from the sea. He looks over at the water and sees a woman drowning a few metres from shore, so he rushes down, dives in and saves the helpless women, and brings her back to the beach. The man looks at the woman and realises that she is very, very hot. She has big boobs, a hot arse and sexy legs.

The woman says to the man, 'You saved my life, anything you want I'll do, anything.'

The man thinks for a while and finally says, 'You couldn't take the dog for a walk, could you?'

A man and his wife have been stranded on a deserted island for many years. One day another man washes up on shore. The new man and the wife are very attracted to each other right away, but realise certain protocols must be observed. The husband, however, is very glad to see the second man.

'Now we will be able to have three people doing eight hour shifts in the watchtower, rather than two people doing twelve-hour shifts.'

The new man is only too happy to help and volunteers to do the first shift. He climbs up the tower and is soon standing watch. Soon the husband and wife start placing stones in a circle to make a fire to cook supper. The second man yells down, 'Hey, no screwing!'

They yell back, 'We're not screwing!'

A few minutes later they start to put driftwood into the stone circle. Again the second man yells down, 'Hey, no screwing!'

Again they yell back, 'We're not screwing!'

Later they are putting palm leaves on the roof of their shack to patch leaks. Once again the second man yells down, 'Hey, I said no screwing!'

They yell back, 'We're not screwing!'

Finally the shift is over so the second man climbs down from the tower and the husband starts to climb up. He's not even halfway up before the wife and the second man are screwing each other's brains out.

The husband looks out from the tower and says, 'Son-of-a-gun. From up here it *does* look like they're screwing.'

GOVERNMENT

Whether it's the taxation department, local government or the highest office in the land, there are plenty of laughs to be had in government. Unfortunately, the laughs are usually unintended.

A new tax inspector is eager to make a name for himself. So he decides to review the tax returns of the local synagogue. He interrogates the rabbi, asking him what the synagogue does with the wax drippings from the Shabbat, Havdallah and Chanukah candles. The rabbi, pleased to show the inspector that nothing goes to waste, responds that the used wax is collected and sent to a candle factory, which in turn sends the temple new candles.

'What about the crumbs from the matzo you eat at Passover?' asks the inspector.

'Simple,' the rabbi responds. 'We collect all the crumbs, send them to the matzo bakery and they send us matzo meal.'

'All right,' says the inspector, refusing to give up. 'I know that you're a mohel as well as a rabbi. What do you do with the leftovers from the circumcisions?'

'Easy,' says the rabbi. 'We send them to the tax office and they send us little pricks like you.'

President George W. Bush is visiting an elementary school and spends time in one of the classrooms. The children are in the middle of a discussion related to words and their meanings. The teacher asks the president if he would like to lead the class in the discussion of the word, 'tragedy'. So the illustrious leader asks the class for an example of a tragedy.

One little boy stands up and offers, 'If my best friend, who lives next door, is playing in the street and a car comes along and runs him over, that would be a tragedy.'

'No,' says Bush, 'that would be an accident.'

A little girl raises her hand, 'If a school bus carrying fifty children drove off a cliff, killing everyone involved, that would be a tragedy.'

'I'm afraid not,' explains Mr President. 'That's what we would call a great loss.'

The room goes silent. No other children volunteer. President Bush searches the room.

'Isn't there someone here who can give me an example of a tragedy?'

Finally, in the back of the room, a small boy raises his hand. In a quiet voice he says, 'If Air Force One, carrying Mr and Mrs Bush, was struck by a missile and blown up to smithereens, by a terrorist like Osama bin Laden, that would be a tragedy.'

'Fantastic,' exclaims Bush, 'that's right. And can you tell me why that would be a tragedy?'

'Well,' says the boy, 'because it wouldn't be an accident, and it certainly wouldn't be a great loss.'

The Queen of England and George W. Bush are riding in the royal carriage down Pall Mall chatting politely when one of the horses breaks wind. The smell is terrible and both the Queen and President Bush are too embarrassed to say anything until the Queen has to break the awkward silence.

'Mr President, I'm so terribly sorry. As you now realise, there are some things over which even the Queen of England has no control.'

Very graciously, President Bush replies, 'Think nothing of it Your Majesty. If you had not said anything, I would have thought it was the horse.'

George W. Bush and Dick Cheney go out to dinner. The waitress asks them what they would like to order. After looking at the menu, Cheney says he would like a piece of prime rib with all the trimmings, and Bush says he would like a quickie. At that, the waitress storms off, shouting over her shoulder how she thought all that horrible behaviour and language was over, now that Bush was president.

So, Bush sits there, looking confused, and Cheney leans over and says, 'Uh, Mr President, that's pronounced "quiche".'

A man is required to report to the taxation department. He asks his accountant for advice on what to wear.

'Wear your shabbiest clothing. Let them think you are a pauper,' says the accountant.

Then he asks his lawyer the same question, but gets the opposite advice.

'Do not let them intimidate you. Wear your most elegant suit and tie,' says his lawyer.

Confused, the man goes to his priest, tells him of the conflicting advice, and requests some resolution of the dilemma.

'Let me tell you a story,' replies the priest. 'A woman, about to be married, asks her mother what to wear on her wedding night.

"Wear a heavy, long, flannel nightgown that goes right up to your neck," she says.

But when she asks her best friend, she gets conflicting advice,

"Wear your most sexy negligee, with a V neck right down to your navel."'

The man protests, 'What does all this have to do with my problem with the taxation department?'

'No matter what you wear,' replies the priest. 'You're going to get screwed.'

RELIGION

*The world of humour would be much the poorer
without priests, rabbis and other religious figures.
And if you ever get the chance to see God perform,
don't miss it. I hear he does a terrific stand-up routine.*

One day in the synagogue, the rabbi is conducting prayers when he hears an argument going on at the back. Yossi and Jacob are involved in a heated discussion.

'Jacob I tell you, black is a colour.'

'No Yossi, black is no colour.'

'Yes, black is a colour!'

The rabbi steps in. 'What is this? We are conducting prayers here and you two are waking the dead. Have a little respect, no?'

'We are sorry Rabbi,' says Yossi, 'but it is a most important question. Dear Rabbi, we know you are a man of great education. You are a teacher of our community. Can you tell us please, is black a colour?'

So the rabbi stops to consider this. 'Well brothers, I can't give you the number or name of the appropriate scripture just now, but yes, I am sure that we Jews believe that black is a colour. Now, may I get back to the prayers?'

And he returns to reading the prayers. Soon he hears another argument from the back of the synagogue.

'White is a colour.'

'No, White is no colour!'

Again, the rabbi steps in. 'Jacob, Yossi, what are you doing? We are in a synagogue trying to pray to our God, the saviour, and you two are still arguing! My friends, please! Stop this.'

'We are sorry Rabbi, truly sorry,' says Yossi again. 'But we have an extremely important question and we must seek your advice. Please Rabbi, can you tell us, is white a colour?'

So the rabbi, trying to maintain his patience with these two, looks for an answer.

'God help me. Yes,' he says, 'white is a colour too. God has also given us white as a colour. Now gentlemen, please, I beg you. May I continue with the prayers?'

He begins again when he hears Yossi say to Jacob, 'You see Jacob? No question, you can trust me. I sold you a colour TV.'

A priest is walking past a pub when he sees a small boy drinking beer and smoking a Cuban cigar. The priest is shocked to the core.

'Why aren't you in school?' he asks the boy.

''Cause I'm only four.'

A man is driving down a deserted stretch of highway when he notices a sign out of the corner of his eye.
It reads: 'Sisters of Mercy House of Prostitution – 10km.'

He thinks it is just a figment of his imagination and drives on without a second thought. Soon, he sees another sign which says: 'Sisters of Mercy House of Prostitution – 5km.'

He realises that these signs are for real. Then he drives past a third sign saying: 'Sisters of Mercy House of Prostitution – Next Right.'

His curiosity gets the best of him and he pulls into the drive. On the far side of the parking lot is a sombre stone building with a small sign next to the door reading: 'Sisters of Mercy'.

He climbs the steps and rings the bell. The door is answered by a nun in a long black habit who asks, 'What may we do for you, my son?'

He answers, 'I saw your signs along the highway, and was interested in possibly doing business.'

'Very well, my son. Please follow me.'

He is led through many winding passages and is soon quite disoriented. The nun stops at a closed door, and tells the man, 'Please knock on this door.'

He does as he is told and the door is answered by another nun in a long habit, holding a tin cup. This nun instructs, 'Please place $50 in the cup, then go through the large wooden door at the end of this hallway.'

He gets $50 out of his wallet and places it in the second nun's cup. He trots eagerly down the hall and slips through the door, pulling it shut behind him. As the door locks behind him, he finds himself back in the parking lot, facing another small sign: 'Go in Peace, You Have Just Been Screwed by the Sisters of Mercy.'

Before they can be ordained, three young men have to undergo an ordeal which will test the chastity of their thoughts. Ordered by a priest to strip, the trio have rubber bands fastened to their private parts and are ushered into a bedroom where a beautiful girl lies naked on the bed.

After a few moments there is a loud *boing!* The first seminarian is told to go to the showers to cool his ardour.

A moment later there is a second loud *boing!* The owner of that rigid member is also sent to the showers.

Minutes pass, and when nothing happened to the third aspiring clergyman, he is congratulated by the priest.

'Well done, my son,' he enthuses. 'Now go and join the others in the shower.'

Boing!

An elderly doctor and a Baptist minister are seated next to each other on a plane. The plane is delayed on the ground due to some technical problems. Just after taking off, the pilot offers his apologies to the passengers and announces that a round of free drinks will be served.

When the charming flight attendant comes round with her trolley, the doctor orders a gin and tonic for himself. The flight attendant then asks the minister whether he wants anything.

He replies, 'Oh No! Thank you. I would rather commit adultery than drink alcohol.'

The elderly doctor promptly hands his gin and tonic back to the flight attendant and says, 'Madam, I did not know there was a choice.'

One morning the Pope awakes in his bed chamber in the Vatican. To his surprise, he notices that he has woken up with a massive erection. Perplexed, he calls on his personal physician.

'Doctor, this should not be possible,' he says, 'I'm the Pope, and I'm celibate! I haven't had one of these for thirty years!'

The doctor replies, 'Well, father, this is a natural phenomenon for all men, and it will happen even to you from time to time.'

The Pope exclaims, 'But you must do something about this. I have Mass in an hour, and this thing isn't going away.'

The doctor replies, 'You have two options. Either I can administer an injection to your penis to make the problem go away, which will hurt and make you feel ill, or you can make love to a woman.'

The Pope says, 'No, I do not want the injection, so get me a nun. But there are three considerations. First, she must be blind so she cannot see who does this thing to her. Second, she must be deaf so she cannot hear who does this thing to her. Third, she's gotta have really big tits.'

Three nuns have been behaving very well, so the mother superior says to them, 'Look sisters you have all behaved really well lately and just for that I want you three to go out and do something bad for a change.'

The first nun comes back and says, 'I robbed a bank.'

The mother superior says, 'That's alright dear, just take a sip from the holy water now.'

The second nun comes back and says, 'I stole a car.'

The mother superior says, 'That's alright dear, just take a sip from the holy water now.'

The third nun comes back and says, 'I pissed in the holy water.'

Two nuns are riding their rickety old bikes down the bumpy back streets of Rome late one summer afternoon. It starts getting quite dark and the two nuns are a little nervous.

The younger nun steers her bicycle closer to the older nun and says, 'You know, I've never come this way before.'

The older nun nods her head knowingly and says, 'It's the cobblestones.'

Four Catholic women are having coffee. The first Catholic woman tells her friends, 'My son is a priest. When he walks into a room, everyone calls him "Father".'

The second Catholic woman chirps, 'My son is a bishop. Whenever he walks into a room, people call him "Your Grace".'

The third Catholic crone says, 'My son is a cardinal. Whenever he walks into a room, he's called "Your Eminence"'.

Since the fourth Catholic woman sips her coffee in silence, the first three women give her a subtle 'Well . . .?'

So she replies, 'My son is six foot two, has plenty of money, broad square shoulders, is terribly handsome, dresses very well, has a tight muscular body, tight hard buns and a very nice bulge. And whenever he walks into a room women gasp, "Oh, my Lord!"'

An Amish woman and her daughter are riding in an open buggy one cold, blustery January day.

The daughter says to the mother, 'My hands are freezing cold.'

The mother replies, 'Put your hands between your legs. The body heat will warm them up.'

So the daughter does, and her hands warm up. The next day, the daughter is riding in the buggy with her boyfriend.

The boyfriend says, 'My hands are freezing cold.'

The daughter says, 'Put them between my legs, the body heat will warm them up.'

The next day, the boyfriend is driving in the buggy with the daughter.

He says, 'My nose is freezing cold.'

The daughter says, 'Put it between my legs. It will warm up.'

He does, and his nose warms up. The next day, the boyfriend is driving again with the daughter and he says, 'My penis is frozen solid.'

The daughter says, 'Put it between my legs, the body heat will warm it up.'

The next day, the daughter is driving in the buggy with her mother, and she says to her mother, 'Have you ever heard of a penis?'

The slightly concerned mother says, 'Sure, why do you ask?'

The daughter says, 'Well, they make one hell of a mess when they thaw out.'

Adam is walking around the Garden of Eden feeling very lonely, so God asks him, 'What is wrong with you?'

Adam tells God he doesn't have anyone to talk to.

God says, 'And that's a problem? OK, I'll find you some company. This company will cook for you day and night, wash your clothes and keep the garden in order; will bear your children and never ask you to get up in the middle of the night to take care of them; will not nag you, will always be the first to admit being wrong when you've had a disagreement and will always agree with every decision you make. The company will never have a headache, and will freely give you sex, love and compassion whenever needed. But it's going to be expensive Adam. It's going to cost you an arm and a leg.'

'An arm and a leg?' says Adam. 'Wow.'

He thinks for a few seconds, then asks, 'Well, what can I get for just a rib?'

God is just about done creating the universe. He has a couple of left-over things in his bag of creations, so he stops by to visit Adam and Eve in the Garden of Eden. He tells the couple that one of the things he has to give away is the ability to stand up and pee.

'It's a very handy thing,' God tells the couple, who he finds hanging around under an apple tree. 'I was wondering if either one of you wanted that ability?'

Adam pops a cork. He jumps up and begs, 'Oh, give that to me! I'd love to be able to do that! It seems the sort of thing a man should do. Oh please, oh please, oh please, let me have that ability. I'd be so great! When I'm working in the garden or naming the animals, I could just let it rip, I'd be so cool. Oh please, God, let it be me who you give that gift to, let me stand and pee, oh please!'

On and on he goes like an excited little boy. Eve just smiles and shakes her head at the display. She tells God that if Adam really wants it so badly, and it sure seems to be the sort of thing that will make him happy, she really doesn't mind if Adam is the one given the ability to stand up and pee. And so God gives Adam this gift. And it is . . . well, good.

'Fine,' God says, looking back into his bag of left-over gifts. 'What's left here for you Eve? Oh yes, multiple orgasms.'

One day in the Garden of Eden, Eve calls out to God, 'Lord, I have a problem!'

'What's the problem, Eve?'

'Lord, I know you've created me and have provided this beautiful garden and all of these wonderful animals, and that hilarious comedic snake, but I'm just not happy.'

'Why is that, Eve?' comes the reply from above.

'Lord, I am lonely. And I'm sick to death of apples.'

'Well, Eve, in that case, I have a solution. I shall create a man for you.'

'What's a "man", Lord?'

'This man will be a flawed creature, with aggressive tendencies, an enormous ego and an inability to empathise or listen to you properly. All in all, he'll give you a hard time. But, he'll be bigger, faster and more muscular than you. He'll also need your advice to think properly. He'll be really good at fighting and kicking a ball about, hunting fleet-footed ruminants, and not altogether bad in the sack.'

'Sounds great,' says Eve, with an ironically raised eyebrow. 'What's the catch, Lord?'

'Well, you can have him on one condition.'

'What's that, Lord?'

'You'll have to let him believe that I made him first.'

A minister dies and is waiting in line at the pearly gates. Ahead of him is a guy who's dressed in sunglasses, a loud shirt, leather jacket and jeans.

St Peter addresses this guy, 'Who are you, so that I may know whether or not to admit you to the kingdom of heaven?'

The guy replies, 'I'm Joe Cohen, taxi-driver.'

St Peter consults his list. He smiles and says to the taxi-driver, 'Take this silken robe and golden staff and enter the kingdom of heaven.'

The taxi-driver goes into heaven with his robe and staff, and it's the minister's turn.

He stands erect and booms out, 'I am Joseph Snow, pastor of Saint Mary's for the last forty-three years.'

St Peter consults his list. He says to the minister, 'Take this cotton robe and wooden staff and enter the kingdom of heaven.'

'Just a minute,' says the minister. 'That man was a taxi-driver and he gets a silken robe and golden staff. How can this be?'

'Up here, we work by results,' says St Peter. 'While you preached, people slept; while he drove, people prayed.'

Bill Gates dies and is up at the pearly gates. St Peter says to him, 'Well, you've got a choice. Have a look around here. Pop down to hell and see what Satan has to offer. Check us out, and then let me know your decision.'

Bill has a look around heaven. There are lots of people singing hymns and praising the Lord. He goes down to hell. There are beautiful beaches, lots of sun, sand and attractive women. He loves it.

He goes back to St Peter and says, 'Look, I know you're really doing good things here, but hell seems more with it. More my kind of scene, you know what I mean? No hard feelings, but I pick hell.'

'No worries. You've got it.'

Bill finds himself back in hell, neck deep in fire and brimstone, suffering eternal torment. He can't work it out.

'Hey! St Peter!' he yells. 'Where have all the beautiful girls and long beaches gone?'

'Sorry if you got confused,' says St Peter. 'That was just the demo version.'

A guy dies and reports immediately at the gates of heaven and St Peter says, 'In checking our records, I find that you have never done anything outstanding enough to get you into heaven.'

'What do you mean?' the guy asks. 'What about when I came to the aid of the little old man who was being pushed around by those motorcycle thugs?'

Obviously impressed, St Peter looks though the record books again. Finding nothing, he says, 'You did that?'

The guy says, 'Yes, I kicked over a couple of bikes and told them to pick on someone their own size.'

St Peter is puzzled. He says, 'There is absolutely no record of it. When did it happen?'

'Oh, about ten minutes ago.'

An attractive young woman with raven-black hair and wide eyes approaches the gates of heaven.

Looking her over, St Peter says, 'And may I ask, young lady, if you are a virgin?'

'I am,' is her demure reply.

Not wanting to appear distrustful but having to be cautious, St Peter calls over an angel to examine her. Several minutes later the angel returns.

'She's a virgin,' the angel states, 'though I'm obliged to inform you that she does have seven small dents in her maidenhead.'

Thanking the angel, St Peter takes his place behind the ledger and faces the girl.

'Well, miss, we're going to admit you. What is your name?'

She replies sweetly, 'Snow White.'

St Peter is manning the pearly gates when forty people from New York City show up. Never having seen anyone from the Big Apple at heaven's door, St Peter says he will have to check with God. After hearing the news, God instructs him to admit the ten most virtuous people from the group.

A few minutes later, St Peter returns to God breathless and says, 'They're gone!'

'What? All of the New Yorkers are gone?' asks God.

'No!' replies St Peter. 'The pearly gates.'

Four nuns all die together. They are lined up at the pearly gates being asked a series of questions by St Peter.

The last question asked is, 'Have you ever touched a penis?'

The first nun replies, 'Once, with the tip of my finger.'

St Peter tells her to dip her finger in holy water, then she can pass into heaven.

The second nun replies, 'Once, I held one in my hand.'

St Peter tells her to place her hand into holy water, then she can pass into heaven.

Suddenly, the nun that's standing fourth in line pushes ahead of the nun who had been third in line. St Peter asks her why she has done such a thing.

She replies, 'St Peter, if you think I'm going to gargle that holy water after she sits her arse in it, you're crazy.'

Jesus is strolling through heaven when he sees an old man sitting on a cloud, staring disconsolately into the distance.

'Old man,' says Jesus, 'this is heaven! Why are you so sad?'

The old man doesn't bother to turn as he says, 'I've been looking for my son and haven't been able to find him.'

Jesus says, 'Tell me about it.'

'Well,' says the old man, still gazing at the sunlit horizon, 'on earth I was a carpenter, and one day my son went away. I never heard from him again, and I was hoping I'd find him here, in heaven.'

His heart pounding suddenly in his chest, Jesus bends over the old man and says, 'Father?'

The old man turns and cries, 'Pinocchio?'

A guy goes to hell and is met by the devil who explains that the punishments of the inmates are changed every thousand years and he is to select his first punishment. The first room has a young guy on the wall being whipped. The new guy is not keen on this and asks to see the next room.

The next room has a middle-aged guy being tortured with fire.

The new guy immediately asks to see the third room. It has a really old guy chained to the wall getting a blow job from a gorgeous blonde. The guy jumps at the chance and selects that room.

The devil walks into the room taps the blonde on the shoulder and says, 'OK, you can stop now. You've been relieved.'

A cowboy dies and, as he was a bad fellow, he goes straight down to hell. When he gets down there the devil is waiting.

The devil says, 'You have three choices for ways to spend your eternity. Do you pick door number one, two or three?'

The cowboy says, 'Let me check what's behind door number one.'

The door opens and he sees hundreds of people standing on their heads on a wood floor.

'I don't want this,' he says, 'let's try door number two'

The door opens and he sees hundreds of people standing on their heads on a hard cement floor.

'Woah! I don't want to spend the rest of my life like that! What's behind door number three?'

The door opens and he sees hundreds of people drinking coffee, and having a good time, but they are all up to their knees in horse poo.

'I'm a cowboy, I'm used to horse dung. I'll go with door number three,' he says.

The devil hands him a cup of coffee and introduces him to the crowd and leaves him to it.

After ten minutes, the devil comes back in and says, 'Coffee break's over. Everybody back on their heads.'

F orrest Gump dies and goes to heaven. The gates are closed, however, and Forrest approaches the gatekeeper. It is St Peter himself.

'Well, Forrest, it's certainly good to see you. We have heard a lot about you. It's now our policy to administer an entrance examination which you must pass before you can get into heaven,' says St Pete.

'Nobody ever told me about any entrance exams,' says Forrest. 'Sure hope the test ain't too hard; life was a big enough test as it was. But I guess, like Mama always used to say, the test will be like a box of chocolates – you never know what you've got until you take a bite. So dish her up to me now. I'm a-ready, St Pete.'

'The test I have for you is only three questions. The first one is, 'What days of the week begin with the letter 'T'? Second, how many seconds are there in a year?, and third, what is God's first name? Take your time, think about it and come back to me when you reckon that you have the answers.'

Forrest goes away to think the questions over. He returns the next day.

St Peter waves him up and asks, 'Now that you have had a chance to think the questions over, tell me your answers.'

Forrest says, 'Well, the first one, how many days of the week begin with the letter 'T'? Shucks, that one's easy. That'd be today and tomorrow!'

The saint's eyes open wide and he exclaims, 'Forrest! That's not what I was thinking, but, you do have a point, and I guess I didn't specify, so I give you credit for that answer. How about the next one. How many seconds in a year?'

'Now that one's harder,' says Forest. 'But, I thunk and thunk about that, and I guess the only answer can be twelve.'

Astounded, St Peter says, 'Twelve! Twelve! Forrest, how in heaven's name could you come up with twelve seconds in a year?'

Forrest says, 'Shucks, there gotta be twelve: January second, February second, March second –'

'Hold it,' interrupts St Peter. 'I see where you're going with it. And I guess I see your point, though that wasn't quite what I had in mind. But I'll give you credit for that one too. Let's go on with the next and final question. Can you tell me God's first name?'

Forrest says, 'Well sure, I know God's first name. Everybody probably knows it. It's Howard.'

'Howard?' asks St Peter. 'What makes you think it's Howard?'

Forrest answers, 'It's in the prayer.'

'The prayer?' asks St Peter. 'Which prayer?'

'The Lord's Prayer,' responds Forest: 'Our Father, who art in heaven, Howard be thy name . . .'

Four priests board a train for a long journey to a church council conference. Shortly into the trip, one priest says 'Well, we've all worked together for many years, but don't really know one another. I suggest we tell each other one of our sins to get better acquainted.'

They look nervously at each other but nod OK.

The first priest says, 'Since I suggested it, I'll go first. With me it's the drink. Once a year I take off my collar and go out of town to a pub and drink myself blind for a few days. Get it out of my system.'

They all look at each other again nervously, but the next priest slowly starts, 'Well, with me, it's the gambling. Periodically, I nick the money out of the poor box and go to the races. Spend it all! But I get it out of my system.'

The third, who is really nervous now reluctantly says, 'This is very difficult. My sin is worse. I take off my collar and go into the red light district, pick out a lass, and spend a week in the saddle. But I really get it out of my system.'

They all look at the fourth priest, waiting, but he doesn't say anything.

One of the others speaks up, 'Come now, we've all told our innermost faults. It's your turn.'

He looks at the others and starts hesitantly 'Well, I'm an inveterate gossip, and I can't wait to get off this train!'

Once upon a time in the kingdom of heaven, God went missing for seven days. Eventually, Michael the Archangel found him.

He inquired of God, 'Where have you been?'

God sighed a deep sigh of satisfaction and proudly pointed downwards through the clouds; 'Look son, look what I have made.'

Archangel Michael looked puzzled and said, 'What is it?'

God replied, 'It's another planet but I'm after putting life on it. I've named it Earth and there's going to be a balance between everything on it. For example, there's North America and South America. North America is going to be rich and South America is going to be poor, and the narrow bit joining them – that's going to be a hot spot. Now look over here. I've put a continent of whites in the north and another one of blacks in the south.'

And then the archangel said, 'And what's that green dot there?'

And God said 'Ahhh that's the Emerald Isle – that's a very special place. That's going to be the most glorious spot on earth; beautiful mountains, lakes, rivers, streams, and an exquisite coastline. These people here are going to be great characters, and they're going to be found travelling the world. They'll be playwrights and poets and singers and songwriters. And I'm going to give them this black liquid which they're going to go mad on, and for which people will come from the far corners of the earth to imbibe. Michael the Archangel gasped in wonder and admiration. But then, seemingly startled, he proclaimed: 'Hold on a second, what about the balance? You said there was going to be a balance.'

God replied wisely. 'Wait until you see the neighbours I'm going to give them.'

Three men die in a car accident on Christmas Eve. They all find themselves at the pearly gates waiting to enter heaven. Here St Peter greets them and tells them that if they wish to enter into heaven they must present something 'Christmassy'.

The first man searches his pockets, and finds some pine needles from the family's Christmas tree. He is let in.

The second man presents a bow and some ribbon, from presents that were opened earlier in that night. So he is also allowed in.

The third man pulls out a pair of black lace panties.

Confused at this last offering, St Peter says in a booming voice, 'I fail to see the relevance. How do these represent Christmas?'

To which the third man sheepishly replies, 'Oh, they're Carol's.'

Father O'Malley, the new priest, is nervous about hearing confessions, so he asks the older priest to sit in on his sessions. The new priest hears a couple of confessions, and then the old priest asks him to step out of the confessional for a few suggestions.

The old priest suggests, 'Cross you arms over your chest, and rub your chin with one hand.'

The new priest tries this and achieves a concerned, thoughtful look.

The old priest says, 'Good. Now try saying things like, "I see, yes, go on, I understand" and "how did you feel about that?"'

The new priest tries saying those things and sounds caring and compassionate.

The old priest says, 'Wonderful! Now, don't you think that's a little better than slapping your knee and saying "No shit? What happened next?"'

A man sick of the outside world decided to join a monastery in Tibet. One of the stipulations for acceptance into this most holy order was that he was only permitted to say two words every five years.

For the first five years he eats rice, sleeps on a wooden bed, and has only one blanket with holes in it. He tends to the fields and looks after livestock everyday.

After five years the head monk comes to him and says he can use his two words to which he replies, 'More blankets.'

Now the man is warm at night on his wooden bed with all his blankets but still he only eats rice and tends to the fields and livestock everyday.

Another five years pass and the head monk comes to him again and says that he can use two more words.

He replies, 'More food.'

He now sleeps on his wooden bed with all his blankets and eats gourmet food every day but he still has to tend to the fields and livestock.

Another five years passes and the head monk comes again to him and says, 'You may use two words now.'

The man replies, 'I'm leaving.'

'Good,' said the head monk, 'all you've done is bloody complain since you got here.'

Jeff and Mike are killed in an accident and as Jeff arrives at the pearly gates, he is met by St Peter.

'Where's my friend Mike?' Jeff asks the old Saint.

St Peter replies, 'Mike wasn't as fortunate as you, instead of heaven, he went in the other direction.'

Jeff is deeply concerned by this and asks, 'Well, could I see Mike just one more time?'

St Peter agrees to this, so they walk over to the edge of heaven and look down. Jeff sees Mike down in hell with a sexy blonde on one side of him and a keg of beer on the other.

'I really don't mean to complain,' Jeff says, 'but Mike seems to be having a pretty nice time down in hell.'

'Look a little closer,' says St Peter. 'The keg has a hole in it, and the blonde doesn't.'

One day Mrs Jones went to have a talk with the minister at the local church.

'Reverend,' she said, 'I have a problem, my husband keeps falling asleep during your sermons. It's very embarrassing. What should I do?'

'I have an idea,' said the minister. 'Take this hat-pin with you. I will be able to tell when Mr Jones is sleeping, and I will motion to you at specific times. When I motion, you give him a good poke in the leg.'

In church the following Sunday, Mr Jones dozed off. Noticing this, the preacher put his plan to work.

'And who made the ultimate sacrifice for you?' he said, nodding to Mrs Jones.

'Jesus!' Jones cried, as his wife jabbed him the leg with the hat-pin.

'Yes, you are right, Mr Jones,' said the minister.

Soon, Mr Jones nodded off again. Again, the minister noticed.

'Who is your redeemer?' he asked the congregation, motioning towards Mrs Jones.

'Oh God!' Mr Jones cried out, as he was stuck again with the hat-pin.

'Right again,' said the minister, smiling.

Before long, Mr Jones again winked off. However, this time the minister did not notice. As he picked up the tempo of his sermon, he made a motion that Mrs Jones mistook as the signal to bayonet her husband with the hat-pin again .

The minister asked, 'And what did Eve say to Adam after she bore him his 99th son?'

Mrs Jones poked her husband, who yelled, 'You stick that goddamned thing in me one more time and I'll break it in half and shove it up your arse!'

Three pastors and their wives were car-pooling their way back from a revival meeting when their van slid off the side of a cliff and sadly, they were all killed. They arrived at the pearly gates together. Peter called the first couple forward and began to examine the journal in which their life story was written. He looked up at the first preacher and spoke sharply.

'You hypocrite!' he boomed, 'All you ever cared about in your life was money! You've hoarded money all your life! You were the wealthiest person in your whole community. In fact, so smitten with money were you that you even went out and married a woman named Penny. Money is evil and will never buy you happiness!'

The preacher and his wife were obviously shaken and meekly cast their eyes down and were chastened.

But St Peter softened and said, 'Well, you did preach the gospel, so I won't send you off to hell but you can't come in the front gate. You must walk all the way around heaven and enter by the back door. Off you go!'

So the couple went shamefully on their way. St Peter then turned to the next pastor and his wife.

'All you ever talked and cared about was alcohol and where you would get your next drink! In fact, you have been drunk nearly every time you preached. You were so consumed with alcohol and drinking that you married a woman named Brandy!'

The pastor hung his head and nodded in shame.

'However, you too preached a powerful sermon, despite being drunk, so you have also been spared the everlasting flames of hell. Nevertheless, you have to walk all the way around heaven and enter in the back way. Off with you!'

The couple slowly shuffled off. He then turned his attention to the third and final couple, pointing an accusing finger at them. But, before he could begin to speak the pastor held up his hand in order to silence St Pete.

He turned to his wife and said, 'We'd better start walking, Fanny.'

Devil:	Why so miserable?
Larry:	What do you think? I'm in hell.
Devil:	Hell's not so bad. We actually have a lot of fun down here. You like a drink, Larry?
Larry:	Sure, I like a drink.
Devil:	Well you're going to love Mondays then. On Mondays that's all we do – drink. Beer, whisky, tequila, Guinness, wine coolers, diet drinks. We drink till we throw up and then we drink some more!
Larry:	Gee that sounds great.
Devil:	You a smoker?
Larry:	You better believe it! I love smoking.
Devil:	OK! You're going to love Tuesdays. On Tuesdays we get the finest Cuban cigars, and smoke our lungs out. If you get cancer – no problem – you're already dead, remember?
Larry:	Wow. That's awesome!
Devil:	I bet you like to gamble.
Larry:	Why, yes, as a matter of fact, I do. Love the gambling.
Devil:	Cause Wednesday you can gamble all you want. Blackjack, Roulette, Poker, Slots, Craps, whatever. If you go bankrupt – who cares, you're dead anyhow.
Devil:	You into drugs?
Larry:	Are you kidding? I love drugs! You don't mean . . .
Devil:	I do! Thursday is drug day. Help yourself to a great big bowl of crack. Or smack. Smoke a bong the size of a submarine. You can do all the drugs you want and if you overdose, that's OK – you're dead – so, who cares! OD as much as you like!
Larry:	Gee whiz, I never realised that hell was such a great place!!
Devil:	See, now you're getting the hang of it! Now Larry, tell me, are you gay?
Larry:	Ah, no.

Devil: Ooooh. Well Larry, I'm afraid you're really gonna hate Fridays.

A wealthy farmer went to church one Sunday. After the service he said to the priest, 'Father, that was a damned good sermon you gave, damned good!'

'I'm happy you liked it,' said the priest. 'But I wish you wouldn't use those terms in expressing yourself.'

'I can't help it,' said the rich farmer. 'I still think it was a damned good sermon. In fact, I liked it so much I put $100 in the collection basket.'

'Holy shit, did you?' replied the priest.

The church service was under way and the collection plate was being passed around.

When the preacher saw a $100 bill in the plate, he was so surprised that he stopped the service and asked, 'Will whoever put the $100 bill in the plate, please stand up?'

A young, gay man in the congregation stood up.

The preacher told him, 'I am so impressed that you would donate such a large sum. Since you put that money in the plate I think that it is only fair that you should choose three hymns.'

Excitedly, the gay guy looked around, and said, 'Well, I'll take him and him and him.'

The good Lord decided to make a companion for Adam. He summoned St Peter to his side.

'My dear Peter,' he said. I have a little job for you. I want you to make a being who is similar to man, yet different, and one who can offer man comfort, companionship and pleasure. I will call this being "woman".'

So St Peter set about creating a being who was similar to man, yet was different in ways that would be appealing, and that could provide physical pleasure to man. When St Peter had finished creating this woman, he summoned the Lord to look at his work.

'Ah, St Peter, once again you have done an excellent job,' said the Lord.

'Thank You, O Great One' replied St Peter. 'I am now ready to provide the brain, nerve endings and senses to this being, this woman. However, I require your assistance on this matter, O Lord.'

'You shall make her brain, slightly smaller, yet more intuitive, more feeling, more compassionate, and more adaptable than man's,' said the Lord.

'What about the nerve endings?' said St Peter. 'How many will I put in her hands?'

'How many did we put in Adam?' asked the Lord.

'Two hundred, O Mighty One,' replied St Peter.

'Then we shall do the same for this woman,' said the Lord.

'And how many nerve endings shall we put in her feet?' enquired St Peter.

'How many did we put in Adam?' asked the Lord.

'Seventy five, O Mighty One,' replied St Peter.

'Do the same for woman,' said the Lord.

'OK. And how many nerve endings should we put in woman's genitals?' inquired St Peter.

'How many did we put in Adam?'

'Four hundred and twenty, O Mighty One,' replied St Peter.

'Do the same for woman, said the Lord. 'Actually, no wait. I've changed my mind. Give her 10,000. I want her to scream my name out loud when she's enjoying herself!'

An old rabbi, on seeing his son graduate from high school, wanted to know what the young man's plans were.

He called his son into his study and questioned him. 'Son, I vish to know, what kind of career are you going to have?'

The rabbi laid on a table three items, a $100 bill, a bottle of whisky and the good book.

He looked to the boy and said, 'Ve need to know your future. If you take the $100 bill, you will become a gambler, and that is very terrible. If you take the whisky, you will become a drunkard and that too is very, very bad. But . . . if you take the good book, you will become a rabbi, like you papa.'

The young lad's mind was blank. He was just out of high school and he did not yet know what he wanted to do with his life. After a few minutes of trying to think, he finally decided there was only one answer.

The boy took the $100 bill and put it in his pocket. He picked up the whisky in one hand and with the other grasped the good book, put it under his arm and quickly left the room.

The old rabbi was stunned. He could not understand what had just happened.

Then all of a sudden his eyes grew wide, he jumped to his feet, and slapping the side of his face he cried, 'Oi Vay . . . he is going to become a Catholic priest!'

God is talking to one of his angels.
He says, 'Boy, I just created a 24-hour period of alternating light and darkness on Earth.'

The angel says, 'What are you going to do now?'

God says, 'Call it a day.'

Two nuns are ordered to paint a room that is going to be redecorated in the convent for a visit by the pope. The last instruction from Mother Superior is that they must not get so much as a drop of paint on their habits. After conferring about this for a while, the two nuns decide to lock the door of the room, strip off their habits, and paint in the nude.

In the middle of the project, there is a knock at the door.

'Who is it?' calls one of the nuns.

'It's the blind man,' replies a voice from the other side of the door.

The two nuns look at each other and shrug, deciding that no harm can come from letting a blind man into the room. They open the door.

'Nice tits,' says the man, 'where do you want the blinds?'

The pope arrives in London for a meeting with Tony Blair. He is running late. As he comes out of the airline terminal he hails a cab.

He says to the Cockney cab-driver, 'I have to be at Number 10 in fifteen minutes.'

'Fifteen minutes, guv'nor? Leave it out. We're at Heathrow. This is London! It takes at least an hour. I can't do it!'

'Well, you get out and let me drive,' says the pope.

The cabbie is a bit taken back by this, but it's the pope, so he jumps into the back seat and the pope gets behind the wheel. The pope is enjoying the experience, flying along, dodging in and out of traffic, when he zooms past a policeman on a motorbike waiting in a side-street.

The cop jumps on his motorbike and pursues the speeding vehicle. Finally, he catches up with it, pulls it over, and asks the driver to wind down the window. When he sees who is driving, he gets on his radio.

'This is road patrol to base I need some help,' says the policeman.

'What's up?' asks headquarters.

'Well I've pulled someone over for speeding and he is obviously very important. What should I do?'

'How important is he? A local politician?' asks headquarters.

'No, bigger than that.'

'The Mayor of London?'

'No, bigger than that.'

'Michael Caine?'

'No, bigger than that.'

'Hell, not the prime minister?'

'No, bigger than that'

'Bigger than that?' asks headquarters in a bewildered tone, 'Bleedin hell, who is it?'

'I don't know,' replies the cop, 'but he's got the pope driving him around.'

Jesus walks into a Holiday Inn, tosses three nails on the counter and asks, 'Can you put me up for the night?'

Three nuns were driving down a highway one day when they lost control of their car and plunged off a cliff. They awoke and found themselves standing before the pearly gates.

St Peter walked toward them and, after greeting them, told them that they would have to answer one question each before they were admitted to the kingdom of heaven. This made the nuns very nervous. They had never heard of this requirement before.

Finally, one nun stepped forward and said, 'St Peter, I'm ready for my question.'

St Peter replied, 'Your question is: Who was the first man on Earth?'

The nun breathed a huge sigh of relief, and said, 'Why, it was Adam.'

The lights flashed, the bells tolled, and the gates of heaven opened. It was a cause of great relief to the others. The second stepped forward without hesitation.

St Peter said, 'And you must tell me who was the first woman on Earth.'

With another great sigh of relief, the nun replied, 'Eve.'

The lights flashed, the bells tolled, and the gates of heaven opened. The third nun was then brimming with excitement. 'I'm ready St Peter!'

St Peter said, 'All right, what was the first thing Eve said to Adam?'

The nun was shocked. 'My goodness, that's a hard one . . .'

The lights flashed, the bells tolled, and the gates of heaven opened.

Three women die together in an accident and go to heaven. When they get there, St Peter says, 'We only have one rule here in heaven, don't step on the ducks.'

So they enter heaven, and sure enough, there are ducks all over the place. It is almost impossible not to step on a duck, and although they try their best to avoid them, the first woman accidentally steps on one. Along comes St Peter with the ugliest man she ever saw.

St Peter chains them together and says 'Your punishment for stepping on a duck is to spend eternity chained to this ugly man!'

The next day, the second woman steps accidentally on a duck, and along comes St Peter, who doesn't miss a thing, and with him is another extremely ugly man. He chains them together with the same admonishment he gave to the first woman.

The third woman has observed all this and, not wanting to be chained for all eternity to an ugly man, is very, very careful where she steps. She manages to go months without stepping on any ducks, but one day St Peter comes up to her with the most handsome man she has ever laid eyes on. Very tall, long eyelashes, muscular and thin. St Peter chains them together without saying a word.

The woman remarks, 'I wonder what I did to deserve being chained to you for all of eternity?'

The guy says, 'I don't know about you, but I stepped on a duck!'

Jesus came across an adulteress crouching in a corner with a crowd around her preparing to stone her to death. He stopped the crowd and said, 'Let he who is without sin cast the first stone.'

Suddenly a woman at the back of the crowd fired off a stone at the adulteress.

Jesus looked over and said, 'Mother! Sometimes you really piss me off!'

As soon as she had finished convent school, a bright young girl named Lena shook the dust of Ireland off her shoes and made her way to New York where, before long, she became a successful performer in show business.

Eventually she returned to her home town for a visit and on a Saturday night she went to confession in the church that she had always attended as a child.

In the confessional Father Sullivan recognised her and began asking her about her work. She explained that she was an acrobatic dancer, and he wanted to know what that meant. She said she would be happy to show him the kind of thing she did on stage. She stepped out of the confessional and within sight of Father Sullivan, she went into a series of cartwheels, leaping splits, handsprings and back-flips.

Kneeling near the confessional, waiting their turn, were two middle-aged ladies. They witnessed Lena's acrobatics with wide eyes, and one said to the other: 'Will you just look at the penance Father Sullivan is giving out this night, and me without me bloomers on!'

Moses, returning from the mountain, spoke to his people: 'The good news is that we got them down to 10. The bad news is that adultery is still one of them.'

A proud Irishman named Pat went to heaven and met St Peter at the pearly gates.

St Peter asked, 'Who are you?' and Pat replied, 'My name is Pat, I'm an Irishman, born on St Patrick's Day, died on St Patrick's Day, while marching in the St Patrick's Day parade.'

St Peter said to Pat, 'Yes, this is true, and a worthy claim! Here's a little green cloud for you to drive around heaven in and here is a harp that, when you push this button here, will play When Irish Eyes Are Smiling. Enjoy it, Pat. Have a good time in heaven.'

Pat jumps on his little green cloud, punches the button, and heads out with a smile on his face and a song in his heart.

He's having a wonderful time in heaven, driving his little green cloud around, but on the third day, he's driving down Expressway H-1 with the harp playing full blast when, all of a sudden, a Jewish man in a pink and white two-tone cloud with tail fins roars past him. And in the back of this cloud is an organ which is playing all sorts of celestial music. Pat makes a U-turn right in the middle of the Heaven Expressway and charges back to the pearly gates.

He says, 'St Peter, my name is Pat, I'm a proud Irishman. I was born on St Patrick's Day, died on St Patrick's Day, marching in the St Patrick's Day parade. I come up here to heaven and I get this tiny, insignificant little green cloud and this little harp that plays only one song, When Irish Eyes Are Smiling. But, there's a Jew over there. He's got a big, beautiful pink and white two-tone cloud and a huge organ that plays all kinds of celestial music and I, Pat the Irishman, want to know why!'

St Peter stands up from his desk. He leans over and motions Pat to come closer. Then he says, 'Pat, shush! He's the boss' son!'

SCHOOLDAYS

Were our schooldays really this amusing?
I don't remember them this way. But then,
I was too busy studying.

For weeks a six-year-old lad keeps telling his first-grade teacher about the baby brother or sister that is expected at his house. One day his mother allows the boy to feel the movements of the unborn child in her belly. The six-year-old is obviously impressed, but makes no comment. Furthermore, he stops telling his teacher about the impending event.

The teacher finally sits the boy down and says, 'Tommy, whatever has become of that baby brother or sister you were expecting at home?'

Tommy bursts into tears and confesses, 'I think Mummy ate it!'

The first-grade teacher is starting a new lesson on multi-syllable words. She thinks it will be a good idea to ask a few of the children for examples of words with more than one syllable.

'Jane, do you know any multi-syllable words?'

After some thought Jane proudly replies, 'Monday.'

'Great Jane. That has two syllables, Mon . . . day. Does anyone know another word?'

'I do! I do!' replies Johnny.

Knowing Johnny's more mature sense of humour she picks Mike instead. 'OK Mike, what is your word.'

'Saturday,' says Mike.

'Great, that has three syllables.'

Not wanting to be outdone, Johnny says, 'I know a four-syllable word. Pick me! Pick me!'

Not thinking he can do any harm with a word that large the teacher reluctantly says, 'OK. Johnny what is your four-syllable word?'

Johnny proudly says, 'Mas . . . tur . . . ba . . . tion.'

Shocked, the teacher, trying to retain her composure says, 'Wow, Johnny. Four syllables! That's certainly is a mouthful.'

'No Ma'am, you're thinking of "blowjob", and that's only two syllables.'

Johnny is always saying that he is too smart for the first grade. He thinks he should at least be in the third grade. One day, his teacher has had enough. She takes Johnny to the principal's office and explains Johnny's request, while Johnny waits in the outer office. The principal tells Johnny's teacher that he will give the boy a test and if Johnny fails to answer any of the special questions he is to go back to the first grade and behave. The teacher agrees. Johnny is brought into the room. The principal tells Johnny his terms and Johnny agrees.

'What is three times three?' asks the principal.

'Nine,' replies Johnny.

'What's six times six?'

'Thirty-six.'

'What's nine times nine?'

'Eighty-one.'

And so it goes with every question the principal thinks a third-grader should know. Johnny appears to have a strong case.

The principal tells the teacher, 'I think Johnny can go on to the third grade.'

The teacher, knowing Little Johnny's tendency toward sexual wisecracks, says to the principal, 'Let me ask him some questions before we make that decision?'

The principal and Johnny both agree, Johnny with a sly look on his face.

The teacher begins by asking, 'What does a cow have four of that I have only two of?'

'Legs,' Johnny answers.

'What is in your pants that you have but I don't have?' asks the teacher.

The principal's eyes open wide! Before he can stop Johnny's expected answer, he says, 'Pockets.'

The principal breathes a sigh of relief and tells the teacher, 'I think we should put Johnny in the fifth grade. I missed the last two questions myself!'

A Teacher asks the children to discuss what their dads do for a living.

Mary says, 'My dad is a lawyer. He puts the bad guys in jail.'

Jack says, 'My dad is a doctor. He makes all the sick people better.'

All the kids in the class have their turn except Stevie.

Teacher says, 'Stevie, what does your dad do?'

Stevie says, 'My dad is dead.'

'I'm sorry to hear that, but what did he do before he died?'

'He turned blue and shat on the carpet.'

YOU'RE A SHOCKER!

The Smiths have no children and decide to use a proxy father to start their family. On the day the proxy father is to arrive, Mr Smith kisses his wife and says, 'I'm off. The man should be here soon.'

Half an hour later, just by chance, a door-to-door baby photographer rings the doorbell, hoping to make a sale.

'Good morning madam. You don't know me but I've come to –'

'Oh, no need to explain. I've been expecting you,' Mrs Smith cuts in.

'Really?' the photographer asks. 'Well, good! I've made a specialty of babies.'

'That's what my husband and I had hoped. Please come in and have a seat. Just where do we start?' asks Mrs Smith, blushing.

'Leave everything to me. I usually try two in the bathtub, one on the couch and perhaps a couple on the bed. Sometimes the living room floor is fun too; you can really spread out.'

'Bathtub, living room floor? No wonder it didn't work for Harry and me.'

'Well madam, none of us can guarantee a good one every time. But if we try several different positions and I shoot from six or seven angles, I'm sure you'll be pleased with the results.'

'I hope we can get this over with quickly,' gasps Mrs Smith.

'Madam, in my line of work, a man must take his time. I'd love to be in and out in five minutes, but you'd be disappointed with that, I'm sure.'

'Don't I know it!' Mrs Smith exclaims.

The photographer opens his briefcase and pulls out a portfolio of his baby pictures. 'This was done on the top of a bus in the middle of London.'

'Oh my god!' Mrs Smith exclaims, tugging at her handkerchief.

'And these twins turned out exceptionally well, when you consider their mother was so difficult to work with.' The photographer hands Mrs Smith the picture.

'She was difficult?' asks Mrs Smith.

'Yes, I'm afraid so. I finally had to take her to Hyde Park to get the job done right. People were crowding around four and five deep, pushing to get a good look.'

'Four and five deep?' asks Mrs Smith, eyes wide in amazement.

'Yes,' the photographer says. 'And for more than three hours too. The mother was constantly squealing and yelling. I could hardly concentrate. Then darkness approached and I began to rush my shots. Finally, when the squirrels began nibbling on my equipment I just packed it all in.'

Mrs Smith leans forward. 'You mean they actually chewed on your, er . . . um . . . ah . . . equipment?'

'That's right. Well madam, if you're ready, I'll set up my tripod so that we can get to work.'

'Tripod?' Mrs Smith looks extremely worried now.

'Oh yes, I have to use a tripod to rest my Canon on. It's much too big for me to hold while I'm getting ready for action. Madam? Madam? . . . Good Lord, she's fainted!'

A professor is sent to darkest Africa to live with a primitive tribe. He spends years with them, teaching them reading, writing, maths and science. One day the wife of the tribe's chief gives birth to a white child.

The members of the tribe are shocked, and the chief pulls the professor aside and says, 'Look here! You're the only white man we've ever seen and this woman gave birth to a white child. It doesn't take a genius to work out what happened!'

The professor thinks quickly, 'No, Chief. You're mistaken. What you have here is a natural occurrence . . . what we in the civilised world call an albino! Look at that field over there. All of the sheep are white except for one black one. Nature does this on occasion.'

The chief is silent for a moment, then says, 'Tell you what. You don't say anything more about the sheep and I won't say anything more about the baby.'

A construction worker on the third floor of a building needs a handsaw. He sees one of the labourers on the first floor and yells down to him, but the man indicates that he cannot hear. So, the guy on the third floor tries to use signals. He points to his eye meaning 'I' then at his knee meaning 'need' then he moves his hand back and forth meaning 'handsaw'.

The man on the first floor nods, then drops his pants and begins to masturbate. The man on the third floor freaks out and runs down to the first floor yelling, 'What the hell is wrong with you! Are you stupid or something? I was saying that I needed a handsaw!'

The labourer looks at the construction worker and says, 'I knew that, I was just trying to tell you that I was coming.'

After a few years of married life, a guy finds that he is unable to perform anymore. He goes to his doctor, and his doctor tries a few things but nothing works.

Finally the doctor says to him, 'This is all in your mind,' and refers him to a psychiatrist.

After a few visits to the shrink, the shrink confesses, 'I am at a loss as to how you can possibly be cured.' Finally the psychiatrist refers him to a witch doctor.

The witch doctor says, 'I can cure this,' and throws

some powder on a flame. There is a flash with billowing blue smoke.

The witch doctor says, 'This is powerful healing but you can only use it once a year! All you have to do is say "one, two, three" and it shall rise for as long as you wish!'

The guy then asks the witch doctor, 'What happens when it's over?'

The witch doctor says, 'All you or your partner has to say is "one, two, three, four" and it will go down. But be warned it will not work again for a year.'

The guy goes home and that night he is ready to surprise his wife with the good news.

So he is lying in bed with her and says, 'One, two, three.'

Suddenly he gets an erection.

His wife turns over and says, 'What did you say "one, two, three" for?'

A representative for a condom company is on her way to an international condom convention. While rushing through the airport, she drops the briefcase carrying her samples, scattering condoms across the floor. She notices a passer-by looking at her as she tries to get the condoms back into her briefcase.

'It's OK,' she says. 'I'm going to a convention.'

A beautiful woman loves growing tomatoes, but can't seem to get her tomatoes to turn red. One day while taking a stroll she comes upon a male neighbour who has the most beautiful garden full of huge red tomatoes.

The woman asks the man, 'What do you do to get your tomatoes so red?'

The man responds, 'Well, twice a day I stand in front of my tomato garden and expose myself, and my tomatoes turn red from blushing so much.'

Well, the woman is so impressed, she decides to try doing the same thing to her tomato garden to see if it works. So twice a day for two weeks she exposes herself to her garden hoping for the best.

One day the man is passing by and asks the woman, 'By the way, How did you make out? Did your tomatoes turn red?'

'No' she replies, 'but my cucumbers are enormous.'

While in the playground with his friend, Alex notices that Jimmy is wearing a brand new, shiny watch.

'Did you get that for your birthday?' asks Alex.

'Nope,' replies Jimmy.

'Well, did you get it for Christmas then?'

Again Jimmy says, 'Nope.'

'You didn't steal it, did you?' asks Alex.

'No,' says Jimmy. 'I went into mum and dad's bedroom the other night when they were "doing the nasty". Dad gave me his watch to get rid of me.'

Alex is extremely impressed with this idea, and extremely jealous of Jimmy's new watch. He vows to get one for himself. That night, he waits outside his parents' bedroom until he hears the unmistakable noises of lovemaking. Just then, he swings the door wide open and boldly strides into the bedroom.

His father, caught in mid-stroke, turns and says angrily, 'What do you want now?'

'I wanna watch,' Alex replies.

Without missing a stroke, his father says, 'Fine. Stand in the corner and watch, but keep quiet.'

A mother and father take their young son to the circus. When the elephants appear, the son is intrigued by them.

He turns to his mother and says, 'Mum, what's that hanging between the elephant's legs?'

The mother is very embarrassed, and says, 'Oh, it's nothing son.'

So the son turns to his father and asks the same question.

The father replies, 'It's the elephant's penis, son.'

So the son says, 'Why did mum say it was nothing?'

The father draws himself up, and says proudly, 'Because I've spoiled that woman, son.'

A man and his young son are in the chemist when the son comes across the condoms and asks his father what they are.

The dad replies, 'Well son, those are condoms and they're for protection when you're having sex.'

The son then picks up one of the packs and asks why it has three condoms in it.

The dad replies, 'Those are for high-school boys. One for Friday, one for Saturday, and one for Sunday.'

The son then picks up one with six condoms and asks, 'Why six?'

The dad replies, 'Well son, those are for uni students. Two for Friday, two for Saturday and two for Sunday.'

The son then notices the twelve-pack of condoms and asks the same question.

The dad replies, 'Son, those are for married men. One for January, one for February, one for March . . .'

J ohn takes his blind date to the carnival.
'What would you like to do first, Kim?' he asks.

'I want to get weighed,' says the girl. They amble over to the weight guesser. The man guesses 55kg. Kim gets on the scale and it reads 53kg and she wins a prize.

Next the couple go on the Ferris wheel. When the ride is over, John again asks Kim what she would like to do.

'I want to get weighed,' she says. Back to the weight guesser they go. Since they have been there before, the man guesses Kim's correct weight, and John loses his dollar. The couple walk around the carnival and again John asks where to next.

'I want to get weighed,' Kim responds.

By this time, John thinks she is really weird and takes her home early, dropping her off with a handshake.

Kim's roommate, Laura, asks, 'How'd it go?'

Kim responds, 'Oh, Waura, it was wousy.'

Two lovers are really into spiritualism and reincarnation. They vow that if either dies, the one remaining will try to contact the partner in the other world exactly thirty days after the death. Unfortunately, a few weeks later, the young man dies in a car crash. True to her word, his sweetheart tries to contact him in the spirit world exactly thirty days later.

At the séance, she calls out, 'John, John, this is Martha. Do you hear me?'

A ghostly voice answers her, 'Yes Martha, this is John. I can hear you.'

Martha tearfully asks, 'Oh John, what is it like where you are?'

'It's great. There are azure skies, a soft breeze, sunshine most of the time, the grass is green and the cows have beautiful eyes.'

'What do you do all day?' asks Martha.

'Well, Martha, we get up before sunrise, eat a good breakfast, and then there's nothing but making love until noon. After lunch, we nap until two and then make love again until about five. After dinner, we go at it again until we fall asleep about 11 p.m.'

Martha is somewhat taken aback. 'Is that what heaven really is like?'

'Heaven? I'm not in heaven, Martha.'

'Well, then, where are you?'

'I'm a bull on a stud farm.'

A young man is showing off his new sports car to his girlfriend. She is thrilled at the speed.

'If I do 250kph, will you take off your clothes?' he smirks.

'OK,' says his adventurous girlfriend.

As he gets up to 250kph, she peels off all her clothes. Unable to keep his eyes on the road, the car skids on some gravel and flips over. The naked girl is thrown clear, but the boyfriend is jammed beneath the steering wheel.

'Go and get help!' he cries.

'But I can't! I'm naked and my clothes are gone!'

'Take my shoe,' he says, 'and cover yourself.'

Holding the shoe over her privates, the girl runs down the road and finds a service station. Still holding the shoe between her legs, she pleads to the service station proprietor for help.

'Please help me! My boyfriend's stuck!'

The proprietor looks at the shoe and says, 'There's nothing I can do. He's in too far.'

A husband and wife decide they need to use code to indicate that they want to have sex without letting their children in on it. They decide on the word 'typewriter'.

One day the husband tells his five-year-old daughter, 'Go tell your mummy that daddy needs to type a letter.'

The child tells her mother what her dad said, and her mum responds, 'Tell your daddy that he can't type a letter right now 'cause there is a red ribbon in the typewriter.'

The child goes back to tell her father what mummy said.

A few days later the mum tells the daughter, 'Tell daddy that he can type that letter now.'

The child tells her father, returns to her mother and announces, 'Daddy said never mind about the typewriter, he already wrote the letter by hand.'

A guy stumbles from a bar with his keys in his hand. A cop sees him and asks, 'Can I help you Sir?'

'Yesshh. Ssshhomebody shtole my carr.'

The cop asks him, 'Well, where did you last see it?'

The guy thinks for a while, 'At the end of dissh key.'

The cop looks at him and notices that his tool is hanging down from his pants.

'Sir, are you aware that you are exposing yourself to the whole world to see?'

The guy looks down woefully and says, 'Oh my goddd. Thheey got my girlfriend too.'

Two women are at their local shopping mall, when one happens to see her husband emerging from a florist shop carrying a large bunch of roses.

'Oh no,' she says 'Looks like I'll have to spread the legs tonight.'

'Why?' asks the other. 'Don't you own a vase?'

A married woman is having an affair. Whenever her lover comes over, she puts her nine-year-old son in the closet. One day the woman hears a car in the driveway and, thinking it's her husband, puts her lover in the closet, as well.

Inside the closet, the little boy says, 'It's dark in here, isn't it?'

'Yes it is,' the man replies.

'You wanna buy a baseball?' the little boy asks.

'No thanks,' the man replies.

'I think you do want to buy a baseball,' the little extortionist continues.

'OK. How much?' the man replies after considering the position he is in.

'Twenty-five dollars,' the little boy replies.

'Twenty-five dollars?' the man repeats but complies to protect his hidden position.

The following week, the lover is visiting the woman again when she hears a car in the driveway and again places her lover in the closet with her little boy.

'It's dark in here, isn't it?' the boy starts off.

'Yes it is,' replies the man.

'Wanna buy a baseball glove?' the little boy asks.

'OK. How much?' the hiding lover responds, acknowledging his disadvantage.

'Fifty dollars,' the boy replies and the transaction is completed.

The next weekend, the little boy's father says, 'Hey, son. Go get your ball and glove and we'll play some catch.'

'I can't. I sold them,' replies the little boy.

'How much did you get for them?' asks the father, expecting to hear the profit in terms of lizards and candy.

'Seventy-five dollars,' the little boy says.

'Seventy-five dollars? That's thievery! I'm taking you to church right now. You must confess your sin and ask for forgiveness,' the father explains as he hauls the child away.

At the church, the little boy goes into the confessional, draws the curtain, sits down, and says, 'It's dark in here, isn't it?'

'Don't you start that shit in here,' the priest says.

A pianist is hired to play background music for a movie. When it is completed he asks when and where he can see the film. The producer sheepishly confesses that it is actually a porno film and it is due out in a month. A month later, the musician goes to a porno theatre to see it. With his collar up and dark glasses on, he takes a seat in the back row, next to a couple who also seem to be in disguise.

The movie is even raunchier than he had feared, featuring group sex, S&M and even a dog. After a while, the embarrassed pianist turns to the couple and says, 'I'm only here to listen to the music.'

'Yeah?' replies the man. 'We're only here to see our dog.'

Pingi the penguin is a long-haul truck driver. One day, while driving across a desert, his truck starts to play up. Spotting a garage in the distance, he coaxes his vehicle to it, and asks the mechanic to have a look at it. Finding the heat of the sun unbearable, as penguins are wont to do, Pingi retreats into the cafe and has a couple of cooling drinks. Still hot, he then has some ice-cream, but as penguins are not built to handle ice-cream (flippers being most unsuitable), most of the ice-cream ends up all over him.

Covered with ice-cream, he wanders back to where the mechanic is finishing up.

'How are things going?' asks Pingi.

'It looks like you've blown a seal,' says the mechanic.

'No,' replies Pingi, 'it's ice-cream.'

A man with a twenty-five-inch penis goes to his doctor to complain that he is unable to get any women to have sex with him. They all tell him that his penis is too long.

'Doctor,' he asks, in total frustration, 'is there any way you can shorten it?'

The doctor replies, 'Medically son, there is nothing I can do. But, I do know this witch who may be able to help you.'

So the doctor gives him directions to the witch. The man calls upon the witch and relays his story.

'Witch, my penis is twenty-five inches long and I can't get any women to have sex with me. Can you help me shorten it?'

The witch stares in amazement, scratches her head, and then replies, 'I think I have a solution to your problem. What you have to do is go to this pond deep in the forest. In the pond, you will see a frog sitting on a log who can help solve your dilemma. First you must ask the frog, will you marry me? Each time the frog declines your proposal, your penis will be five inches shorter.'

The man's face lights up and he dashes off into the forest.

Finding the frog, he says, 'Will you marry me?'

The frog looks at him dejectedly and replies, 'No.'

The man looks down and suddenly his penis is five inches shorter.

'Wow,' he screams out loud. 'This is great. But it's still too long at twenty inches, so I'll ask the frog to marry me again.'

'Frog, will you marry me?' the guy shouts.

The frog rolls its eyes back in its head and screams back, 'No!'

The man feels another twitch in his penis, looks down, and it is another five inches shorter.

The man laughs, 'This is fantastic.' He looks down at his penis again, fifteen inches long, and reflects for a moment. Fifteen inches is still a monster, just a little less would be ideal.

Grinning, he looks across the pond and yells out, 'Frog will you marry me?'

The frog looks back across the pond shaking its head, 'How many damn times do I have to tell you? No, no and for the last time, no!'

A guy buys a second-hand Harley Davidson which is almost in mint condition. Before riding off, he asks the owner how he managed to keep it in such good shape.

'Well,' says the owner, 'it's pretty simple. Just make sure that if the bike is outside and it's going to rain, rub Vaseline on the chrome. It protects it from the rain.'

The next night, the guy goes over to his girlfriend's house for dinner. It's the first time he's been there and she meets him on the doorstep.

'Honey,' she says, 'I gotta tell you something about my parents before you go in. When we eat dinner, we don't talk. In fact, the person who says anything during dinner has to do the dishes.'

'No problem,' he says. And in they go.

The boyfriend is astounded. Right smack in the middle of the living room is a huge stack of dirty dishes. In the family room, another huge stack of dishes. Piled up the stairs, dirty dishes. In fact, everywhere he looks, dirty dishes. They sit down to dinner and, sure enough, no-one says a word. As dinner progresses, the boyfriend decides to take advantage of the situation. So he leans over and kisses his girlfriend. No-one says a word. So he decides to reach over and fondle her breasts. He looks at her parents, but still they keep quiet. So he stands up, grabs his girlfriend, strips her naked, and they make love right on the dinner table. Still, no-one says a word.

'Her mum's kinda cute,' he thinks. So he grabs his girlfriend's mum and has his way with her right there on the dinner table. Again, total silence. Then, a few raindrops hit the window and the boyfriend realises it's starting to rain. He thinks he'd better take care of the motorcycle, so he pulls the Vaseline from his pocket. Suddenly the father stands up and shouts, 'All right, all right! I'll do the damn dishes.'

Time after time, night after night Tom just can't last long while having sex with his wife. He feels horrible, he feels like he is disappointing her.

She constantly reassures him saying, 'Honey, don't worry about it. It's alright.'

But he decides that he is going to do whatever he can to remedy the problem. After a day or two of thought, Tom decides to ask his doctor.

The doctor looks at him and says, 'Believe it or not, it's not an uncommon problem. Have you ever tried masturbating before you have sex with your wife?'

Tom replies, 'No.'

'Well,' the doctor continues, 'if you do, it will take you longer to come when you're having sex with your wife.'

Tom smiles and says, 'Thanks doc, I'll give it a try.'

The next day while Tom is at work, he receives a call from his wife. She warns him that she is extremely horny and that she is going to attack him the moment he walks through the door.

This gets him excited, but then he realises that if she attacks him when he walks through the door, he won't be able to try out the doctor's suggestion.

Tom tries to think of somewhere he can go to try his new technique. He can't do it at his desk. The mail room is too risky. So is the toilet. He decides he will just pull over on his way home, get under his truck and act like he's working on it, nobody will know.

Tom leaves work and gets about halfway home before he decides he's found just as good a place as any to do what he must do. He pulls over, gets under his truck and starts masturbating, eyes closed imaging that it's his wife giving him a hand job. After a few minutes he feels someone hit him on the leg.

Startled, Tom yells out, 'What? Who's there?'

A reply comes sharply, ' I'm the sheriff, mind if I ask what you're doin'?'

Tom has to think fast, 'It appears I have an oil leak or something, I'm just checking it out.'

The sheriff replies, 'Oh, OK. But you might also want to check your parking brake while you're down there, your truck rolled down the hill five minutes ago.'

A husband suspects his wife is having an affair. He needs to go on a business trip for several days, so he decides to set a trap for her. He puts a bowl of milk under the bed. From the bed springs, he suspends a spoon. He has it calibrated so that her weight on the bed will not drop the spoon into the milk. But, if there is any more weight than that, the spoon will drop into the milk and he will detect it upon his return home.

He comes home several days later. The first thing he does is reach under the bed and retrieve the bowl. It's full of butter.

A convicted murderer escapes from prison after spending twenty-five years inside. While on the run, he breaks into a house and ties up a young couple who have been sleeping in the bedroom. He ties the man to a chair on one side of the room and ties the woman to the bed. He gets on the bed right over the woman, and appears to be kissing her neck. Suddenly he gets up and leaves the room, though not the house.

As soon as possible the husband makes his way across the room to his bride, his chair in tow, and whispers, 'Honey, this guy hasn't seen a woman in years. I saw him kissing your neck. Just cooperate and do anything he wants. If he wants to have sex with you, just go along with it and pretend you like it. Whatever you do don't fight him or make him mad. Our lives depend on it! Be strong and I love you.'

After spitting out the gag in her mouth, the half-naked wife says, 'Darling, I'm so relieved you feel that way. You're right, he hasn't seen a woman in years, but he wasn't kissing my neck. He was whispering in my ear. He said he thinks you're really cute and asked if we kept the Vaseline in the bathroom. Be strong and I love you, too.'

It is George the mailman's last day on the job after thirty-five years of carrying the mail through all kinds of weather to the same neighbourhood. When he arrives at the first house on his route he is greeted by the whole family there, who roundly and soundly congratulate him and send him on his way with a tidy gift envelope. At the second house they present him with a box of fine cigars. The folks at the third house hand him a selection of terrific fishing lures.

At the fourth house, a strikingly beautiful woman in a revealing negligee meets him at the door. She takes him by the hand, gently leads him through the door (which she closes behind him), and leads him up the stairs to the bedroom where she blows his mind with the most passionate love he has ever experienced. When he has had enough they go downstairs, where she fixes him a giant breakfast: eggs, potatoes, ham, sausage, blueberry waffles, and freshly squeezed orange juice. When he is truly satisfied she pours him a cup of steaming coffee. As she is pouring, he notices a dollar bill sticking out from under the cup's bottom edge.

'All this was just too wonderful for words,' he says, 'but what's the dollar for?'

'Well,' she says, 'last night, I told my husband that today would be your last day, and that we should do something special for you. I asked him what to give you. He said, "Screw him. Give him a dollar." The breakfast was my idea.'

A middle-aged man and woman meet, fall in love, and decide to get married. On their wedding night they settle into the bridal suite at their hotel and the bride says to her new groom, 'Please promise to be gentle . . . I am still a virgin.'

The startled groom asks, 'How can that be? You've been married three times before.'

The bride responds, 'Well you see it was this way: My first husband was a psychiatrist and all he ever wanted to do was talk about it. My second husband was a gynaecologist and all he ever wanted to do was look at it. My third husband was a stamp collector and all he ever wanted to do was . . . God I miss him.'

Three prostitutes are living together: a mother, a daughter and a grandmother. One night the daughter comes home looking very down.

'How did you do tonight, dear?' asks her mother.

'Not too good.' replies the daughter, 'I only got $20 for a blow job.'

'Wow!' says the mother, 'In my day, we were glad to get $5 for a blow job!'

'Good God!' says the grandmother. 'In my day, we were glad just to get something warm in our stomachs!'

A couple are having a quickie in the back of a car in a dark lane.

The man says to the woman, 'This is fantastic, but why are your ankles banging against my ears?'

'I've still got my tights on.'

Bill Bodgy is a travelling toy salesman who is going through a period of low sales. He arrives one morning at the door of a large mansion, and is met by a nine-year-old boy. He enquires if either of the boy's parents are home, and receives a negative reply. He tells the boy that he is selling the latest thing in trail bikes, and will come back later in order to speak to the boy's parents. The boy tells him not to bother, since he is too advanced for that sort of thing. The salesman tries to push his product, and then foolishly agrees that if he can do everything the boy can do, the boy will ask for a bike for Christmas. If not, then Bill must give him a bike. First of all, the boy jumps onto the roof of a nearby shed, balances along the ridge, and jumps off with a somersault. Thanking his lucky stars he has kept fit, Bill copies him. Next the boy does five handstands on the lawn, with the same response from Bill. The boy then takes Bill into the house, and into a rear bedroom, in which a stunning twenty-five-year-old girl is lying in bed.

'My cousin Jackie,' explains the boy. 'She's a flight attendant with Qantas, and has just come off an international flight and taken a couple of sleeping pills. Nothing will wake her. Is this deal still on?'

Somewhat apprehensive, but desperate for a sale, Bill agrees. The boy pulls down the bedclothes to reveal a skimpy bikini nightie. He then replaces the bedclothes, and invites Bill to copy his actions. Sweat breaking from his brow, Bill does as invited. The boy then pulls down the bedclothes a second time, and slides the nightie top up to reveal the most immaculate pair of tits. Bill does the same, now trembling. The boy then slides down the bottom half of the nightie, to reveal all. Shaking like a leaf, Bill follows suit.

The boy then takes out his dick, folds it in half, and announces, 'I'll have a red one with racing handles.'

Three sisters decide to get married on the same day to save their parents the expense of separate weddings. As a further step to reduce the price tag, the three sisters resolve to spend their honeymoon night at home. Later that night, their mother can't sleep, so she goes to the kitchen for a cup of tea. On her way, she tiptoes by her oldest daughter's bedroom and hears her screaming.

The mother thinks to herself, 'That's normal, especially on her wedding night.'

She sneaks by her second-oldest daughter's room and hears her laughing.

'That's normal too,' she says, smiling to herself.

Finally, she slips by her youngest daughter's room where she doesn't hear a peep, but she thinks nothing of it. The next morning in the kitchen, after the husbands have gone out, the woman asks her eldest daughter about last night's noises.

'Well Mum,' she replies, 'you always said if it hurt I should scream.'

'You're absolutely right sweetheart,' the mother assures her, and turns to her middle daughter.

'Now why were you laughing?' she asks.

'You always said if it tickled, I could laugh,' she answers.

'True enough, honey.' The mother smiles, remembering her newlywed days.

'Now it's your turn, baby,' she says, turning to her youngest daughter. 'Why was it so quiet in your room last night?'

'Mum, don't you remember? You always told me never to talk with my mouth full.'

A couple are going through some tough times, so they agree that the woman will walk the streets for a night and see if she can make a bit of money. The guy drops her off on a corner in a rough area of town and drives off. The next morning he picks her up and finds her with her hair a mess, make-up smudged and obviously needing a lot of rest.

She climbs in the car and excitedly says, 'Look honey, I made $40.50.'

'Which of the buggers gave you fifty cents?' he asks.

'All of them!' she says.

A hippie gets onto a bus and sits next to a nun in the front seat. The hippie looks over and asks the nun if she will have sex with him. The nun, surprised by the question, politely declines and gets off at the next stop.

When the bus starts on its way the driver says to the hippie, 'I can tell you how you can get that nun to have sex with you.'

The hippie says that he'd love to know, so the bus driver tells him that every Tuesday evening at midnight the nun goes to the cemetery and prays to God. 'If you went dressed in a robe and glow in the dark paint mask she would think you are God and you could command her to have sex with you.'

The hippie decides this is a great idea, so the next Tuesday he goes to the cemetery and waits for the nun to show up. At midnight, sure enough, the nun shows up and begins praying. The hippie jumps out from hiding and says, 'I am God! I have heard your prayers and I will answer them, but . . . first you must have sex with me.'

The nun agrees but asks for anal sex so she might keep her virginity, because she is married to the church. The hippie agrees to this and has his way with the nun.

After the hippie finishes he stands up and rips off the mask and shouts, 'Ha! Ha! Ha! I'm the hippie!'

Then the nun jumps up and shouts, 'Ha! Ha! Ha! I'm the bus driver!'

Blondie is sitting on a beach in Florida, attempting to strike up a conversation with the attractive gentleman reading on the blanket beside hers.

'Hello, Sir,' she says, 'Do you like movies?'

'Yes, I do,' he responds, then returns to his book.

Blondie persists, 'Do you like gardening?'

The man again looks up from his book. 'Yes, I do,' he says politely before returning to his reading.

Undaunted, Blondie asks, 'Do you like pussycats?'

With that, the man drops his book and pounces on Blondie, ravishing her as she's never been ravished before.

As the cloud of sand begins to settle, Blondie drags herself to a sitting position and pants, 'How did you know that was what I wanted?'

The man thinks for a moment and replies, 'How did you know my name was Katz?'

Jim phones his office in the morning and says to his boss, 'Boss, I'm not coming in today, I'm sick.'

His boss says, 'Exactly how sick are ya?'

Jim replies, 'Well, I'm in bed with my sister!'

A king and a queen rule a large kingdom. The king is short in vital parts and the queen has to seek solace with every Tom, Dick and Harry. After some time, the king grows suspicious of the queen's escapades and wants to punish the subjects willing to risk their lives for a fling with her.

He seeks the services of his court magician to help identify the culprits. The magician builds an invisible contraption that is attached to the queen's waist. The mechanism is simple, it slices any elongated object that ventures anywhere within an inch of the queen's waist.

Having set his trap the king sets off on a hunting trip and returns to his palace, after spending a sleepless week, burning with curiosity. Immediately after his arrival he summons the queen's private bodyguards to his foyer and dispatches all his attendants. He orders them to undress. All of them have lost their penises! He next summons the palace guards and the result is the same. By mid-afternoon he realises that there is not a single male soul in the vicinity who had not made a valiant attempt only to be left without a penis.

The only man left is his minister and, to his surprise, the king finds him to be the only man who has a penis left.

Pleased with his minister's loyalty, he asks him what punishment would befit all the others. In reply, he receives only a blubbering sound from the minister's mouth.

THE INNOCENCE
OF KIDS

*Those innocent little comments that kids come
out with are so amusing. The frightening
thing is, they're usually the truth.*

A father asks his ten-year-old son, Johnny, if he knows about the
birds and the bees.

'I don't want to know,' Johnny says, bursting into tears.

Confused, the father asks Johnny what is wrong.

'Oh Daddy,' Johnny sobs. 'At age six I got the "there's no Santa"
speech. At age seven I got the "there's no Easter bunny" speech.
Then at age eight you hit me with the "there's no tooth fairy"
speech! If you're going to tell me now that grown-ups don't really
screw, I've got nothing left to live for.'

A couple have two little boys, ages eight and ten, who are
excessively mischievous. The two are always getting into
trouble and their parents are sure that if any mischief occurs in
their town, their two young sons are in some way involved. The
parents are at their wits' end as to what to do about their sons'
behaviour. The mother has heard that a clergyman in town has
been successful in disciplining children in the past, so she asks
her husband if he thinks they should send the boys to speak
with the clergyman.

The husband says, 'We might as well. We need to do
something before I really lose my temper.'

The clergyman agrees to speak with the boys, but asks to

THE INNOCENCE OF KIDS

see them individually. The eight-year-old goes to meet with him first.

The clergyman sits the boy down and asks him sternly, 'Where is God?'

The boy makes no response, so the clergyman repeats the question in an even sterner tone, 'Where is God?'

Again the boy makes no attempt to answer, so the clergyman raises his voice even more and shakes his finger in the boy's face, 'Where is God!'

At that the boy bolts from the room and runs directly home slamming himself in his closet.

His older brother follows him into the closet and says, 'What happened?'

The younger brother replies, 'We are in *big* trouble this time. God is missing. And they think we did it!'

Little Joe sees his daddy's car pass the playground and go into the woods. Curious, he follows the car and sees Daddy and Aunt Susie in a passionate embrace.

Joe finds this exciting and can barely contain himself as he runs home and starts to tell his mother, 'Mummy, Mummy, I was at the playground and Daddy and –'

Mummy tells him to slow down. She wants to hear the story.

So Joe tells her, 'I was at the playground and I saw Daddy go into the woods with Aunt Susie. I went back to look and he was giving Aunt Susie a big kiss, then he helped her take off her shirt, then Aunt Susie helped Daddy take his pants off, then Aunt Susie laid down on the seat, then Daddy –'

At this point, Mummy cut him off and said, 'Joe, this is such an interesting story, suppose you save the rest of it for supper time. I want to see the look on Daddy's face when you tell it tonight.'

At the dinner table, Mummy asks Joe to tell his story. Joe starts his story, describing the car going into the woods, the undressing, laying down on the seat, and '. . . then Daddy and

Aunt Susie did that same thing that Mummy and Uncle Bill used to do when Daddy was in the navy.'

Mikey and Jane are only ten years old, but they just know that they are in love. One day they decide that they want to get married, so Mikey goes to Jane's father to ask him for her hand. Mikey bravely walks up to him and says, 'Mr Smith, Jane and I are in love and I want to ask you for her hand in marriage.'

Thinking that this is the cutest thing, Mr Smith replies, 'Well Mikey, you are only ten. Where will you two live?'

Without even taking a moment to think about it, Mikey replies, 'In Jane's room. It's bigger than mine and we can both fit there nicely.'

Still thinking this is just adorable, Mr Smith says with a huge grin, 'OK then how will you live? You're not old enough to get a job. You'll need to support Jane.'

Again, Mikey instantly replies. 'Our allowance. Jane makes $5 a week and I make $10 a week. That's about $60 a month, and that'll do us just fine.'

By this time Mr Smith is a little shocked that Mikey has put so much thought into this. So, he thinks for a moment, trying to come up with something that Mikey won't have an answer for.

After a second, Mr Smith says, 'Well Mikey, it seems like you have got everything worked out. I just have one more question for you. What will you do if the two of you should have little ones of your own?'

Mikey just shrugs his shoulders and says, 'Well, we've been lucky so far.'

A boy wakes up in the middle of the night and goes to the bathroom. On the way back to bed, he passes his parents room. When he looks in, he notices the covers bouncing.

He calls to his dad, 'Hey Dad, what are you doing?'

Dad answers, 'Playing cards.'

The boy asks, 'Who's your partner?'

Dad answers, 'Your mum.'

The boy then passes by his older sister's room. Again, he notices the covers bouncing.

He calls to his sister, 'Hey Sis, what are you doing?'

The sister answers, 'Playing cards.'

The boy asks, 'Who's your partner?'

She answers, 'My boyfriend.'

A little later, dad gets up and goes to the bathroom. As he passes the boy's room, he notices the covers bouncing.

He calls to his son, 'What are you doing?'

The boy answers, 'Playing cards.'

Dad asks, 'Really? Who's your partner?'

The boy answers, 'You don't need a partner if you have a good hand.'

A few months after his parents divorce, Little Johnny passes by his mum's bedroom and sees her rubbing her body and moaning, 'I need a man, I need a man!'

Over the next couple of months, he sees her doing this several times. One day, he comes home from school and hears her moaning. When he peeks into her bedroom, he sees a man on top of her.

Little Johnny runs into his room, takes off his clothes, throws himself on his bed, starts stroking himself, and moans, 'Ohh, I need a bike! I need a bike!'

Little Johnny comes home from Catholic school with a black eye.

His father sees it and says, 'Johnny, how many times do I have to tell you not to fight with the other boys?'

'But Dad, it wasn't my fault. We were all in church saying our prayers. We all stood up and my teacher in front of me had her dress in the crack of her bum. I reached over and pulled it out. That's when she hit me.'

'Johnny,' the father says, 'you don't do those kinds of things to women.'

Sure enough, the very next day Johnny comes home with the other eye black and blue. Johnny's father says, 'Johnny, I thought we had a talk.'

'But Dad,' Johnny says, 'It wasn't my fault. There we were in church saying our prayers. We all stood up and my teacher in front of us had her dress in the crack of her bum. Then Louie, who was sitting next to me, saw it and he reached over and pulled it out. Now I know she doesn't like this, so I pushed it back in.'

Little Johnny, on a particularly reckless day, is playing in the backyard. Soon, some honeybees start swirling around, annoying little Johnny. He stomps on them in his temper.

His father catches him trampling the honeybees and, after a brief moment of thought, he says, 'That's it! No honey for you for one month!'

Later that afternoon, Johnny ponders some butterflies, and soon starts catching them and crushing them under his feet.

His father again catches him and, after a brief moment of thought, says, 'No butter for you for one month!'

Early that evening, Johnny's mother is cooking dinner, and gets jumpy when cockroaches start scurrying around the kitchen floor. She begins stomping on them one by one until all the cockroaches are dead. Johnny's mother looks up to find Johnny and his father watching her.

Johnny says, 'Are you going to tell her, Daddy, or should I?'

Two little boys go into a grocery store. One is nine, one is four. The nine-year-old grabs a box of tampons from the shelf and carries it to the register.

The cashier asks, 'Oh, these must be for your mum, huh?'

The nine-year-old replies, 'Nope, not for my mum.'

Without thinking, the cashier responds, 'Well, they must be for your sister then?'

The nine-year-old quips, 'Nope, not for my sister either.'

The cashier has now become curious. 'Oh. Not for your mum and not for your sister, who are they for?'

The nine-year-old says, 'They're for my four-year-old little brother.'

The cashier is surprised. 'Your four-year-old little brother?'

The nine-year-old explains, 'Well yeah, they say on TV if you wear one of these you can swim or ride a bike and my little brother can't do either of them!'

LAWYERS

This section is included despite the fact that lawyers may decide to sue for defamation. But then they've got to prove that the jokes about them are not true. And they couldn't do that, could they?

What do lawyers use for birth control?
Their personalities.

What can a goose do that a duck can't, and a lawyer should?
Stick his bill up his arse.

Four surgeons are taking a coffee break and are discussing their work.

The first says, 'I think accountants are the easiest to operate on. You open them up and everything inside is numbered.'

The second says, 'I think librarians are the easiest to operate on. You open them up and everything inside is in alphabetical order.'

The third says, 'I like to operate on electricians. You open them up and everything inside is colour-coded.'

The fourth one says, 'I like to operate on lawyers. They're heartless, spineless, gutless, and their heads and their arse are interchangeable.'

A lawyer and a blonde are sitting next to each other on a long flight. The lawyer leans over to her and asks if she would like to play a fun game. The blonde just wants to take a nap, so she politely declines and rolls over to the window to catch a few winks. The lawyer persists and explains that the game is really easy and a lot of fun.

He explains, 'I ask you a question, and if you don't know the answer, you pay me $5, and vice-versa.'

Again, she politely declines and tries to get some sleep. The lawyer, now somewhat agitated, says, 'OK, if you don't know the answer you pay me $5, and if I don't know the answer, I will pay you $500.' He reckons that since she is a blonde that he will easily win the match. This offer catches the blonde's attention and, realising that there will probably be no end to this torment unless she plays, agrees to the game.

The lawyer asks the first question. 'What's the distance from the earth to the moon?'

The blonde doesn't say a word, reaches in to her purse, pulls out a $5 note and hands it to the lawyer. Now, it's the blonde's turn.

She asks the lawyer, 'What goes up a hill with three legs, and comes down with four?'

The lawyer looks at her with a puzzled look. He takes out his laptop computer and searches all his references. He taps into the air-phone with his modem and searches the Net and the Library of Congress. Frustrated, he sends emails to all his co-workers and friends he knows. All to no avail. After over an hour, he wakes the blonde and hands her $500. The blonde politely takes the $500 and turns away to get back to sleep.

The lawyer, who is more than a little miffed, wakes the blonde and asks, 'Well, so what *is* the answer?'

Without a word, the blonde reaches into her purse, hands the lawyer $5, and goes back to sleep.

What's the difference between a lawyer and a rooster? When a rooster wakes up in the morning, its primal urge is to cluck defiance.

How can you tell when a lawyer is lying?
His lips are moving.

How many lawyers does it take to roof a house?
Depends on how thin you slice them.

What would happen if you locked a zombie in a room full of lawyers?
He would starve to death.

What do you call a lawyer with an IQ of fifty?
Senator.

What do you call a lawyer gone bad?
Your honour.

What do you call 5000 dead lawyers at the bottom of the ocean?
A good start!

What do you have when a lawyer is buried up to his neck in sand?
A shortage of sand.

One day, a teacher, a garbage collector, and a lawyer all die and go to heaven. St Peter is there but is having a bad day since heaven is getting crowded. When they get to the gate, St Peter informs them that there will be a test to get into heaven – they each have to answer a single question.

To the teacher, he says, 'What was the name of the ship that crashed into the iceberg and sank with all its passengers?'

The teacher thinks for a second and then replies, 'That would be the *Titanic*, right?'

St Peter lets him through the gate. Then he turns to the garbage man, and, thinking that heaven doesn't really need all the stink that this guy would bring into it, decides to make the question a little harder, 'How many people died on the ship?'

The garbage man guesses, '1228.'

'That happens to be right; go ahead.'

St Peter turns to the lawyer, 'Name them.'

A wealthy lawyer has a summer house in the country, to which he retreats for several weeks of the year. Each summer, the lawyer invites a friend to spend some time at his place.

On one occasion, he invites a Czechoslovakian friend to stay with him. The friend, eager to get a freebie from a lawyer, agrees. They have a splendid time in the country – rising early and enjoying the great outdoors. Early one morning, the lawyer and his Czechoslovakian companion go out to pick berries for their morning breakfast. As they go around the berry patch, gathering blueberries and raspberries in tremendous quantities, along come two huge bears – a male and a female. Well, the lawyer, seeing the two bears, immediately dashes for cover. His friend, though, isn't so lucky, and the male bear reaches him and swallows him whole. The lawyer runs back to his Mercedes, tears into town as fast has he can, and gets the local backwoods sheriff. The sheriff grabs his shotgun and dashes back to the berry patch with the lawyer. Sure enough, the two bears are still there.

'He's in that one!' cries the lawyer, pointing to the male, while visions of lawsuits from his friend's family dance in his head. The sheriff looks at the bears and, without batting an eye, levels his gun, takes careful aim, and shoots the female.

'What'd ya do that for!' exclaims the lawyer, 'I said he was in the other!'

'Exactly,' replies the sheriff, 'but would *you* believe a lawyer who told you that the Czech was in the male?'

A local charity office realises that it has never received a donation from the town's most successful lawyer.

A local volunteer calls to solicit a donation, saying, 'Our research shows that even though your annual income is over a million dollars, you do not give one penny to charity. Wouldn't you like to give back to your community by donating some money to our worthy cause?'

The lawyer thinks for a moment and says, 'First, did your research show that my mother is dying after a long, painful illness and has huge medical bills far beyond her ability to pay?'

Embarrassed, the volunteer mumbles, 'Uh, no.'

'Secondly, that my brother, a disabled veteran, is blind and confined to a wheelchair and is unable to support his wife and six children?'

The stricken volunteer rep begins to stammer an apology but is cut off.

'Thirdly, that my sister's husband died in a dreadful traffic accident,' the lawyers voice rises in indignation, 'leaving her penniless with a mortgage and three children?'

The humiliated volunteer, completely beaten, says simply, 'I had no idea.'

The lawyer then says '. . . and if I don't give any money to *them*, why should I give any to you?'

An old man is on his death bed. He wants badly to take all his money with him. He calls his priest, his doctor and his lawyer to his bedside.

'Here's $30 000 cash to be held by each of you. I trust you to put this in my coffin when I die so I can take all my money with me.'

At the funeral, each man put an envelope in the coffin. Riding away in a limousine, the priest suddenly breaks into tears and confesses that he only put $20 000 into the envelope because he needs $10 000 for a new baptistery.

'Well, since we're confiding in each other,' says the doctor, 'I only put $10 000 in the envelope because we need a new machine at the hospital which costs $20 000.'

The lawyer is aghast. 'I'm ashamed of both of you,' he exclaims. 'I want it known that when I put my envelope in that coffin, it held my personal cheque for the full $30 000.'

Two tigers are stalking through a jungle in Asia. Suddenly, the one to the rear reaches out with his tongue, and licks the posterior of the tiger in front of him.

The startled front tiger turns and says, 'Cut it out.'

The rear tiger apologises, and they continue onward.

About five minutes later, it happens again.

The front tiger turns, growling, 'I said stop it.'

The rear tiger again apologises, and they continue. Another five minutes pass, and again the front tiger feels the unwanted tongue.

The front tiger turns, giving the rear tiger a ferocious glare, and angrily hisses, 'What is it with you?'

The rear tiger replies, 'I'm sorry. I really didn't mean to offend you. But I just ate a lawyer and I'm trying to get the taste out of my mouth!'

Do you know how to save a drowning lawyer? No? Good!

Chicago sends its police chief, fire chief, and city attorney to a municipal management conference in Indiana. While driving through a rural area, their car breaks down, and they seek assistance at a nearby farmhouse. The farmer tells them that the local garage is closed, and that they are welcome to spend the night, but that he only has one spare bed. He tells them that somebody can sleep on his couch, but that one of them would have to spend the night in his barn.

The police chief announces that he will volunteer to sleep in the barn. A short time later there is a knock at the door. It's the police chief, complaining that he can't sleep. There are pigs in the barn, and they remind him of insults that have been yelled at him, and he is too disturbed to sleep.

The fire chief says that he will trade with the police chief, and goes out to the barn. A short time later, there is another rapping at the door. It's the fire chief, who complains that the cows in the barn remind him of Mrs O'Leary's cow, which started the great Chicago fire. He has tried to sleep, but keeps having nightmares where they are kicking over lanterns and setting the barn ablaze.

The city attorney declares, 'You two are such babies. I will go sleep in the barn.'

Everything seems fine, until a few minutes later, there's another knock at the door. When the occupants answer it, they find the very indignant cows and pigs.

Two lawyers go into a café and order two drinks. Then they produce sandwiches from their briefcases and start to eat.

The waiter becomes quite concerned and marches over and tells them, 'You can't eat your own sandwiches in here.'

The lawyers look at each other, shrug their shoulders and exchange sandwiches.

What's the difference between a lawyer and a trampoline? You take off your shoes to jump on a trampoline.

What's the difference between a dead skunk in the road and a dead lawyer in the road?

There are skid marks in front of the skunk.

A solicitor from Dublin, while hunting in the west, brought down a fowl, which landed in a farmer's field. As the lawyer climbed over the wall to retrieve the bird, the elderly owner appeared, asking what he was doing.

The litigator replied, 'I shot that bird you see lying there, and now I'm about to pick it up.'

'This is my property you crossing into, and I'm telling you, yer not coming over,' said the old man.

'I'll have you know that I'm one of the best solicitors in all of Ireland, and if you don't let me retrieve my bird, I'll take ye to court for everything y'own!'

'Well now, being as how you're not from around here, you don't know how we settle things like this. You see now, here we use the three-kick method.'

'And what would that be?' asked the lawyer.

'First I kick you three times and then you do the same to me, and back and forth like that till one of us gives up.'

The attorney thought this over, and quickly decided he could easily take on the old codger, and agreed to the local custom. The old farmer walked slowly over to the lawyer. With his first kick he planted the toe of his heavy boot in the solicitor's groin dropping him to his knees. The second blow nearly wiped the lawyer's nose off his face. The attorney was flat on the ground when the farmer's third kick to the kidney almost finished him.

The lawyer dug deep for his every bit of will, dragged himself standing, and said, 'OK you old bugger, now it's my turn.

The old farmer just smiled and said, 'No, I believe I'll give up now. You can have the bird.'

A man was forced to take a day off from work to appear in court for a minor traffic summons. He grew increasingly restless as he waited hour after endless hour for his case to be heard. When his name was called late in the afternoon, he stood before the judge, only to hear that court would be adjourned for the rest of the afternoon and he would have to return the next day.

'What for?' he unwisely snapped at the magistrate.

His Honour, equally irked by a tedious day, roared, 'Twenty dollars for contempt of court. That's why!'

Then, noticing the man checking his wallet, the magistrate said, 'That's all right. You don't have to pay now.'

The young man replied, 'I'm just seeing if I have enough for two more words.'

'So let me get this straight,' the prosecutor says to the defendant, 'you came home from work early and found your wife in bed with a strange man.'

'That's correct,' says the defendant.

'You then take out a pistol and shoot your wife, killing her.'

'That's correct.'

'Then my question to you is, why did you shoot your wife and not her lover?' asked the prosecutor.

'It seemed easier, than shooting a different man every day.'

The pope and a lawyer find themselves together before the pearly gates. After a little polite small talk, St Peter shows up to usher them to their new heavenly station. After passing out wings, harps, halos and such, St Peter shows them to their new lodgings.

Peter brings them down on the front lawn of a huge palatial estate with all sorts of lavish trappings. This, Peter announces, is where the lawyer will be spending eternity.

'Holy Mary,' the pope thinks, 'If he's getting a place like this, I can hardly wait to see my heavenly reward!'

Peter leads the way but the landscape below begins to appear more and more mundane until they finally land on a street lined with dull brownstone houses. Pete indicates that the third stairs on the left will take the pope to his new domicile and turns to leave, wishing the pope the best.

The pope is quite taken aback and cries out, 'Hey Peter! What's the deal here? You put that lawyer in a beautiful estate home and I, spiritual leader of the whole world, end up in this dive?'

'Look here old fellow, this street is practically encrusted with spiritual leaders from many times and from many religions. We're putting you here with them so you can all get together and discuss dogma and philosophy. That other guy gets an elegant estate, because he's the first lawyer ever to make it up here.'

Avery successful lawyer parked his brand-new BMW in front of his office, ready to show it off to his colleagues. As he got out, a truck passed too close and completely tore the door off the driver's side. The counsellor immediately grabbed his mobile phone, dialled emergency, and within minutes a policeman pulled up. Before the officer had a chance to ask any questions, the lawyer started screaming hysterically. His BMW, which he had just picked up the day before, was now completely ruined and would never be the same, no matter what the panel-beater did to it.

When the lawyer finally wound down from his ranting and raving, the officer shook his head in disgust and disbelief. 'I can't believe how materialistic you lawyers are,' he said.

'You are so focused on your possessions that you don't notice anything else.'

'How can you say such a thing?' asked the lawyer.

'Don't you know that your left arm is missing from the elbow down? It must have been torn off when the truck hit you.'

'Ahhh!' screamed the lawyer. 'Where's my Rolex?'

O'Reilly, a dishonest lawyer, bribed a man on his client's jury to hold out for a charge of manslaughter, as opposed to the charge of murder which was brought by the state.

The jury was out for several days before they returned with the manslaughter verdict. When O'Reilly paid the corrupt juror, he asked him if he had a very difficult time convincing the other jurors to see things his way.

'I sure did,' the juror replied, 'the other eleven wanted to acquit.'

Q: What happens to a lawyer when he takes Viagra?
A: He gets taller.

LAW ENFORCEMENT

*Laws are in place for one reason only. To turn the
general population against those who enforce the law.*

The stockbroker is nervous about being in prison because his
cellmate looks like a real thug.

'Don't worry,' the gruff-looking fellow says, 'I'm in here for a
white-collar crime too.'

'Well, that's a relief,' sighs the stockbroker. 'I was sent to
prison for fraud and insider trading.'

'Oh nothing fancy like that for me,' grins the convict. 'I just
murdered a couple of priests.'

A man is driving down the road with twenty penguins in the
back seat. The police stop him and say that he can't drive
around with the penguins in the car and he should take them to
the zoo. The man agrees and drives off. The next day the same
man is driving down the road with twenty penguins in the back
again.

He is stopped by the same police officer who says, 'Hey!
I thought I told you to take those penguins to the zoo.'

The man replies, 'I did. Today I'm taking them to the movies.'

The police complimented me on my driving today. They left a
note on my windscreen that said 'Parking Fine.'

Twenty puppies were stolen from a pet shop. Police are
warning people to look out for anyone selling hot dogs.

A squad car driver was covering a quiet beat out in the sticks, when he was amazed to find a former police lieutenant covering the same beat.

He stopped the car and asked, 'Why, Smithson, this wouldn't be your new beat way out here in the sticks, would it?'

'That it is,' Smithson replied grimly, 'ever since I arrested Judge O'Shea on his way to the masquerade ball.'

'You mean you pinched his honour?'

'How was I to know that his convict suit was only a costume?'

'Well, that's life. There's a lesson in here somewhere.'

'That there is,' replied Smithson. 'Never book a judge by his cover.'

A farmer was involved in a terrible road accident with a large truck. He ended up in court fighting for a big compensation claim.

'I understand you're claiming damages for the injuries you're supposed to have suffered?' said the counsel for the insurance company.

'Yes, that's right,' replied the farmer.

'You claim you were injured in the accident, yet I have a signed police statement that says when the attending police officer asked you how you were feeling, you replied, "I've never felt better in my life." Is that the case?'

'Yeah, but –'

'A simple yes or no will suffice.'

'Yes,' replied the farmer quietly.

Then it was the turn of the farmer's counsel to ask the questions.

'Please tell the court the exact circumstance of events following the accident when you made your statement of health,' his lawyer said.

'Certainly,' replied the farmer. 'After the accident my

horse was thrashing around with a broken leg and my poor old dog was howling in pain. This cop comes along, takes one look at my horse and shoots him dead. Then he goes over to my dog, looks at him and shoots him dead too. Then he comes straight over to me, with his gun still smoking, and asks me how I was feeling. Now, mate, what the hell would you have said to him?'

A young skinhead started a job on a farm. The boss sent him to the back paddocks to do some fencing work, but come evening, he was half an hour late.

The boss got on the CB radio to check if he was all right.

'I've got a problem, boss. I'm stuck 'ere. I've hit a pig!'

'Ah well, these things happen sometimes,' the boss said. 'Just drag the carcass off the road so nobody else hits it in the dark.'

'But he's not dead, boss. He's got tangled up on the bull-bar, and I've tried to untangle him, but he's kicking and squealing, and he's real big boss. I'm afraid he's going to hurt me!'

'Never mind,' said the boss. 'There's a .303 under the tarp in the back. Get that out and shoot him. Then drag the carcass off the road and come on home.'

'OK, boss.'

Another half an hour went by, but there was still not a peep from the kid. The boss got back on the CB. 'What's the problem, son?'

'Well, I did what you said boss, but I'm still stuck.'

'What's up? Did you drag the pig off the road like I said?'

'Yeah boss, but his motorcycle is still jammed under the truck.'

A highway patrolman waited outside a popular bar, hoping for a bust. At closing time everyone came out and he spotted his potential quarry. The man was so obviously inebriated that he could barely walk. He stumbled around the parking lot for a few minutes, looking for his car. After trying his keys on five other cars, he finally found his own vehicle.

He sat in the car a good 10 minutes, as the other patrons left. He turned his lights on, then off, wipers on, then off. He then started to pull forward into the grass, then he stopped.

Finally, when he was the last car, he pulled out onto the road and started to drive away. The patrolman, waiting for this, turned on his lights and pulled the man over. He administered the breathalyser test, and to his great surprise, the man blew a 0.00.

The patrolman was dumbfounded. 'This equipment must be broken!' he exclaimed.

'I doubt it,' said the man. 'Tonight I'm the designated decoy!'

A man in his 40s bought a new BMW and went out on the interstate for a nice evening drive. The top was down, the breeze was blowing through what was left of his hair, and he decided to open her up.

As the needle jumped up to 140kph, he suddenly saw flashing red and blue lights behind him.

'There's no way they can catch a BMW,' he thought to himself and opened her up further.

The needle hit 150, 160 . . . then the reality of the situation hit him.

'What the hell am I doing?' he thought and pulled over.

The cop came up to him, took his licence without a word, and examined it and the car. 'It's been a long day,' said the cop, 'this is the end of my shift, and it's Friday the 13th. I don't feel like more paperwork, so if you can give me an excuse for your driving that I haven't heard before, you can go.'

The guy thinks for a second and says, 'Last week my wife ran off with a cop. I was afraid you were trying to give her back.'

'Have a nice weekend,' said the officer.

COURTROOM CAPERS

*There are millions of jokes about judges, lawyers
and other people in the legal profession.
Some of them are even set in a courtroom.*

An English anthropologist is doing research in an isolated
African village, and the tribal chief asks if he would like to
attend a trial his people are conducting that afternoon.

'You'll be surprised,' says the chief, 'at how well we've copied
your country's legal procedures. You see, we have read accounts
of many English trials in your newspapers, and incorporated
them into our judicial system.'

When the Englishman arrives at the wooden courthouse, he
is truly amazed to see how closely the African court officials
resemble those in England. The counsels are suitably attired in
long black robes and the traditional white powdered wigs. Each
argues his case with eloquence and in proper judicial language.
But he can't help being puzzled by the occasional appearance of
a bare-breasted native woman running through the crowd
waving her arms frantically.

After the trial, the anthropologist congratulates his host on
what he has seen and then asks, 'What was the purpose of
having a semi-nude woman run through the courtroom during
the trial?'

'I really don't know,' confesses the chief, 'but in all the
accounts we read in your papers about British trials, there was
invariably something about "an excited titter running through
the gallery."'

Two young guys are picked up by the cops for smoking dope and appear in court before the judge.

The judge says, 'You seem like nice young men, and I'd like to give you a second chance rather than jail time. I want you to go out this weekend and try to show others the evils of drug use and get them to give up drugs forever. I'll see you back in court Monday.'

On Monday, the two guys are back in court, and the judge says to the first one, 'How did you do over the weekend?'

'Well, Your Honour, I persuaded seventeen people to give up drugs forever.'

'Seventeen people? That's wonderful. What did you tell them?'

'I used a diagram, Your Honour. I drew two circles like this and told them this big circle is your brain before drugs and this small circle is your brain after drugs.'

'That's admirable. And you, how did you do?' the judge asks the second boy.

'Well, Your Honour, I persuaded 150 people to give up drugs forever.'

'One hundred and fifty people! That's amazing! How did you manage to do that?'

'Well, I used a similar approach. I said, This small circle is your arsehole before prison . . .'

A husband and wife are divorcing and are in the process of arguing in front of a judge over custody of the children. The mother is asked to give her side of the story and explains that since she has brought the children into this world, she should retain custody of them. The judge nods his head in agreement, then turns to the man for his side of the story.

The man thinks for a few moments, then stands and says, 'Judge, when I put a quarter in a candy machine and a candy bar comes out, does it belong to me or the machine?'

Three frogs are arrested and brought into the courtroom for sentencing.

The judge asks the first frog, 'What's your name?'

'Frog.'

'What were you arrested for?'

'Blowing bubbles in the water.'

Then he asks the second frog, 'What's your name?'

'Frog.'

'What were you arrested for?'

'Blowing bubbles in the water.'

Then he asks the third frog, 'What's your name?'

'Bubbles.'

MAKING MUSIC

*I thought musicians worked together in cooperation
and harmony. That was, until I started reading
these jokes. They hate each other!*

How many country and western singers does it take to change a light bulb?

Three. One to change the bulb and two to sing about the old one.

How many sound men does it take to change a light bulb?
'One, two, one, two . . .'

How many jazz musicians does it take to change a light bulb?
Don't worry about the changes. We'll fake it!

What happens if you play blues music backwards?
Your wife returns to you, your dog comes back to life, and you get out of prison.

What do you get when you play New Age music backwards?
New Age music.

What's the difference between a puppy and a country music singer-songwriter?
Eventually the puppy stops whining.

Why do musicians have to be awake by six o'clock?
Because most shops close by six thirty.

What would a musician do if he won a million dollars?
Continue to play gigs until the money ran out.

What's the definition of an optimist?
A folk musician with a mortgage.

Donald MacDonald from the Isle of Skye is admitted to
Oxford University, and is now living in his first year of
residence there. His clan is very excited that one of their own
has made it into the upper class of education, but they are
concerned how he'll do in 'that strange land'. After the first
month, his mother comes to visit, with reinforcements of
whiskey and oatmeal.
'And how do you find the English students, Donald?'
she asks.
'Oh, Mother,' he replies, shaking his head sadly, 'they're such
terrible, noisy people. The one on that side keeps banging his
head against the wall, and won't stop, and the one on the other
side screams and screams and screams away into the night.'
'But Donald! How do you manage with those dreadful noisy
English neighbours?'
'Well, mother, I just ignore 'em. I just stay here and play my
bagpipes.'

What's the definition of a gentleman?
Someone who can play the bagpipes, but doesn't.

Musician: Did you hear my last recital?
Friend: I hope so.

What's the difference between a moose and a blues band?
The moose has the horns up front and the arsehole
behind.

Why did the Philharmonic disband?
Excessive sax and violins.

Two musicians are driving down a road. All of a sudden they notice the Grim Reaper in the back seat. Death informs them that they had an accident and they are both dead. But, before he takes them into eternity, he is able to grant each musician one last request to remind them of their past life on earth. The first musician says he was a country and western singer and would like to hear eight choruses of *Achy-Breaky Heart* as a last hoorah.

The second musician says, 'I was a jazz musician. Kill me now!'

A man walks up to a pianist in a bar. The man has a wad of bills in his hand and asks if the pianist can play a jazz chord. The pianist does as requested.

'No, no,' the man says. 'A jazz chord.'

The pianists does a bit of improvising but the man doesn't like that either.

'No, no, no! A jazz chord. You know, "a jazz chord, to say, ah love you."'

What is the difference between the men's final at Wimbledon and a high-school musical?
The tennis final has more men.

What is the difference between a world war and a high-school musical?
The musical causes more suffering.

What is the difference between a high-school musical director and a chimpanzee?
It's scientifically proven that chimpanzees are able to communicate with humans.

THE STRING SECTION

A violinist says to his wife, 'Oh, baby, I can play you just like my violin.'
His wife replies, 'I'd rather have you play me like a harmonica!'

Why are harps like elderly parents?
Both are unforgiving and hard to get in and out of cars.

THE KEYBOARD SECTION

The doorbell rings and the lady of the house discovers a workman, complete with tool chest, on her front porch.
'Madam,' he announces, 'I'm the piano tuner.'
The lady exclaims, 'Why, I didn't send for a piano tuner.'
The man replies, 'I know you didn't, but your neighbours did.'

What do you get when you drop a piano down a mine shaft?
A flat minor.

What do you get when you drop a piano on an army base?
A flat major.

Why was the piano invented?
So musicians have somewhere to put their beers.

THE WOODWIND SECTION

Two musicians are walking down the street, and one says to the other, 'Who was that piccolo I saw you with last night?'
The other replies, 'That was no piccolo, that was my fife.'

What is the difference between a clarinet and an onion?
Nobody cries when you chop a clarinet into little pieces.

A community orchestra is plagued by attendance problems. Several musicians are absent at each rehearsal. As a matter of fact, every player in the orchestra has missed several rehearsals, except for one very faithful oboe player. Finally, as the dress rehearsal draws to a close, the conductor takes a moment to thank the oboist for her faithful attendance.

She, of course, humbly responds, 'It's the least I could do, since I won't be at the performance.'

Q: How do you get two piccolos to play in unison?
A: Shoot one.

BRASS SECTION

What do you call a trombonist with a beeper and a mobile telephone?
An optimist.

What kind of calendar does a trombonist use for his gigs?
Year at a Glance.

Q: What's the difference between a baritone saxophone and a chain saw?
A: The exhaust.

How can you tell which kid on a playground is the child of a trombonist?
He doesn't know how to use the slide, and he can't swing.

What is the difference between a French horn section and a '57 Chevy?
You can tune a '57 Chevy.

How many tuba players does it take to change a light bulb?
Three! One to hold the bulb and two to drink 'till the room spins.

How do you fix a broken tuba?
With a tuba glue.

These two tuba players walk past a bar . . .
Well, it could happen!

PERCUSSION SECTION

Why are orchestra intermissions limited to twenty minutes?
So you don't have to retrain the drummers.

What did the drummer get on his IQ test?
Drool.

How do you know when a drummer is knocking at your door?
The knock slows down.

Did you hear about the time the bass player locked his keys in the car?
It took two hours to get the drummer out.

What's the difference between a drummer and a drum machine?
With a drum machine you only have to punch the information in once.

A customer walks into a new store on the block that sells brains. There are three glass cases, each containing a nice, wet, quivering brain. The first one says 'Astrophysicist' and it costs $10. The second says, 'Avon salesman' and costs $1000.

The third says, 'Drummer' and costs $10 000. The customer is confused, and questions the salesperson.

'I don't get it. Why would I want a drummer's brain for $10 000 when I can get an astrophysicists' for $10?'

The salesman replies, 'Because it's never been used.'

Two girls are walking along when they hear, 'Psst! Down here!' They both look down and see a frog sitting beside the road. The frog says to them, 'Hey, if you kiss me I'll turn into a world-famous drummer and make you both rich and famous!'

The two girls looked at each other, and one of them reaches down and grabs the frog and stuffs it in her pocket.

The other girl says, 'What did you do that for?'

The first replies, 'I'm not stupid. I know a talking frog is worth heaps more than a famous drummer.'

A guy walks into a shop.

'You got one of them Marshall Hiwatt AC30 amplification thingies and a Gobson StratoBlaster geetar with a Fried Rose tremulo?'

'You're a drummer, aren't you?'

'Duh, yeah. How'd you know?'

'This is a travel agency.'

Hey, did you hear about the drummer who finished high school?

Me neither.

How is a drum solo like a sneeze?

You can tell it's coming, but you can't do anything about it.

A man dies and goes to heaven. Contrary to what he expected, heaven is essentially a really long hallway with doors on either side, each with a short IQ range listed on it. Inside, the rooms are perfectly tailored so that the conversation will match the intelligence of the people in them.

He opens the 170 door. 'Well,' comes the conversation inside, 'I've always found Fourier transforms to be a rather limited way of interconverting what are fundamentally –'

He slams the door. Too rich for him.

He heads down the hall a bit to the 115 zone and opens the door. 'I just read *Generation X*,' comes a voice, 'and though Coupland doesn't do too badly in identifying his generation's fundamental angst, I was a bit confused by –'

Slam! Not bad, but now the man is getting curious, and wants to see what is further down the scale. He tries 95. 'Hey, did you read the paper today? Says interest rates will go up again –'

Slam! How about 60? 'Huh. Thought *Married with Children* last night was pretty funny. Didn't get the bit about the hooters, though –'

Slam! It is getting pretty bad. He tries 35. The people inside are looking at one another and drooling.

Finally, he comes to the one marked with a 10. He hesitates, fearing what he will see when he opens it. But he does, seeing only two guys inside.

'So,' one says to the other, 'what size sticks do you use?'

VOCALIST SECTION

If you threw a violist and a soprano off a cliff, which one would hit the ground first?

Who cares?

What's the difference between a soprano and a terrorist?
You can negotiate with a terrorist.

What's the difference between a soprano and a piranha?
The lipstick.

What's the difference between a soprano and a pit bull?
The jewellery.

How can you tell that there's a vocalist at your front door?
She's forgotten the key and doesn't know when to come in.

How many sopranos does it take to change a light bulb?
One. She holds the bulb and the world revolves around
her.

What's the difference between a soprano and a Porsche?
Most musicians have never been in a Porsche.

A jazz musician dies and goes to heaven. He is told, 'Hey man,
welcome! You have been elected to the Jazz All-Stars of
Heaven – right up there with Satchmo, Miles, Django, all the
greats. We have a gig tonight. Only one problem. God's girlfriend
gets to sing.'

Once a young tenor named Springer,
Got his testicles caught in a wringer.
 He hollered in pain
 As they rolled down the drain,
 'There goes my career as a singer!'

What do you see if you look up a soprano's skirt?
A tenor.

How many bass singers does it take to change a light bulb?
None. They're so macho they prefer to walk in the dark and
bang their shins.

GUITARS AND BANJOS

How can you tell the difference between banjo songs?
By the names.

How do you get a guitar player to play softer?
Give him some sheet music.

What did the guitarist do when his teacher told him to turn his amplifier on?
 He caressed it softly and told it that he loved it.

How many bass guitarists does it take to change a light bulb?
Don't bother. Just leave it out. No-one will notice.

Q: What do a vacuum cleaner and an electric guitar have in common?
A: Both suck when you plug them in.

ACCORDION SECTION

What's the difference between an Uzi and an accordion?
The Uzi stops after twenty rounds.

What's an accordion good for?
Learning how to fold a map.

CONDUCTING SECTION

What's the difference between a symphony conductor and Dr Scholl's footpads?
 Dr Scholl's footpads buck up the feet.

What's the difference between an opera conductor and a baby?

A baby sucks its fingers.

What is the ideal weight for a conductor?
About one kilogram, including the urn.

A musician calls the symphony office to talk to the conductor.
'I'm sorry, he's dead,' comes the reply.

The musician calls back twenty-five times, always getting the same reply from the receptionist. At last she asks him why he keeps calling.

'I just like to hear you say it.'

A man and his son are walking through a cemetery. The boy asks, 'Look Daddy, they buried two people in the same grave.'

The father says, 'Two people? Let me see.'

So the father takes a look, and sure enough, the marker says, 'Here lies a symphony conductor and a humble man.'

A guy is so dumb his teacher gives him two sticks and he becomes a drummer. But he loses one, so he becomes a conductor.

Q: Why is a conductor like a condom?
A: It's safer with one, but more fun without.

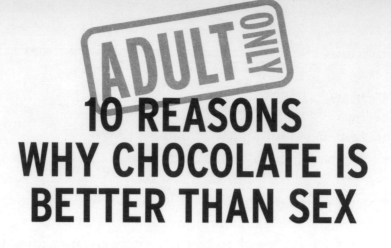

10 REASONS WHY CHOCOLATE IS BETTER THAN SEX

1. Chocolate satisfies even when it has gone soft.

2. You can have chocolate in front of your mother.

3. If you bite the nuts too hard the chocolate won't mind.

4. The word 'commitment' doesn't scare off chocolate.

5. You can have chocolate on top of your workbench or desk during working hours without upsetting your co-workers.

6. You don't get hairs in your mouth with chocolate.

7. With chocolate there's no need to fake it.

8. Chocolate doesn't make you pregnant.

9. When you have chocolate it does not keep your neighbours awake.

10. With chocolate, size doesn't matter.

ON THE FARM

It must be the country air, or the silence, or the . . .
Actually, it's the people who live on farms that
make them such an ideal location for a joke.

A ventriloquist goes for a walk in the country and sees a farmer sitting on his porch with his dog. The ventriloquist asks the farmer if he can talk to the dog.

'Dogs don't talk,' the farmer tells him.

'Well, can I try?'

'Sure, go ahead. Though you're wasting your time.'

'Hey dog, how's it goin'?' asks the ventriloquist.

'Doin' all right,' replies the dog.

The farmer is shocked, while the ventriloquist proceeds to trick the farmer.

'Is this your owner?' the ventriloquist asks pointing at the farmer.

'Yep,' the dog replies.

'How's he treat you?'

'Real good. He walks me twice a day, feeds me great food, and takes me to the lake once a week to play.'

Next, the ventriloquist asks if he can speak to the farmer's horse.

'Horses don't talk,' the farmer says.

Again, the ventriloquist insists until the farmer agrees.

'Hey horse, how's it goin'?' the ventriloquist asks.

'Cool,' the horse replies.

The farmer looks even more astonished than when the dog spoke.

'Is this your owner?' the ventriloquist asks pointing at the farmer.

'Yep,' the horse replies.

'How's he treat you?'

'Pretty good, thanks for asking. He rides me regularly, brushes me down often, and keeps me in the barn to protect me from the elements.'

The ventriloquist then turns to the farmer again and asks, 'Mind if I talk to your sheep?'

The farmer gesticulates wildly and is hardly able to talk. Nevertheless, he manages to blurt out, 'Them sheep ain't nothin' but liars, every darned one of 'em!'

A young lad from the city goes to visit his uncle, a farmer. For the first few days, the uncle shows him all the usual things, chickens, cows, crops, etc. After three days, however, it is obvious that the nephew is getting bored, and the uncle is running out of things to amuse him. Finally, the uncle has an idea.

'Why don't you grab a gun, take the dogs and go shooting?'

This seems to cheer the nephew up, and with enthusiasm, off he goes, dogs in tow. After a few hours, the nephew returns.

'How did you enjoy that?' asks the uncle.

'It was great!' exclaims the nephew. 'Got any more dogs?'

A farmer hires a uni student one summer to help around the farm.

At the end of the summer the farmer says, 'Son, since you have done such a fine job here this summer, I am going to throw a party for you.'

The uni student says, 'Great!'

So the farmer says, 'Well you better be able to handle a few beers because there will be lots of drinking.'

The student says, 'I can drink just as much as anyone else.'

And the farmer adds, 'There is also going to be a lot of fightin' so I hope you are ready.'

So the student responds, 'I have been working hard all summer and I think I'm in pretty good shape.'

'One more thing,' says the farmer. 'Did I mention that there will be lots of sex?'

'You beauty!' shouts the student. 'I have been out here all summer and I have been dying for some action. What should I wear to this party?'

The farmer says, 'Nothing fancy. It's just going to be me and you.'

An extraordinarily handsome man decided he has the God-given responsibility to marry the perfect woman so they can produce children beyond comparison. With this as his mission he begins searching for the perfect woman. After a diligent, but fruitless, search up and down the east coast, he starts to head west. Shortly thereafter he meets a farmer who has three stunningly gorgeous daughters that positively take his breath away. So he explains his mission to the farmer, asking for permission to marry one of them.

The farmer simply replies, 'They're all lookin' to get married, so you came to the right place. Look them over and select the one you want.'

The man dates the first daughter. The next day the farmer asks for the man's opinion.

'Well,' says the man, 'she's just a weeeeee bit, not that you can hardly notice, but pigeon-toed.'

The farmer nods and suggests the man date one of the other girls; so the man goes out with the second daughter. The next day, the farmer again asks how things went.

'Well,' the man replies, 'She's just a weeeee bit, not that you can hardly tell, cross-eyed.'

The farmer nods and suggests he date the third girl to see if things are any better. So he does.

The next morning the man rushes in exclaiming, 'She's perfect, just perfect! She's the one I want to marry.'

So they are wed right away. Months later a baby is born. When the man visits the nursery he is horrified. The baby is the ugliest, most pathetic human you can imagine. He rushes to his father-in-law asking how such a thing could happen considering the parents.

'Well,' explains the farmer, 'she was just a weeeee bit, not that you could hardly tell, pregnant when you met her.'

HUNTING AND FISHING

*There's something about people who go hunting
and fishing. I'm not saying they've got a screw
loose or anything but . . .*

Two hunters are out looking for pheasant when they come
upon the local farmer's daughter, sitting naked on a fence,
sunning herself.

The first hunter asks, 'Are you game?'

She replies, 'I sure am, Honey!'

So the second hunter shoots her.

A guy is on his honeymoon near his favourite fishing lake. He
fishes from dawn to dark with his favourite fishing guide.
One day the guide mentions that the man seems to be spending
his honeymoon fishing.

'Yes, but you know how I love to fish' the man replies.

'But aren't you newlyweds supposed to be into something
else?' the guide asks.

'Yes, but she's got gonorrhoea; and you know how I love to
fish.'

A few hours later the guide says, 'I understand, but that's not
the only way to have sex.'

'I know, but she's got diarrhoea; and you know how
I love to fish.'

The following day the guide says, 'Sure, but that's still not the
only way to have sex.'

'Yeah, but she's got pyuria; and you know how I love to
fish.'

Late that afternoon, thoroughly frustrated the guide comments, 'I guess I'm not sure why you'd marry someone with health problems like that.'

'It's 'cause she's also got worms; and you know I just love to fish.'

Two hunters bump into each other every afternoon after a day's hunting. And every afternoon, one of the hunters has a bearskin, while the other has nothing. Eventually, the empty-handed hunter asks the other hunter how he manages to catch a bear each day.

'It's easy,' says the hunter.

'I go over to one of those holes in the mountain, stand in front of it and shout, "you stupid fat, ugly bear, get your stinking arse out off this hole!," then the bear comes out and I shoot it. Easy as.'

'I'll try that,' the other hunter says.

The next day, the first hunter comes out of the woods with a bear skin and bumps into the other hunter who is crawling around on his hands and knees, covered in blood and missing a leg.

'What happened to you man?'

'Aargh, I did what you told me to do. I went to a hole, started shouting and swearing at the bear and guess what happened?'

'What?'

'A bloody train came out.'

Two hunters are dragging their dead deer back to their car. Another hunter approaches pulling his along too.

'Hey, I don't want to tell you how to do something, but I can tell you that it's much easier if you drag the deer in the other direction. Then the antlers won't dig into the ground.'

After the third hunter leaves, the two decide to try it.

A little while later one hunter says to the other, 'You know, that guy was right. This is a lot easier!'

'Yeah, but we're getting farther from the truck,' the other adds.

WHY FISHING IS BETTER THAN SEX

- When you go fishing and you catch something, that's good. If you're having sex and you catch something, that's bad.

- Fish don't compare you to other fishermen and don't want to know how many other fish you have caught.

- In fishing you lie about the one that got away. With sex you lie about the one you caught.

- You can catch and release a fish without having to lie and promise to still be friends after you've let it go.

- You don't have to change your line to keep catching fish.

- You can catch a fish on a twenty-cent night crawler. If you want to catch a woman you're talking at least dinner and a movie.

- Fish don't mind if you fall asleep while you're fishing.

UNIVERSITY LIFE

It's a wonder anyone ever gets through uni.

An autopsy lecturer is giving an introductory lecture to a class of students. Standing over a corpse, he addresses the class.

'There are two things you need to make a career in medical forensics. First, you must have no fear.'

Having said that, he shoves his finger up the corpse's arsehole then licks it.

'Now you must do the same,' he tells the class.

After a couple of minutes of uneasy silence, the class do as instructed.

'Second,' the lecturer continues, 'you must have an acute sense of observation. For instance, how many of you noticed that I put my middle finger up this man's anus, but licked my index finger?'

A pre-med student takes an examination and the last question is: Give four advantages of breast milk.

The student begins to answer the question:

1. No need to sterilise bottles
2. Healthier for the child
3. Available whenever necessary

But the fourth point eludes him. When there are only a couple of minutes left to finish the exam he gets desperate and answers:

4. Available in attractive containers

On the first day of uni, the Dean addresses the students, pointing out some of the rules. 'The female dormitory will be out-of-bounds for all male students, and the male dormitory for all female students. Anybody caught breaking this rule will be fined $20 the first time. Anybody caught breaking this rule the second time will be fined $60. Being caught a third time will cost you a fine of $180. Are there any questions?'

A male student in the crowd inquires, 'How much for a season pass?'

Agirl goes into the doctor's office for a check-up. As she takes off her blouse, he notices a red 'H' on her chest.

'How did you get that mark on your chest?' asks the doctor.

'Oh, my boyfriend went to Harvard and he's so proud of it that he never takes off his Harvard sweatshirt, even when we make love,' she replies.

A couple of days later, another girl comes in for a check-up. As she takes off her blouse, he notices a blue 'Y' on her chest.

'How did you get that mark on your chest?' asks the doctor.

'Oh, my boyfriend went to Yale and he's so proud of it that he never takes off his Yale sweatshirt, even when we make love,' she replies.

A couple of days later, another girl comes in for a check-up. As she takes off her blouse, he notices a red 'M' on her chest.

'Do you have a boyfriend at Michigan?' asks the doctor.

'No, but I have a girlfriend at Wisconsin. Why do you ask?'

Avisiting lecturer is giving a seminar on the supernatural. To get a feel for his audience, he asks, 'How many people here believe in ghosts?'

About ninety students raise their hands.

'Well that's a good start. Out of those of you who believe in ghosts, do any of you think you've ever seen a ghost?'

About forty students raise their hands.

'That's really good. I'm really glad you take this seriously. Has anyone here ever talked to a ghost?'

Fifteen students raise their hands.

'That's a great response. Has anyone here ever touched a ghost?'

Three students raise their hands.

'That's fantastic. But let me ask you one question further. Have any of you ever made love to a ghost?'

One student in the back raises his hand. The lecturer is astonished. He takes off his glasses, takes a step back, and says, 'Son, all the years I've been giving this lecture, no-one has ever claimed to have slept with a ghost. You've got to come up here and tell us about your experience.'

The student replies with a nod and a grin, and begins to make his way up to the podium.

The lecturer says, 'Well, tell us what it's like to have sex with a ghost.'

The student replies, 'Ghost? Damn. From back there I thought you said "goats"!'

DOCTORS AND NURSES

*There's nothing at all funny about sickness and
death. Unless it's happening to someone else.*

A guy goes to see a doctor and after a series of tests the doctor
comes in and says, 'I've got some good news and some bad
news.'

'What's the bad news?' asks the patient.

'The bad news is that, unfortunately, you've only got three
months to live.'

The patient is shocked, 'Oh my god! Well what's the good
news then, doctor?'

The doctor points over to the secretary at the front desk, 'You
see that blonde with the big tits, tight arse and legs that go all
the way up to heaven?'

The patient says, 'Yes.'

The doctor smiles and replies, 'I'm banging her!'

M r Smith goes to the doctor's office to collect his wife's test
results.

'I'm sorry, Sir,' says the receptionist, 'but there has been a bit
of a mix-up and we have a problem. When we sent your wife's
sample to the lab, the samples from another Mrs Smith were
sent as well and we are now uncertain which one is your wife's.
Frankly, that's either bad or terrible.'

'What do you mean?' asks Mr Smith.

'Well, one Mrs Smith has tested positive for Alzheimer disease
and the other for AIDS. We can't tell which your wife's is.'

'That's terrible! Can we take the test over?'

'Normally, yes. But your medical insurance fund won't pay for these expensive tests more than once.'

'Well, what am I supposed to do now?' asks Mr Smith.

'The doctor recommends that you drop your wife off in the middle of town. If she finds her way home, don't sleep with her.'

A proctologist has grown tired of his career and decides to go back to study. After thinking about what he wants to do with the rest of his life, he decides to go to trade school to become a garage mechanic. After struggling through the first course, he takes the final exam. When he gets the results back he is amazed to find he got 200%.

'How in the world did I pass? I thought I was going to flunk this thing,' he says in wonder.

'Well,' replies the instructor, 'I gave you fifty points for getting the engine rebuilt, I gave you fifty points because it ran, and the other 100 points was from doing it all through the muffler.'

A man goes to an urologist and tells him that he is having a problem and that he is unable to get his penis erect. After a complete examination, the doctor tells the man that the muscles around the base of his penis are damaged from a prior viral infection and there is nothing he can do for him. However, he knows of an experimental treatment that might be applicable, if the man is willing to take the risk. The treatment consists of implanting muscle tissue from an elephant's trunk into the man's penis.

The man thinks about it for a while. The thought of going through life without ever experiencing sex again is just too much for him to bear. So, with the assurance that there will be no cruelty or adverse effect on the elephant, the man decides to go for it. A few weeks after the operation, he is given the green light to use his newly renovated equipment. As a result, he plans a romantic evening with his girlfriend and takes her to one of the best restaurants in the city. However, in the middle of dinner, he feels a stirring between his legs that continues to the point of being extremely painful. To release the pressure, he unzips his fly and immediately his penis springs from his pants, goes to the top of the table, grabs a potato, and then returns to his pants.

His girlfriend is stunned at first, but then with a sly smile on her face says, 'That was incredible. Can you do that again?'

With his eyes watering, he replies, 'I think I can, but I'm not sure if I can fit another potato up my arse.'

In a doctor's surgery, Merv sits waiting patiently to see Dr Strangeways. Suddenly, a nun rushes out of his surgery in tears. Somewhat taken aback, Merv goes in next.

'Morning doctor. That nun looked very upset.'

'Yeah, I told her she was pregnant.'

'A nun? Pregnant?'

'Oh, she isn't really. But it sure as hell cured her hiccups.'

A man visits his doctor for his regular check-up. The doctor is not too pleased with what he finds and asks the man to send his wife to see him. The wife goes to see the doctor who tells her that her husband has a very serious heart condition.

'Don't be too alarmed though,' the doctor reassures her. 'With the right treatment he can live a long and happy life. You will have to give him every attention. Treat him very gently. Don't ask him to do any work around the house. No lawn mowing or anything like that. In fact, you must pamper his every whim. Cook his favourite dishes. Never get cross with him when he gets difficult – and he will. Always do whatever it is he feels like doing. Spoil him totally and you will have your husband for a very long time.'

When she arrives home, the husband says, 'What did the doctor say?'

The wife replies, 'You're going to die.'

A woman comes home from the doctor.

'What did the doctor say?' her husband asks.

'He said I have the figure of an eighteen-year-old,' she replies.

'What did he say about your big fat arse,' quips the husband.

'Your name didn't come up.'

An old country doctor goes way out to the boondocks to deliver a baby. It is so far out that there is no electricity. When the doctor arrives, no-one is home except for the labouring mother and her five-year-old child. The doctor instructs the child to hold a lantern up high so he can see while he helps the woman deliver the baby. The child does so, the mother pushes, and after a little while, the doctor lifts the newborn baby by the feet and spanks him on the bottom to get him to take his first breath.

'Hit him again,' the child says. 'He shouldn't have crawled up there in the first place.'

A tired doctor is awakened by a phone call in the middle of the night.

'Please, you have to come right over,' pleads a distraught young mother. 'My child has swallowed a contraceptive.'

The physician dresses quickly, but before he can get out the door, the phone rings again.

'You don't have to come over after all,' the woman says with a sigh of relief. 'My husband just found another one.'

A man's wife has been in a coma for several days following a particularly nasty knock on the head. As usual, one of the nurses in the hospital is giving her a wash in bed. As she washes down the woman's body, she sponges her pubic hair. Out of the corner of her eye the nurse thinks she has seen the woman's eyebrows shudder. Not quite sure, she tries again. This time, she actually did see some movement.

'Doctor, Doctor,' she calls, 'I saw some movement!'

The Doctor comes into the room and tries as well. Once more, they both see movement around the woman's eyes.

'Well this is good news,' says the doctor. 'I think we should call her husband and let him know.'

They call her husband and tell him that they have seen some movement. When he arrives, they explain that by touching the woman's pubic hair, they were seeing some sort of reaction in her facial muscles. The doctor suggests that the husband might like to try something a little more adventurous in order to provoke a stronger reaction.

'I suggest that we leave the room and that you try a little oral sex,' he says.

The husband agrees and is left alone in the room. Several moments later, all the emergency alarms and buzzers are activated. The doctor and a host of nurses run into the wife's room where they see the husband zipping up his jeans.

'Oops,' he says, 'I think I choked her.'

A woman goes to her doctor for a follow-up visit after the doctor has prescribed testosterone for her. She is a little worried about some of the side effects she is experiencing.

'Doctor, the hormones you've been giving me have really helped, but I'm afraid that you're giving me too much. I've started growing hair in places that I've never grown hair before.'

The doctor reassures her. 'A little hair growth is a perfectly normal side effect of testosterone. Just where has this hair appeared?'

'On my balls.'

A man runs to the doctor and says, 'Doctor, you've got to help me. My wife thinks she's a chicken.'

The doctor says, 'How long has she had this condition?'

'Two years,' says the man.

'Then why did it take you so long to come and see me?'

The man shrugs his shoulders, 'We needed the eggs.'

A man walks into the doctor's surgery and flips his penis onto the desk and says, 'I'd like you to have a look at this Doc.'

The doctor looks and says, 'I can see nothing wrong with it.'

'I know, but it's a bloody beauty isn't it?'

Two doctors are in a hospital hallway one day complaining about Nurse Molly.

'She's incredibly mixed up,' says one doctor. 'She does everything absolutely backwards. Just last week, I told her to give a patient 2mg of morphine every ten hours, she gave him 10mg every two hours. He damn near died on us.'

The second doctor says, 'That's nothing. Earlier this week, I told her to give a patient an enema every twenty-four hours. She tried to give him twenty-four enemas in one hour. The guy damn near exploded.'

Suddenly they hear a bloodcurdling scream from down the hall.

'Oh my God!' says the first doctor, 'I just realised I told Nurse Molly to prick Mr Smith's boil.'

A man walks into a crowded doctor's office.

As he approaches the desk the receptionist asks, 'Yes Sir, may we help you?'

'There's something wrong with my dick,' he replies.

The receptionist is shocked and says, 'You shouldn't come into a crowded office and say things like that.'

'Why not? You asked me what was wrong and I told you,' he says.

'We do not use language like that here,' she says. 'Please go outside and come back in and say that there's something wrong with your ear or whatever.'

The man walks out, waits several minutes and re-enters. The receptionist smiles smugly and asks, 'Yes?'

There's something wrong with my ear,' he states.

The receptionist nods approvingly.

'And what is wrong with your ear, Sir?'

'I can't bloody piss out of it,' the man replies.

An old man goes to the doctor for his yearly physical, his wife tagging along.

When the doctor enters the examination room, he tells the old man, 'I need a urine sample, a stool sample and a sperm sample.'

The old man, being hard of hearing, looks at his wife and yells, 'What?' What did he say? What's he want?'

His wife yells back, 'He needs your underwear.'

An elderly married couple go to the doctor for their annual medical check-ups.

After the examination, the doctor says to the elderly man, 'You appear to be in good health. Do you have any medical concerns that you would like to discuss with me?'

'In fact, I do,' says the man. 'After I have sex with my wife for the first time, I am usually hot and sweaty. And then, after I have sex with my wife the second time, I am usually cold and chilly.'

'This is very interesting,' replies the doctor. 'Let me do some research and get back to you.'

After examining the elderly woman, the doctor says, 'Everything appears to be fine. Do you have any medical concerns that you would like to discuss with me?'

The woman replies that she has no questions or concerns.

The doctor then asks, 'Your husband had an unusual concern. He claims that he is usually hot and sweaty after having sex with you the first time and then cold and chilly after the second time. Do you know why?'

'Oh that old buzzard!' she replies. 'That's because the first time is usually in summer and the second time is usually in winter.'

One day a young married couple are in their bedroom making love. All of a sudden a bumble bee enters the bedroom window. As the young woman parts her legs the bee enters her vagina.

The woman starts screaming, 'Oh my god, help me, there's a bee in my vagina.'

The husband immediately takes her to the local doctor and explains the situation.

The doctor thinks for a moment and says, 'Hmm, tricky situation. But I have a solution to the problem if young Sir will permit.'

The husband is very concerned and agrees that the doctor can use whatever method he likes to get the bee out of his wife's vagina.

The doctor says, 'OK, what I'm gonna do is rub some honey over the top of my penis and insert it into your wife's vagina. When I feel the bee getting closer to the tip of my dick I shall withdraw it and the bee should hopefully follow my penis out of your wife's vagina.'

The husband nods and gives his approval.

The young woman says, 'Yes, yes, whatever, just get on with it.'

So the doctor, after covering the tip of his penis with honey, inserts it into the young woman's vagina.

After a few gentle strokes, the doctor says, 'I don't think the bee has noticed the honey yet. Perhaps I should go a bit deeper.'

So the doctor goes deeper. After a while the doctor begins shafting the young woman very hard indeed. The young woman begins to quiver with excitement, she begins to moan and groan aloud.

'Oh doctor, doctor!' she shouts.

The doctor, concentrating very hard, looks like he is enjoying himself. He then put his hands on the young woman's breasts and starts making loud noises.

The husband, at this point, suddenly becomes very annoyed and shouts, 'Now wait a minute, what the hell do you think you're doing?'

The doctor, still concentrating, replies, 'Change of plan, I'm gonna drown the bastard.'

Queen Elizabeth II is visiting one of New York's finest hospitals and during her tour of the wards she passes a room where one of the male patients is masturbating.

'Oh God,' says the Queen. 'That's disgraceful, what is the meaning of this?'

The doctor leading the tour explains, 'I am sorry your Royal Highness, but this man has a very serious condition where his testicles fill up rapidly with semen. If he doesn't do what he is doing at least five times per day, he could swell up and he might die'

'Oh, I am sorry,' says the Queen. 'I was unaware that such a medical condition existed.'

On the same floor they soon pass another room where a young, blonde nurse is performing oral sex on another patient.

'Oh my God,' says the Queen. 'What's happening here?'

The doctor replies, 'Same problem, better health plan.'

Three elderly men are at the doctor's office for a memory test. The doctor asks the first man, 'What is three times three?'

'Two hundred and seventy four,' he replies.

The doctor rolls his eyes and looks up at the ceiling, and says to the second man, 'It's your turn. What is three times three?'

'Tuesday,' replies the second man.

The doctor shakes his head sadly, then asks the third man, 'OK, your turn. What's three times three?'

'Nine,' says the third man.

'That's great!' says the doctor. 'How did you get that?'

'Simple,' he says, 'just subtract 274 from Tuesday.'

Two elderly couples are enjoying a friendly conversation when one of the men asks the other, 'Fred, how was the memory clinic you went to last month?'

'Outstanding,' Fred replies. 'They taught us all the latest psychological techniques – visualization, association. It made a huge difference for me.'

'That's great! What was the name of the clinic?'

Fred goes blank. He thinks and thinks, but can't remember. Then a smile breaks across his face and he asks, 'What do you call that red flower with the long stem and thorns?'

'You mean a rose?'

'Yes, that's it!' He turns to his wife. 'Rose, what was the name of that clinic?'

YOU MIGHT BE A NURSE IF . . .

. . . when using a public toilet, you wash your hands with soap for a full minute and turn off the faucets with your elbows.

. . . men assume you must be great in bed because of the nine billion porn movies about nurses.

. . . everyone, including complete strangers, tells you about each and every ache and pain they have.

. . . you want to put your foot through the TV screen every time you see a nurse on a soap opera doing nothing but talking on the phone and flirting with doctors.

. . . you can watch the goriest movie and eat anything afterwards, even spaghetti with lots of tomato sauce.

. . . you use a plastic 30cc medicine cup for a shot glass.

How many nurses does it take to change a light bulb? As many as the doctor orders.

How many triage nurses does it take to change a light bulb? One, but the bulb will have to spend four hours in the waiting room.

Doctor: I've got very bad news – you've got cancer and Alzheimer's.
Patient: Well, at least I don't have cancer.

A man walks into a doctor's office. He has a cucumber up his nose, a carrot in his left ear and a banana in his right ear.
'What's the matter with me?' he asks the doctor.
The doctor replies, 'You're not eating properly.'

A young woman goes to her doctor complaining of pain.
'Where are you hurting?' asks the doctor.
'I hurt all over,' says the woman.
'What do you mean, all over?' asks the doctor, 'be a little more specific.'
The woman touches her right knee with her index finger and yells, 'Ow, that hurts.'
Then she touches her left cheek and again yells, 'Ouch! That hurts, too.'

Then she touches her right earlobe.

'Ow, even *that* hurts,' she cried.

The doctor checks her thoughtfully for a moment and tells her his diagnosis, 'You have a broken finger.'

A SHORT HISTORY OF MEDICINE

'Doctor, I have an ear ache.'

2000 B.C.:   'Here, eat this root.'

1000 B.C.:   'That root is heathen, say this prayer.'

1850 A.D.:   'That prayer is superstition, drink this potion.'

1940 A.D.:   'That potion is snake oil, swallow this pill.'

1985 A.D.:   'That pill is ineffective, take this antibiotic.'

2000 A.D.:   'That antibiotic is artificial. Here, eat this root!'

A woman, calling Mount Sinai Hospital, says, 'Hello, I want to know if a patient is getting better.'

The voice on the other end of the line says, 'What is the patient's name and room number?'

She says, 'Yes, darling! She's Sarah Finkel, in Room 302.'

The man on the phone says, 'Oh, yes. Mrs Finkel is doing very well. In fact, she's had two full meals, her blood pressure is fine, she's going to be taken off the heart monitor in a couple of hours and if she continues this improvement, Dr Cohen is going to send her home Tuesday.'

The woman says, 'Thank God! That's wonderful! Oh! That's fantastic! That's wonderful news!'

'From your enthusiasm, I take it you must be a close family member or a very close friend!'

She says, 'I'm Sarah Finkel in 302. Cohen, my doctor, doesn't tell me a word!'

An old fellow comes into the hospital, truly on death's door due to an infected gallbladder. The surgeon who removed the gallbladder is adamant that his patients be up and walking in the hall the day after surgery, to help prevent blood clots forming in the leg veins. The nurses walk the patient in the hall as ordered, and after the third day the nurse tells the doctor how he complains bitterly each time they do. The surgeon tells them to keep walking him.

After a week, the patient is ready to go. His children come to pick him up and thank the surgeon profusely for what he has done for their father. The surgeon is pleased and appreciates the thanks, but tells them that it was really a simple operation and he was lucky to get him in time.

'But doctor, you don't understand,' they say, 'Dad hasn't walked in over a year!'

Patient: I always see spots before my eyes.
Doctor: Didn't the new glasses help?
Patient: Sure, now I see the spots much clearer.

A veterinarian is feeling ill and goes to see her doctor. The doctor asks her all the usual questions about symptoms, how long they have been occurring, etc.

She interrupts him, 'Hey look, I'm a vet. I don't need to ask my patients these kinds of questions: I can tell what's wrong just by looking. Why can't you?'

The doctor nods, looks her up and down, writes out a prescription, and hands it to her.

'There you are. Of course, if that doesn't work, we'll have to have you put down.'

THINGS YOU DON'T WANT TO HEAR DURING SURGERY:

- Oops!

- That was some party last night. I can't remember when I've been that drunk.

- Damn! Page 47 of the manual is missing!

- Better save that. We'll need it for the autopsy.

- Come back here with that! Bad dog!

- Wait a minute, if this is his spleen, then what's that?

- Hand me that . . . uh . . . that uh . . . that thingy.

- If I can just remember how they did this on ER last week.

- Ya know, there's big money in kidneys. Hell, the guy's got two of 'em.

- Everybody stand back! I lost my contact lens!

- Sterile, shcmerile. The floor's clean, right?

- What do you mean he wasn't in for a sex change!

- Nurse, did this patient sign the organ donation card?

- Don't worry. I think it's sharp enough.

- I don't know what it is, but hurry up and pack it in ice.

- Let's hurry, I don't want to miss *Baywatch*.

- That laughing gas stuff is pretty cool. Can I have some more of that?

- Fire! Fire! Everyone get out!

At a medical convention, a male doctor and a female doctor start eyeing each other. The male doctor asks the female doctor to dinner and she accepts. As they sit down at the restaurant, she excuses herself to go and wash her hands.

After dinner, one thing leads to another and they end up in her hotel bedroom. Just as things get hot, the female doctor interrupts and says she has to go and wash her hands. When she comes back they go for it. After the sex session, she gets up and says she is going to wash her hands.

As she comes back the male doctor says, 'I bet you are a surgeon.'

She confirms and asks how he knew.

'Easy, you're always washing your hands.'

She then says, 'I bet you're an anaesthesiologist.'

'Wow, how did you guess?' asks the male doctor.

'I didn't feel a thing.'

A guy has been suffering from severe headaches for years with no relief. After trying all the usual cures he's referred to a headache specialist by his family doctor. The doctor asks him what his symptoms are.

'I get these blinding headaches; kind of like a knife across my scalp and –'

He is interrupted by the doctor, 'And a heavy throbbing right behind the left ear.'

'Yes! Exactly! How did you know?'

'Well I am the world's greatest headache specialist, you know.

But I myself suffered from that same type of headache for many years. It is caused by a tension in the scalp muscles. This is how I cured it: Every day I would give my wife oral sex. When she came she would squeeze her legs together with all her strength and the pressure would relieve the tension in my head. Try that every day for two weeks and come back and let me know how it goes.'

Two weeks go by and the man comes back.

'Well, how do you feel?' asks the doctor.

'Doc, I'm a new man! I feel great! I haven't had a headache since I started this treatment! I can't thank you enough. And, by the way, you have a lovely home.'

Doc, I can't stop singing the green, green grass of home.'
'That sounds like Tom Jones syndrome.'
'Is it common?'
'It's not unusual.'

A guy walks into the psychiatrist wearing only cling-film for shorts.
The shrink says, 'Well, I can clearly see you're nuts.'

Doc, I've got a cricket ball stuck up my backside.'
'How's that?'
'Don't you start.'

Bloke goes to the doctors with a lettuce leaf sticking out of his arse.
'Hmmmm, that's strange,' says the doctor.
Bloke replies, 'That's just the tip of the iceberg'.

Dentist: Say 'Aahh'.
Patient: Why?
Dentist: My dog's died.

A guy goes in to see a psychiatrist.

'Doc, I don't seem to be able to make any friends, so I need help from you, you fat bastard!'

A man came to hospital after a serious accident.

'Doctor, doctor, I can't feel my legs!' he shouted.

'I know you can't, I've cut your arms off.'

M an goes to the doc, with a strawberry growing out of his head.

'I'll give you some cream to put on it,' says the doctor.

P atient: Doctor, doctor, an Alsatian bit me on the finger.
Doctor: Which one?
Patient: I don't know. All Alsatians look the same to me.

D avid, a keen fisherman, had driven by a lake many times and had seen a lot of anglers pulling in plenty of fish, so he decided to give his luck a try. On his first day of fishing he had no luck at all but another fisherman near him was scooping in one fish after another. He had to know the secret.

'Excuse me sir, but would you mind telling me what sort of bait you are using?' he asked.

The other man looked around a bit embarrassed. 'Well, I am a surgeon, and quite by accident I found that human tonsils work very well.'

David thanked the surgeon and left. The next day, he returned to the lake, but still had no luck with his ordinary bait. He noticed there was another man reeling in fish after fish.

'Excuse me,' asked David, 'but could you suggest a bait that I could try?'

'Well, I can, but I am not sure it will do you any good. I'm a surgeon and I'm using a bit of human appendix.'

It seemed that the fish in this lake would require a little more effort than normal, but David was willing to give the lake one more try. On the third day, David still had no luck. There was yet another man near him bringing in fish left and right. David wanted to confirm what he already knew.

'Excuse me sir, but are you a doctor?'

'No,' replied the man. 'I'm a Rabbi.'

'Doctor, doctor, my hands are killing me.'
'Take them off your throat.'

'Doctor, doctor, how long have I got?'
'10.'
'10 what? 10 months? 10 weeks?'
'10, 9, 8, 7 . . .'

'Doctor, doctor, have you got something for a migraine?'
'Take this hammer and hit yourself on the head.'

ADULT ONLY

WHY DID THE CHICKEN CROSS THE ROAD?

Martin Luther King Jr:
I envision a world where all chickens will be free to cross roads without having their motives called into question.

Grandpa:
In my day, we didn't ask why the chicken crossed the road. Someone told us that the chicken crossed the road, and that was good enough for us.

Saddam Hussein:
This was an unprovoked act of rebellion and we were quite justified in dropping fifty tons of nerve gas on it.

Fox Mulder:
You saw it cross the road with your own eyes. How many more chickens have to cross before you believe it?

Freud:
The fact that you are at all concerned that the chicken crossed the road reveals your underlying sexual insecurity.

Einstein:
Did the chicken really cross the road or did the road move beneath the chicken?

Bill Clinton:
I did not cross the road with *that* chicken. What do you mean by chicken? Could you define chicken please?

Louis Farrakhan:
The road, you will see, represents the black man. The chicken crossed the 'black man' in order to trample him and keep him down.

The Bible:
And God came down from the heavens, and He said unto the chicken, 'Thou shalt cross the road.' And the chicken crossed the road, and there was much rejoicing.

Colonel Sanders:
What? I missed one?

EATING OUT

*Jokes about food go back a very long way.
I'm sure the first joke ever told was something
along the lines of 'Eve, there's a worm in this apple'
'Well don't yell it out or they'll all want one.'*

A woman is feeling a bit down in the dumps and decides to treat herself to a meal at a very expensive restaurant. She manages to get a table, even though the place is very busy, and she enjoys a delicious meal on her own. Aware of her financial limitations, she doesn't go overboard but does make sure she enjoys herself. When the head waiter brings the bill, she's horrified to see the total – $250! She didn't expect this at all. Realising there's no point complaining, she hands over her credit card.

When the waiter returns with the slip for her to sign, she asks him, 'Would you mind holding my breasts while I sign my name please?'

The waiter is taken aback. In all his years in the job he's never been asked that before. But he is always eager to please the customer and he obliges. When the woman gets up to leave, the waiter's curiosity gets the better of him. He catches up with her at the door.

'I'm sorry to bother you Miss but I'd like to know why you asked me to do that just now.'

'Oh it's quite simple really,' she replies, 'I love to have my breasts held when I'm being screwed!'

A man and a woman are having dinner in a fine restaurant. Their waitress, taking another order at a table a few paces away, notices that the man is slowly sliding down his chair and under the table, with the woman acting unconcerned. The waitress watches as the man slides all the way down his chair and out of sight under the table. Still, the woman dining across from him appears calm and unruffled, apparently unaware that her dining companion has disappeared.

After the waitress finishes taking the order, she comes over to the table and says to the woman, 'Pardon me, Ma'am, but I think your husband just slid under the table.'

The woman calmly looks up at her and replies firmly, 'No he didn't. He just walked in the door.'

'What flavours of ice cream do you have?' inquires the customer.

'Vanilla, strawberry and chocolate,' answers the new waitress in a hoarse whisper.

Trying to be sympathetic, the customer asks, 'Do you have laryngitis?'

'No,' replies the new waitress with some effort, 'just . . . erm . . . vanilla, strawberry and chocolate.'

A traveller becomes lost in the Sahara desert. Realising his only chance for survival is to find civilization, he begins walking. Time passes, and he becomes thirsty. More time passes, and he begins feeling faint.

He is on the verge of passing out when he spies a tent about 500m in front of him. Barely conscious, he reaches the tent and calls out, 'Water!'

A Bedouin appears in the tent door and replies sympathetically, 'I am sorry, Sir, but I have no water. However, would you like to buy a tie?'

With this, he brandishes a collection of exquisite silken neckwear.

'You fool,' gasps the man. 'I'm dying! I need water!'

'Well, Sir,' replies the Bedouin, 'if you really need water, there is a tent about 2km south of here where you can get some.'

Without knowing how, the man summons sufficient strength to drag his parched body the distance to the second tent. With his last bit of strength he tugs at the door of the tent and collapses.

Another Bedouin, dressed in a costly tuxedo, appears at the door and enquires, 'May I help you Sir?'

'Water!' is the feeble reply.

'Oh, Sir,' replies the Bedouin, 'I'm sorry, but you can't come in here without a tie!'

Waiter, there's a fly in my soup!
Force of habit, Sir. Our chef used to be a tailor.

Waiter, there's a fly in my soup!
Couldn't be, Sir. The cook used them all in the raisin bread.

Waiter, there is a fly in my soup!
Sorry Sir, maybe I missed it when I removed the other three.

Waiter, there's a dead fly in my soup!
What do you expect for $5 – a live one?

Waiter, waiter, there's a bee in my soup.
Yes Sir, it's the fly's day off.

Waiter, this coffee tastes like dirt!
Yes Sir, that's because it was only ground this morning.

A waiter brings a customer the steak he ordered, with his thumb over the meat.

'Are you crazy?' yells the customer, 'What are you doing with your hand on my steak?'

'What?' asks the waiter, 'You want it to fall on the floor again?'

H ow many waiters does it take to change a light bulb? None, a burned out bulb can't catch a waiter's eye.

H ow many waitresses does it take to change a light bulb? Three. Two to stand around bitching about it and one to go get the manager.

H ow many cafeteria staff does it take to change a light bulb? 'Sorry, we closed eighteen seconds ago, and I've just cashed up.'

GROWING OLD GRACEFULLY

It's great fun making fun of the elderly.
They're too frail to fight back.

An eighty-five-year-old man marries a beautiful twenty-five-year-old woman. Because her new husband is so old the woman decides that on their wedding night they should have separate suites. She is concerned that the old fellow could over-exert himself. After the festivities she prepares herself for bed and for the knock on the door she is expecting. Sure enough the knock comes and there is her groom ready for action. They start making love and all goes well. He then leaves her room and she prepares to go to sleep for the night. After a few minutes there's a knock on the door and there is the old man again, ready for more action. Somewhat surprised she consents to further sex which is again successful. When it is over, the octogenarian bids her a fond goodnight and leaves. She is very tired now and is close to sleep when, again, there is a knock at the door. There he is, fresh as a twenty-five-year-old and ready for more action. Once again they make love.

As they're lying alongside each other afterwards, the young bride says to him, 'I am really impressed that a guy your age has enough juice to go for it three times. I've been with guys less than half your age that were only good for one . . . you're great.'

The man looks confused, and turns to her and says, 'Have I been in here before?'

After forty years of marriage, Frankenstein and the Bride of Frankenstein come to a stand-still in their love life. Each night Frankenstein comes home from work, eats his dinner, and sits in front of the television until he falls asleep. Dissatisfied with this arrangement, the Bride decides to see a therapist.

'He's never in the mood,' complains the Bride.

'Try a romantic candlelit dinner,' suggests the therapist.

The next day, the Bride returns to the therapist with a frown on her face.

'He's still not in the mood,' she complains.

'This time,' the therapist recommends, 'try something more seductive. Put on some sexy lingerie and lure him into the bedroom.'

But the Bride returns to the therapist the following day complaining that her monster of a husband is still not in the mood.

As a final piece of advice, the therapist says, 'You should try to recreate the moment that first sparked your romance.'

The next day the Bride returns with a huge grin on her face.

'Thank you so much,' she says to the therapist. 'Last night, I forced Frankenstein to come outside in the middle of the lightening storm. And right there, in our backyard, he made love to me like it was our very first time.'

'Making love in a lightening storm put him in the mood?' asks the therapist.

'Well,' says the Bride of Frankenstein, 'I tied a kite to his penis.'

Two old ladies are walking through a museum and get separated. When they run into each other later the first old lady says, 'My! Did you see that statue of the naked man back there?'

The second old lady replies, 'Yes! I was absolutely shocked! How can they display such a thing! My gosh the penis on it was so large!'

And the first old lady blurts out, 'And cold, too!'

A couple have been married for fifty years. They are sitting at the breakfast table one morning when the old gentleman says to his wife, 'Just think, honey, we've been married for fifty years.'

'Yeah,' she replies, 'just think, fifty years ago we were sitting here at this breakfast table together.'

'I know,' the old man says, 'we were probably sitting here naked as jaybirds fifty years ago.'

'Well,' Granny snickers, 'what do you say . . . should we get naked?'

So the two strip to the buff and sit down at the table.

'You know, honey,' the little old lady whispers, 'my nipples are as hot for you today as they were fifty years ago.'

'I'm not surprised,' replies Gramps. 'One's in your coffee and the other is in your oatmeal.'

A police car pulls up in front of grandma's house and grandpa gets out. The polite policeman explains to grandma that the poor gentleman was lost in the park and couldn't find his way home.

'Oh dear,' says grandma, 'You've been going to that park for over thirty years. How could you get lost?'

Leaning close to grandma, so that the policeman can't hear, grandpa whispers, 'I wasn't lost. I was just too tired to walk home.'

An old lady and an old man are sitting in their retirement home. The man turns to the woman and says, 'I bet you can't tell how old I am.'

She says, 'OK.'

She then unzips his fly, feels around for a while and finally says, 'You're seventy-three.'

'That's amazing!' the man exclaims. 'How did you know?'

She replies, 'You told me yesterday.'

A guy goes to his grandmother's house and takes one of his friends with him. While he's talking to his grandmother, his friend starts eating the peanuts on the coffee table and finishes them off.

As they are leaving, the friend says, 'Thanks for the peanuts.'

She says, 'Yeah, since I lost my dentures I can only suck the chocolate off 'em.'

A n eighty-five-year-old man visits his doctor to get a sperm count. The man is given a jar and told to bring back a sample. The next day he returns to the doctor with an empty jar.

'What happened?' asks the doctor.

'Well,' the old man starts, 'I asked my wife for help. She tried with her right hand, then she tried with her left – nothing. Then she tried with her mouth, first with her teeth in, then with her teeth out, still nothing. We even called Evelyn, the lady next door, but still nothing.'

The doctor bursts out, 'You asked your neighbour?'

'Yep, no matter what we tried we couldn't get that damn jar open.'

A n old lady in a nursing home is wheeling up and down the halls in her wheelchair making sounds like she's driving a car.

As she's going down the hall, an old man jumps out of a room and says, 'Excuse me Ma'am but you were speeding. Can I see your drivers licence?'

She digs around in her purse a little, pulls out a candy wrapper, and hands it to him. He looks it over, gives her a warning and sends her on her way. Up and down the halls she goes again.

Again, the same old man jumps out of a room and says, 'Excuse me Ma'am but I saw you cross over the centre line back there. Can I see your registration please?'

She digs around in her purse, pulls out a store receipt and hands it to him. He looks it over, gives her another warning and sends her on her way. She zooms off again up and down the halls weaving all over. As she comes to the old man's room again, he jumps out. He's stark naked and has an erection.

The old lady in the wheelchair looks up and says, 'Oh, no, not the breathalyser again!'

An older lady is lonely, and decides that she needs a pet to keep her company. So off to the pet shop she goes. Forlornly, she searches but nothing seems to catch her interest, except one ugly frog. As she walks by the barrel he is in, he looks up and winks at her.

He whispers, 'I'm lonely too, buy me and you won't be sorry.'

The old lady thinks, why not? She hasn't found anything else. So, she buys the frog and takes it to her car.

Driving down the road the frog whispers to her, 'Kiss me, you won't be sorry.'

So, the old lady thinks what the hell, and kisses the frog.

Immediately the frog turns into an absolutely gorgeous, sexy, handsome, young prince. Then the prince kisses her back, and you know what the old lady turns into?

The first motel she can find.

BEING OVER 60 HAS ITS ADVANTAGES

- No one expects you to run into a burning building.
- People call at 9pm and ask, 'Did I wake you?'
- People no longer view you as a hypochondriac.
- There's nothing left to learn the hard way.
- You can eat dinner at 4pm.
- You can live without sex, but not without glasses.
- You enjoy hearing about other people's operations.
- You get into a heated argument about pension plans.

- You have a party and the neighbours don't even realise it.
- You quit trying to hold your stomach in, no matter who walks into the room.
- You sing along with the elevator music.
- Your investment in health insurance is finally beginning to pay off.
- Your joints are more accurate weather gauges than the Bureau of Meteorology.
- Your secrets are safe with your friends because they can't remember them either.

Two old ladies were outside their nursing home having a smoke, when it started to rain. One of the ladies pulled out a condom, cut off the end, put it over her cigarette, and continued smoking.

'What's that?' asked the other lady.

'A condom.'

'Where'd you get it?'

'You can get them at any drugstore.'

The next day, the second lady hobbled into the local drugstore and announced to the pharmacist that she wanted to buy a package of condoms. The guy looked at her kind of strangely (she was, after all, in her 80s), but politely asked what brand she preferred.

'Doesn't matter,' she replied, 'as long as it fits a Camel.'

The drugs that we use when we're ailing
Go by different names for retailing
Tylenol's acetamenophen.
Advil's Ibuprofen.
And Viagra is Mycoxafailing . . .

Eighty-year-old Jessie bursts into the rec room of the men's retirement home. She holds her clenched fist in the air and announces, 'Anyone who can guess what's in my hand can have sex with me tonight!'

An elderly gentleman in the rear shouts out, 'An elephant?'

Jessie thinks a minute and says, 'Close enough.'

The wealthy old gentleman and his wife were celebrating their 35th wedding anniversary and their three grown sons joined them for dinner. The old man was rather irritated when he discovered none of the boys had bothered to bring a gift, and after the meal, he drew them aside.

'You're all grown men,' he said, 'and old enough to hear this. Your mother and I have never been legally married.'

'What?' gasped one of the sons, 'Do you mean to say we're all bastards?'

'Yes,' snapped the old man, 'and cheap ones, too!'

A woman saw a little wrinkled up man rocking in a chair on his porch.

'I couldn't help noticing how happy you look. What's your secret for a happy life?' she asked him.

'I smoke three packs of cigarettes a day. I also drink a case of whisky a week, eat lots of fatty foods, and never ever take any exercise.'

'That's amazing. Exactly how old are you?'

'Twenty-six.'

A SAD TALE

My nookie days are over,
my pilot light is out.
What used to be my sex appeal,
is now my water spout.
Time was when, of its own accords,
from my trousers it would spring.

But now I have a full time job,
just to find the blasted thing.
It used to be embarrassing,
the way it would behave.
For every single morning,
it would stand and watch me shave.
But now as old age approaches,
it sure gives me the blues.
To see it hang its withered head,
and watch me tie my shoes.

THE BELL CURVE OF LIFE

At age 4   success is not peeing in your pants.
At age 10   success is making your own meals.
At age 12   success is having friends.
At age 18   success is having a driver's licence.
At age 20   success is having sex.
At age 35   success is having money.
At age 50   success is having money.
At age 60   success is having sex.
At age 70   success is having a driver's licence.
At age 75   success is having friends.
At age 80   success is making your own meals.
At age 85   success is not peeing in your pants.

DEATH AND DYING

*This section is for those people who, like me, find funerals
to be far more enjoyable and jolly than weddings.*

A ninety-year-old woman decides that she's seen and done everything, and the time has come to depart from this world. After considering various methods of doing away with herself, she comes to the conclusion that the quickest and surest method is to shoot herself through the heart. The trouble is, she isn't certain about exactly where her heart is, so she phones her doctor and asks him. He tells her that her heart is located two inches above her left nipple. So she shoots herself in the left kneecap.

A n old maid lives in a tiny village. In spite of her old age, she is still a virgin and she is very proud of it. She knows her last days are getting closer, so she tells the local undertaker that she wants the following inscription on her tombstone: 'Born as a virgin, lived as a virgin, died as a virgin.'

Not long after, the old maid dies peacefully, and the undertaker tells his men what the lady has said. The men go to carve it in, but as the lazy no-goods they are, they think the inscription is unnecessarily long.

They simply write: 'Returned unopened'.

B ecky is on her deathbed with her husband, John, maintaining a steady vigil by her side. As he holds her fragile hand, his warm tears run silently down his face, splashing onto her face, and rousing her from her slumber. She looked up and her pale lips began to move slightly.

'My darling John,' she whispers.

'Hush, my love,' he says. 'Go back to sleep. Shhh. Don't talk.'

But she is insistent. 'John,' she says in her tired voice. 'I have to talk. I have something I must confess to you.'

'There's nothing to confess,' replies the weeping John. 'It's all right. Everything's all right, go to sleep now.'

'No, no. I must die in peace, John,' she says. 'I slept with your brother, your best friend and your father.'

John musters a pained smile and strokes her hand.

'Hush now Becky, don't torment yourself. I know all about it,' he says. 'Why do you think I poisoned you?'

One of the workers at the brewery falls in a huge vat of beer and drowns. At the funeral, his wife is crying, 'Oh, Ben, Ben, you never had a chance.'

His foreman says, 'What do you mean, 'never had a chance'? He got out twice to take a piss.'

A funeral service is being held in a synagogue for a woman who has just passed away. At the end of the service the pallbearers are carrying the casket out, when they accidentally bump into a wall, jarring the casket.

They hear a faint moan. They open the casket and find that the woman is still alive.

She lives for ten more years and then dies. A ceremony is again held at the same synagogue and at the end of the ceremony the same pallbearers are again carrying the casket.

As they are walking out, the husband cries, 'Watch out for that wall!'

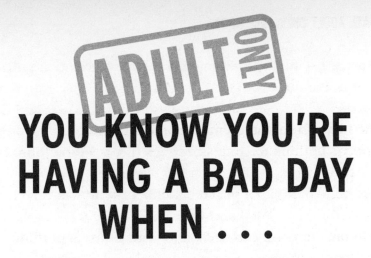

YOU KNOW YOU'RE HAVING A BAD DAY WHEN . . .

- You call suicide prevention and they put you on hold.

- You get to work and find a *60 Minutes* news team waiting in your office.

- You find your son's GI Joe doll dressed in drag.

- You turn on the evening news and they are showing emergency routes out of the city.

- Your twin sister forgets your birthday.

- Your four-year-old tells you that it's almost impossible to flush a grapefruit down the toilet.

- You have to sit down to brush your teeth in the morning.

- You start to pick up the clothes you wore home from the party last night . . . and there aren't any.

- It costs more to fill up your car than it did to buy it.

- You wake up to the soothing sound of running water . . . and remember that you just bought a waterbed.

- Your car payment, house payment, and girlfriend are three months overdue.

- Everyone avoids you the morning after the company office party.

- Your blind date turns out to be your ex-wife.

- You compliment the boss' wife on her unusual perfume and she isn't wearing any.

- Nothing you own is actually paid for.

- You go on your honeymoon to a remote little hotel and the desk clerk, bell hop, and manager have a 'Welcome Back' party for your new spouse.

- Airline food starts to taste good.

- Your mother approves of the person you are dating.

- Your doctor tells you that you are allergic to chocolate chip cookies.

- You realise that you have memorised the back of your cereal box.

- You take longer to get over sex than you did to have it.

- Everyone loves your drivers licence picture.

- You realise that the phone number on the bathroom wall of the bar is yours.

- Your kids start treating you the same way you treated your parents.

- The gypsy fortune teller offers to refund your money.

- People think you are forty . . . and you really are.

- Your new lover calls to tell you 'Last night was terrific.' And you remember that you were home by yourself.

- Everyone is laughing but you.

A LOAD OF OLD BALLS

*Sport is about the challenge, teamwork and fair play.
The hell it is! It's about making fun of those who
support teams that your team always beats.*

A man has the best seat in the stadium for the Grand Final. As he sits down, another man comes down and asks if anyone is sitting in the seat next to him.

'No,' he says, 'The seat is empty.'

'That's incredible,' says the man. 'Who in their right mind would have a seat like this for the Grand Final, the biggest sporting event in the world, and not use it?'

The man says, 'Well, actually, the seat belongs to me. I was supposed to come with my wife, but she passed away. This is the first Grand Final we haven't been to together since we got married in 1985.'

'Oh . . . I'm sorry to hear that. That's terrible. But couldn't you find someone else – a friend or relative, or even a neighbour to take the seat?'

The man shakes his head. 'No. They're all at the funeral.'

A champion jockey is about to enter a major steeplechase race on a new horse.

The horse's trainer meets him before the race and says, 'All you have to remember with this horse is that every time you approach a jump, you have to shout, "Alllleee Ooop!" really loudly in the horse's ear. Providing you do that, you'll be fine.'

The jockey thinks the trainer is mad but promises to shout the command. The race begins and they approach the first hurdle. The jockey ignores the trainer's ridiculous advice and the horse crashes straight through the centre of the jump but somehow manages to stay on its feet. They carry on and approach the second hurdle. The jockey, somewhat embarrassed, whispers 'alleeee ooop' in the horse's ear. The same thing happens – the horse crashes straight through the centre of the jump but again just stays on its feet. At the third hurdle, the jockey thinks, 'It's no good, I'll have to do it,' and yells, 'Allleee Ooop!' really loudly.

Sure enough, the horse sails over the jump with no problems. This continues for the rest of the race, but due to the earlier problems the horse only finishes third. The trainer is fuming and asks the jockey what went wrong.

The jockey tries to protect himself and replies, 'Nothing is wrong with me, it's this bloody horse. What is he, deaf or something?'

The trainer replies, 'Deaf? Deaf? He's not deaf, he's blind.'

Before the final match, the American wrestler's trainer comes to him and says, 'Now don't forget all the research we've done on this Russian. He's never lost a match because of this "pretzel" hold he has. Whatever you do, don't let him get you in this hold. If he does, you're finished.'

The wrestler nods in agreement.

Now, to the match: The American and the Russian circle each other several times looking for an opening. All of a sudden the Russian lunges forward, grabbing the American and wrapping him up in the dreaded pretzel hold. A sigh of disappointment goes up from the crowd, and the trainer buries his face in his hands for he knows all is lost. He can't bring himself to watch the ending.

Suddenly there is a scream, a cheer from the crowd, and the trainer raises his eye just in time to see the Russian flying up in the air. The Russian's back hits the mat with a thud, and the

American weakly collapses on top of him, getting the pin and winning the match.

The trainer is astounded. When he finally gets the American wrestler alone, he asks, 'How did you ever get out of that hold? No-one has ever done it before!'

The wrestler answers, 'Well, I was ready to give up when he got me in that hold, but at the last moment, I opened my eyes and saw this pair of balls right in front of my face. I thought I had nothing to lose, so with my last bit of strength I stretched out my neck and bit those babies just as hard as I could. You'd be amazed how strong you get when you bite your own balls.'

A young woman has been taking golf lessons. She has just started playing her first round of golf when she suffers a bee sting. The pain is so intense that she decides to return to the clubhouse.

Her golf pro sees her come into the clubhouse and asks, 'Why are you back in so early? What's wrong?'

'I was stung by a bee.'

'Where?' he asks.

'Between the first and second hole,' she replies.

He nods knowingly and says, 'Apparently your stance is too wide.'

A guy stands over his tee shot for what seems an eternity, looking up, looking down, measuring the distance, figuring the wind direction and speed, driving his partner nuts.

Finally his exasperated partner says, 'What's taking so long? Hit the blasted ball!'

The guy answers, 'My wife is up there watching me from the clubhouse. I want to make this a perfect shot.'

'Forget it man. You don't stand a snowball's chance in hell of hitting her from here.'

A very attractive couple are playing golf and the wife hits a beautiful, long shot – right through the window of a house. Horrified, the couple go to the house to apologise and offer to pay for the damage. A tall, handsome man answers the door.

'Come in! Come in!' he cries.

The couple, embarrassed by the smiling welcome, confess to breaking the window.

'I know, I know,' says the man. 'And I'm pleased you did.'

The couple exchange confused glances.

'You see that urn?' the man continues, pointing to what had been an antique masterpiece but is now lying in pieces on the floor.

'Oh no!' the wife cries. 'Don't tell me I've broken that too!'

'Don't be worried,' says the man. 'You see I've been in that urn for years and years. I'm a genie and you have set me free.'

The couple just stare at him in amazement.

'Now,' says the genie. 'I have the power to grant three wishes. Why don't we share them. One each.'

Turning to the wife he says, 'What is your greatest wish?'

'Well,' she says hesitantly, 'I would like to think I could have peace of mind and a quiet, calm life forever.'

'Done!' says the genie. 'And what about you Sir?'

The husband doesn't waste a minute to reply. 'I would like to have enough money to live a life of total luxury, to be able to afford expensive cars, take super cruises and live in the best stateroom on the ship, and have a grand house – with servants.'

'Done!'

The husband looks extremely pleased and asks the genie his wish.

The genie looks slightly embarrassed. 'That's rather delicate actually.' He turns to the wife and says, 'Do you mind if I speak to your husband alone for a moment?'

'Not at all,' she says.

The genie takes the husband aside. 'You have a very beautiful wife. I know I shouldn't ask this but my wish would be to spend just one night alone with her. What do you think?'

'Well I'm not sure,' says the husband. 'I'd have to discuss it with her and see how she feels about it.'

'Naturally,' says the genie.

The couple gave the proposition some thought and then the wife says that the genie is, after all, giving them a lifetime of peace, security and luxury. Maybe it isn't really too big an ask – just one night.

'If you're OK with it, I am,' says the husband.

'Actually,' says the wife with a smile, 'he's not unattractive you know. I'm really quite happy to oblige.'

The genie and the wife have a wonderful night together and the next morning the genie says, 'I really want to thank you. I've had a marvellous time with you and I think you quite enjoyed it too.'

'Oh I did,' says the wife.

Please, the genie says, 'Do you mind if I ask you just one question? How old is your husband?'

'Forty-three.'

At this the genie raises his eyebrows. 'And he still believes in genies?'

Three men are playing in a golf tournament: one is an eye surgeon, one is a priest and the other is an engineer. The club captain comes through checking the field and asks if everything is going alright.

'No,' they say. 'Those men ahead are dreadfully slow and holding up the field.'

'Oh, be patient with them,' says the captain. 'They're blind.'

'That's terrible,' says the eye surgeon. 'Send them to me and I'll see if there's anything I can do for them.'

The priest says, 'I'll pray for them.'

The engineer says, 'Why can't they play at night?'

The antenatal class is in full swing with pregnant women and their partners learning how to breathe properly and how to provide support at birth.

At one point, the teacher announces, 'Ladies, exercise is good for you. Walking is especially beneficial. And, gentlemen, it wouldn't hurt you to take the time to go walking with your partner!'

One man raises his arm to ask a question.

'Yes?' asks the teacher.

'Is it all right if she carries a golf bag while we walk?'

A man and his friend meet at the clubhouse and decide to play a round of golf together. The man has a little dog with him and on the first green, when the man holes out a 10m putt, the little dog starts to yip and stands up on its hind legs.

The friend is quite amazed at this clever trick and says, 'That dog is really talented. What does he do if you miss a putt?'

'Somersaults,' says the man.

'Somersaults?' says the friend, 'That's incredible. How many does he do?'

'Hmmm,' says the man. 'That depends on how hard I kick him in the arse.'

A couple of women are playing golf one sunny afternoon. The first of the twosome tees off and watches in horror as the ball heads directly toward a foursome of men playing the next hole. Sure enough, the ball hits one of the guys, and he immediately clasps his hands together at his crotch, falls to the ground, and rolls around in agony. The woman rushes over and immediately begins to apologise. She then explains that she is a physical therapist and offers to help ease his pain.

'Ummph, ooh, nooo, I'll be alright . . . I'll be fine in a few minutes,' he replies as he remains in the foetal position, still clasping his hands together at his crotch. But she persists and he finally allows her to help him. She gently takes his hands away and lays them to the side, loosens his pants and puts her hands inside, beginning to massage him.

'Does that feel better?' she asks.

'Ohhh, yeah. It feels really great,' he replies. 'But my thumb still hurts like hell!'

God, Jesus and John the Baptist are playing golf up in heaven. On the first tee, John the Baptist leads off and hits a big blast right down the middle; it rolls to a stop about 270m out, a perfect lie. Jesus steps up next and kills the ball, sending it about 300m straight, perfect lie. God steps up and waggles and wiggles and then badly hooks his ball into the trees. As it flies in, a huge oak is struck by lightning and splits, one half falling into the path of the oncoming ball and knocking it into the fairway. As it comes to a rest, a bare 50m out, a squirrel darts out of the woods on the other side and grabs the ball and takes off towards the left-side woods. Before he gets in, an eagle swoops down and grabs the squirrel, carrying it aloft down the fairway. Just as it passes over the green, the eagle is pelted by hailstones, whereupon it drops the squirrel (still clutching the ball) onto the green about 1m from the hole. Dazed, the squirrel spits the ball out where it rolls up and stops on the lip of the cup. Suddenly there is an earthquake! The ball drops in . . . a hole in one!

Jesus stares at John the Baptist with a pissed-off look, then turns to God and says, 'Dad? We gonna play golf, or are you just gonna screw around?'

Three women are out playing golf one day and one of them hits her ball into the woods. She goes into the woods to looks for it and finds a frog in a trap.

The frog says to her, 'If you release me from this trap, I will grant you three wishes.'

The woman frees the frog and the frog says, 'Thank you, but I failed to mention that there is a condition to your wishes – that whatever you wish for, your husband will get ten times more or better.'

The woman says, 'That's OK,' and for her first wish she wants to be the most beautiful woman in the world.

The frog warns her, 'You do realise this wish will also make your husband the most handsome man in the world, an Adonis, and that women will flock to him.'

The woman replies, 'That's OK, because I will be the most beautiful woman and he will only have eyes for me.'

So, *poof!* She's the most beautiful woman in the world.

For her second wish, she wants to be the richest woman in the world.

The frog says, 'That will make your husband the richest man in the world and he will be ten times richer than you.'

The woman says, 'That's OK because what is mine is his, and what is his is mine.'

So, *poof!* She's the richest woman in the world.

The frog then inquires after her third wish and she answers, 'I'd like a mild heart attack.'

A man is about to tee off on the golf course when he feels a tap on his shoulder and a man hands him a card that reads, 'I am a deaf-mute. May I play through, please?'

The first man angrily gives the card back, and communicates that no, he may *not* play through, and that his disability did not give him such a right.

The first man whacks the ball onto the green and leaves to finish the hole.

Just as he is about to sink the ball into the hole he is hit in the head with a golf ball, laying him out cold.

When he comes to a few minutes later, he looks around and sees the deaf-mute sternly looking at him, one hand on his hip, the other holding up four fingers.

One fine day in Ireland, a guy is out golfing and gets up to the 16th hole. He tees up and cranks one. Unfortunately, it goes into the woods on the side of the fairway. He goes looking for his ball and comes across a little guy with a huge bump on his head and the golf ball lying right beside him.

'Goodness,' says the golfer, and revives the poor little guy.

Upon awakening, the little guy says, 'Well, you caught me fair and square. I am a leprechaun. I will grant you three wishes.'

'I can't take anything from you, I'm just glad I didn't hurt you too badly,' says the guy, and walks away.

Watching the golfer depart, the leprechaun says, 'Well, he was a nice enough guy, and he did catch me, so I have to do something for him. I'll give him the three things that I would want. I'll give him unlimited money, a great golf game, and a great sex life.'

A year goes past and the same golfer is out golfing on the same course at the 16th hole. He gets up and hits one into the same woods and goes off looking for his ball. When he finds the ball he sees the same little guy and asks how he is doing.

The leprechaun says, 'I'm fine. And might I ask how your golf game is?'

'It's great! I hit under par every time.'

'I did that for you. And might I ask how your money is holding out?'

'That's the amazing thing, every time I put my hand in my pocket, I pull out a hundred dollar note.'

'I did that for you. And might I ask how your sex life is?'

Now the golfer looks at him a little shyly and says, 'Well, maybe once or twice a week.'

Floored the leprechaun stammers, 'Only once or twice a week?'

The golfer looks at him sheepishly and says, 'Well, that's not too bad for a Catholic priest in a small parish.'

GOLF IS BETTER THAN SEX BECAUSE:

- If you damage a ball it is easy to replace it with a new one.
- The lay is always different.
- A hole in one is applauded.

Golfer: Well, I have never played this badly before!
Caddy: I didn't realise you had played before, sir.

Golfer: Notice any improvement today, Jimmy?
Caddy: Yes, ma'am. You've had your hair done.

Golfer: Caddy, do you think it is a sin to play golf on Sunday?

Caddy: The way you play, sir, it's a crime any day of the week!

Golfer: I'd move heaven and earth to be able to break 100 on this course.

Caddy: Try heaven. You've already moved a fair amount of earth.

Man blames fate for other accidents that befall him, but takes full responsibility for a hole in one.

SOCCER

Q: How does David Beckham change a light bulb?
A: He holds it in the air, and the world revolves around him.

A primary teacher starts a new job at a school on Merseyside and, trying to make a good impression on her first day, explains to her class that she is a Liverpool fan. She asks her students to raise their hands if they, too, are Liverpool fans. Everyone in the class raises their hand except one little girl.

The teacher looks at the girl with surprise and says: 'Mary, why didn't you raise your hand?'

'Because I'm not a Liverpool fan,' she replies.

The teacher, still shocked, asks: 'Well, if you're not a Liverpool fan, then who are you a fan of?'

'I'm a Manchester United fan, and proud of it,' Mary replies.

The teacher cannot believe her ears. 'Mary, why are you a United fan?'

'Because my mum and dad are from Manchester, and my mum is a United fan and my dad is a United fan, so I'm a United fan too!'

'Well,' says the teacher, in an annoyed tone, 'that's no reason for you to be a United fan. You don't have to be just like your parents all of the time. What if your mum was a prostitute and your dad was a drug addict and a car thief, what would you be then?'

'Then,' Mary smiles, 'I'd be a Liverpool fan.'

ACTUAL SPORTS QUOTES

'Nobody in football should be called a genius. A genius is a guy like Norman Einstein.'
– Football commentator and former player Joe Theismann 1996.

'You guys line up alphabetically by height' and 'You guys pair up in groups of three, then line up in a circle.'
– Bill Peterson, a Florida state football coach.

'That's so when I forget how to spell my name, I can still find my bloody clothes.'
– Stu Grimson, Chicago Blackhawks left wing, explaining why he keeps a colour photo of himself above his locker.

'I can't really remember the names of all the nightclubs that we went to.'
- Shaquille O'Neal replying to a question about whether he had visited the Parthenon during his visit to Greece.

'He's a guy who gets up at 6am regardless of what time it is.'
- Lou Duva, veteran boxing trainer, on the Spartan training regime of heavyweight Andrew Golota.

'I'm not allowed to comment on lousy officiating.'
- Jim Finks, New Orleans Saints general manager, when asked after a loss what he thought of the refs.

'It's basically the same, just darker.'
- Alan Kulwicki, stock car racer, on racing Saturday nights as opposed to Sunday afternoons.

'I told him, "Son, what is it with you. Is it ignorance or apathy?" He said, "Coach, I don't know and I don't care."'
- Frank Layden, Utah Jazz president, on a former player.

'He treats us like men. He lets us wear earrings.'
- Torrin Polk, University of Houston receiver, on his coach, John Jenkins.

'I'd run over my own mother to win the Super Bowl.'
- Joe Jacoby of the Skins.

'To win, I'd run over Joe's mum too.'
- Matt Millen of the Raiders.

RUGBY

An English family of Rugby supporters head out one Saturday to do their Christmas shopping. While in the sports shop, the son picks up a Scotland rugby shirt and says to his sister, 'I've decided to be a Scotland Supporter and I would like this for Christmas.'

His sister thinks the colours are cute, but is outraged by this, and promptly whacks him round the head and says, 'Go talk to Mum.'

So off goes the little lad with the blue rugby shirt in hand and finds his mother. 'Mum?'

'Yes My darling?' she says.

'I've decided I'm going to be a Scotland supporter and I would like this shirt for Christmas.'

The mother is outraged at this, promptly whacks him around the head and says, 'Go talk to your father.'

Off he goes with the rugby shirt in hand and finds his father. 'Dad?'

'Yes Johnny my boy?'

'I've decided I'm going to be a Scotland supporter and I would like this shirt for Christmas.'

The father is outraged and promptly whacks his son around the head and says, 'No son of mine is ever going to be seen in that!'

About half an hour later, they're all back in the car and heading towards home.

The father turns to his son and says 'Son, I hope you've learned something today?'

The son says, 'Yes, indeed I have dad.'

'Good son, what is it?'

The son replies, 'I've only been a Scotland supporter for an hour and already I hate you English bastards.'

The last time the pope was in Australia he found himself contemplating the beauty of a river deep in the wilds of the Northern Territory when a sudden commotion on the far shore attracted his attention. There, in the jaws of a massive crocodile was a man wearing a New Zealand All Black jersey, desperately struggling to get free.

Right at that moment, three blokes wearing Australian Wallaby jerseys roared into view on a speedboat. The first bloke fired a harpoon into the crocodile's ribs, while the other two reached and pulled the Kiwi from the river and, using long clubs, beat the croc to death. They bundled the bleeding, semi-conscious man into the speedboat along with the dead croc and then prepared for a hasty retreat.

The pope was amazed by this, and summoned them to the shore. Curious, they went over, and the pope said to them: 'I give you my best papal blessing for your brave actions. I had heard that there is a racist xenophobic divide between Australia and New Zealand but now I have seen with my own eyes that this is not true. I can see that your two societies are true examples of racial harmony and could serve as a model for other nations to follow.'

He blessed them and drove off in a cloud of dust.

As he departed, the harpoonist turned to the other Aussies and asked: 'Who the bloody hell was that?'

'That', one answered, 'was his Holiness the Pope. He is in direct contact with God and has access to all God's wisdom.'

'Well,' the harpoonist replied, 'He knows nothing about croc hunting! Now,' he continued, pointing to the bloke in the All Black jersey, 'will this bait still work, or do we need to get another one?'

Wiremoocow, a New Zealander, landed in England to watch the All Blacks and was not feeling well, so he decided to see a doctor.

'Hey doc, I don't feel so good, eh' said Wiremoocow.

The doctor gives him a thorough examination and informs Wiremoocow that he has prostate problems, and that the only cure is an immediate testicular removal.

'No way doc, I'm here for the rugby' replied Wiremoocow 'I'm gitting a sicond opinion. 'ey!'

The second English doctor gave Wiremoocow the same diagnosis and also advised him that testicular removal was the only cure.

Not surprisingly, Wiremoocow refused the treatment. He was devastated but, with only hours to go before the All Blacks opening game he found an expatriate Kiwi doctor and decided to get one last opinion from someone he could trust.

The Kiwi doctor examined him and said, 'Wiremoocow, you huv prostate suckness, 'ey'.

'What's the cure thin doc, 'ey?' asked Wiremoocow hoping for a different answer.

'Wull, Wiremoocow', said the Kiwi doctor 'Wi're gonna huv to cut off your balls.'

'Phew, thunk gud for thut!' said Wiremoocow, 'those Pommy bastards wanted to take my test tickets off me!'

Johnnie Wilkinson goes into the England changing room to find all his team mates looking a bit glum.

'What's up?' he asks.

'Well, we're having trouble getting motivated for this game,' says one guy. 'We know it's important but we've just beaten the All Blacks and Australia in consecutive weeks and let's be honest, it's only South Africa. They're shite and we can't be bothered.'

Johnnie looks at them and says 'Well, the way I've been playing recently, I reckon I can beat them by myself, you lads can go down the pub.'

So Johnnie goes out to play South Africa by himself and the rest of the England team go off for a few jars. After a few pints they wonder how the game is going, so they get the landlord to put the telly on.

A big cheer goes up as the screen reads 'England 7 – South Africa 0 (Wilkinson – 10 minutes – Converted Try)'.

Wilkinson is beating South Africa all by himself! The telly goes off and a few more pints later the game is forgotten until someone remembers, 'It must be full time now, let's see how Johnnie got on.'

They put the telly back on.

'Result from the Stadium: England 7 (Wilkinson 10 minutes) South Africa 7 (Pause 79 minutes).'

They can't believe it, Johnnie has single-handedly got a draw against South Africa and maintained England's unbeaten run at home! They rush back to the Stadium to congratulate him. They find him in the dressing room, still in his gear, seated with his head in his hands. He refuses to look at them.

'I've let you down, I've let you down.' says Johnnie.

'Don't be daft, you got a draw against South Africa, all by yourself. And they only scored at the very, very end!' say the rest of the team.

'No, No, I have let you down,' says Wilkinson, 'I've let you and the whole country down . . . I got sent off after 12 minutes.'

Each member of a rugby union team was issued with an individual heart-rate monitor, similar to a watch, which, after exercise, could download data into a computer to measure resting heart rates, heart rates during exercise, rate of recovery etc.

In addition to the scheduled team training, each player was required to do a session by themselves each day, wearing the heart-rate monitor.

When one of the players, Johnny, handed in his monitor and the information was downloaded, the medical staff became seriously alarmed. They urgently called Johnny and asked if he had done his additional training.

'Yes.' he replied, looking a little strained.

'What did you do?' they asked.

'A big sprint session down at my local park,' he replied. 'Why, what's the problem?'

'The monitor reported 300 beats per minute – at that rate the human body cannot survive.'

'What do you mean the human body? I strapped the monitor on my Rottweiler and made him chase balls for the session.'

30 THINGS *NOT* TO SAY DURING SEX

ADULT ONLY

1. You woke me up for that?
2. Did I mention the video camera?
3. Try breathing through your nose.
4. Person 1: This is your first time . . . right?
   Person 2: Yeah . . . today
5. Do you accept Visa?
6. On second thoughts, let's turn off the lights.
7. Hope you're as good looking when I'm sober.
8. But I just brushed my teeth.
9. I want a baby!
10. *(In a ménage à trois)* Why am I doing all the work?
11. When is this supposed to feel good?
12. You're good enough to do this for a living!
13. But my cat always sleeps on that pillow.
14. Did I tell you my Aunt Martha died in this bed?
15. No, really . . . I do this part better myself!
16. It's nice being in bed with a woman I don't have to inflate!
17. You're almost as good as my ex!
18. Do you know the definition of statutory rape?
19. Now I know why she dumped you.
20. What tampon?
21. I have a confession to make . . .
22. I was so horny tonight I would have taken a duck home!
23. Were you by any chance repressed as a child?
24. I really hate women who actually think sex means something!

25. I'll tell you who I'm fantasising about if you tell me who you're fantasising about.
26. Oprah Winfrey had a show about men like you!
27. Have you seen *Fatal Attraction*?
28. Keep it down, my mother is a light sleeper.
29. Hey, when is it going to be my friend's turn?
30. How long do you plan to be 'almost there'?

LAUGHING AT DISABILITIES

*Making fun of people with disabilities is the bottom
of the barrel. But that's what we're about, scraping
the very bottom of the bad taste joke barrel.*

A blind man is describing his favourite sport, parachuting.
When asked how he is able to parachute, he says that just
about everything is done for him.

'I am placed in the door with my guide dog and told when to
jump. My hand is placed on my release ring for me and out I go
with the dog.'

'But how do you know when you are going to land?' he is
asked.

'I have a very keen sense of smell, and I can smell the trees
and grass when I am 100m from the ground,' he answers.

'But how do you know when to lift your legs for the final
arrival on the ground?' he is again asked.

He quickly answers, 'Oh, the dog's leash goes slack.'

A blind man walks into a store with his guide dog. All of a
sudden, he picks up the leash and begins swinging the dog
over his head.

The manager runs up to the man and asks, 'What are you
doing?'

The blind man replies, 'Just looking around.'

Two dwarfs decide to treat themselves to a vacation in Las Vegas. At the hotel bar, they're dazzled by two women, and wind up taking them to their separate rooms. The first dwarf is disappointed, however, as he's unable to reach a certain physical state that would enable him to join with his date. His depression is enhanced by the fact that, from the next room, he hears cries of 'One, two, three . . . Huh!' all night long.

In the morning, the second dwarf asks the first, 'How did it go?'

The first whispers back, 'It was so embarrassing. I simply couldn't get an erection.'

The second dwarf shakes his head.

'You think that's embarrassing? I couldn't even get on the bed!'

A guy stops in to visit his friend who is paralysed from the waist down. His friend says, 'My feet are cold. Would you get me my sneakers for me?'

The guy goes upstairs, and there are his friend's two gorgeous daughters.

He says, 'Hi, girls. Your dad sent me up here to screw you.'

The first daughter says, 'That's not true.'

He says, 'I'll prove it.'

He yells down the stairs, 'Both of them?'

His friend yells back, 'Of course, both of them!'

Two guys meet after not having seen each other for many, many years.

The first guy asks the second guy, 'How have things been going?'

The second guy, speaking very slowly tells the first guy, 'I w..a..s.. a..l..m..o..s..t m..a..r..r..i..e..d.'

The first guy says in amazement 'Hey! you don't stutter any more.'

'Y..e..s I w..e..n..t t..o a d..o..c..t..o..r a..n..d h..e t..o..l..d m..e t..h..a..t i..f I s..p..e..a..k s..l..o..w..l..y I w..i..l..l n..o..t s..t..u..t..t..e..r.'

The first friend congratulates him on not stuttering anymore and asks why he is no longer engaged to his girlfriend.'

'W..e..l..l m..y f..i..a..n..c..e..e a..n..d I w..e..r..e s..i..t..t..i..n..g o..n h..e..r p..o..r..c..h a..n..d t..h..e d..o..g w..a..s s..c..r..a..t..c..h..i..n..g h..i..s b..a..c..k a..n..d I t..o..l..d h..e..r t..h..a..t w..h..e..n w..e a..r..e m..a..r..r..i..e..d s..h..e c..a..n d..o t..h..a..t f..o..r m..e a..n..d s..h..e t..h..r..e..w t..h..e r..i..n..g i..n m..y f..a..c..e.'

'Why should she throw the ring in your face for that?' asks the first friend.

'W..e..l..l I s..p..e..a..k s..o s..l..o..w..l..y t..h..a..t b..y t..h..e t..i..m..e s..h..e l..o..o..k..e..d a..t t..h..e d..o..g. h..e w..a..s l..i..c..k..i..n..g h..i..s b..a..l..l..s.'

A guy is standing at a urinal when he notices that he is being watched by a midget. Although the little fellow is staring at him intently, the guy doesn't get uncomfortable until the midget drags a small stepladder up next to him, climbs it, and proceeds to admire his privates at close range.

'Wow,' comments the midget, 'Those are the nicest balls I have ever seen!'

Surprised and flattered, the man thanks the midget and starts to move away.

'Listen, I know this is a rather strange request,' says the little fellow, 'but I wonder if you would mind if I touched them?'

Again the man is rather startled, but seeing no real harm in it, he obliges the request.

The midget reaches out, gets a tight grip on the man's balls, and says, 'OK, hand me your wallet or I'll jump off the ladder!'

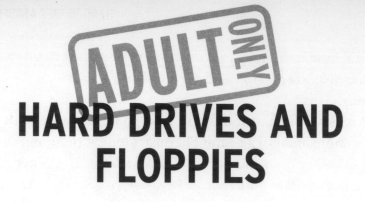

HARD DRIVES AND FLOPPIES

Why are there so many jokes about computer geeks? I guess it's because they're a sitting target.

A helicopter is flying above Seattle when an electrical malfunction disables all of the aircraft's navigational and communications equipment. Due to the cloud and haze, the pilot can't determine his location, or the course to the nearest airport. Finally, he sees a tall building and flies towards it. He circles, makes a handwritten sign that says 'Where Am I?' and holds it up in the helicopter's window.

The people in the building respond quickly. They write their own sign and hold it up in the window. It says 'You Are in a Helicopter.'

The pilot smiles, waves, turns the aircraft around and heads directly for Seattle airport.

After they land on the ground, the co-pilot asks the pilot how the 'You Are in a Helicopter' sign had helped him determine their position.

'Easy,' says the pilot. 'The information they gave me was technically correct, but totally useless, so I knew that had to be the Microsoft building.'

One day Bill complains to his friend, 'My elbow really hurts, I guess I should see a doctor.'

His friend offers, 'Don't do that. There's a computer at the chemist that can diagnose anything quicker and cheaper than a doctor. Simply put in a sample of your urine and the computer will diagnose your problem and tell you what you can do about it. It only costs $10.'

Bill reckons he has nothing to lose, so he fills a jar with a urine sample and goes to the chemist. Finding the computer, he pours in the sample and deposits the $10. The computer starts making some noise and various lights start flashing. After a brief pause out pops a small slip of paper on which is printed: 'You have tennis elbow. Soak your arm in warm water. Avoid heavy lifting. It will be better in two weeks.'

Late that evening, while thinking how amazing this new technology is and how it will change medical science forever, Bill begins to wonder if this machine can be fooled. He decides to give it a try. He mixes together some tap water, a stool sample from his dog and urine samples from his wife and daughter. To top it off, he masturbates into the concoction.

He goes back to the chemist, locates the machine, pours in the sample and deposits the $10. The computer again makes the noise and prints out the following message: 'Your tap water is too hard. Get a water softener. Your dog has worms. Get him vitamins. Your daughter is using cocaine. Put her in a rehabilitation clinic. Your wife is pregnant with twin girls. They aren't yours. Get a lawyer. And if you don't stop jerking off, your tennis elbow will never get better.'

An artist, a lawyer, and a computer scientist are discussing the merits of a mistress. The artist tells of the passion and the thrill which comes with the risk of being discovered. The lawyer warns of the difficulties. It can lead to guilt, divorce and bankruptcy. Not worth it. Too many problems.

The computer scientist says, 'It's the best thing that's ever happened to me. My wife thinks I'm with my mistress. My mistress thinks I'm home with my wife, and I can spend all night on the computer.'

There are three engineers in a car: an electrical engineer, a chemical engineer and a Microsoft engineer. Suddenly the car just stops by the side of the road, and the three engineers look at each other wondering what can be wrong.

The electrical engineer suggests stripping down the electronics of the car and trying to trace where a fault might have occurred.

The chemical engineer, not knowing much about cars, suggests that the fuel might be becoming emulsified and getting blocked somewhere.

Then, the Microsoft engineer, not knowing much about anything, comes up with a suggestion, 'Why don't we close all the windows, get out, get back in, open the windows again, and maybe it'll work!'

Jesus and Satan have a discussion as to who is the better programmer. This goes on for a few hours until they come to an agreement to hold a contest, with God as the judge.

They sit themselves at their computers and begin. They both type furiously, lines of code streaming up the screen, for several hours straight. Seconds before the end of the competition, a bolt of lightning strikes, taking out the electricity. Moments later, the power is restored, and God announces that the contest is over.

He asks Satan to show what he has come up with. Satan is visibly upset, and cries, 'I have nothing. I lost it all when the power went out.'

'Very well, then,' says God, 'let us see if Jesus fared any better.'

Jesus enters a command, and the screen comes to life in a vivid display, the voices of an angelic choir pour forth from the speakers. Satan is astonished.

He stutters, 'B-b-but how? I lost everything, yet Jesus' program is intact. How did he do it?'

God smiles all-knowingly, 'Jesus saves.'

A computer programmer happens across a frog in the road. The frog pipes up, 'I'm really a beautiful princess and if you kiss me, I'll stay with you for a week.'

The programmer shrugs his shoulders and puts the frog in his pocket.

A few minutes later, the frog says, 'OK, OK, if you kiss me, I'll give you great sex for a week.'

The programmer nods and puts the frog back in his pocket.

A few minutes later, 'Turn me back into a princess and I'll give you great sex for a whole year!'

The programmer smiles and walks on.

Finally, the frog says, 'What's wrong with you? I've promised you great sex for a year from a beautiful princess and you won't even kiss a frog?'

'I'm a programmer,' he replies. 'I don't have time for sex. But a talking frog is pretty neat.'

TWELVE STEP PROGRAM OF RECOVERY FOR WEB ADDICTS

1. I will have a cup of coffee in the morning and read my *paper* newspaper like I used to, before the Web.

2. I will eat breakfast with a knife and fork and not with one hand typing.

3. I will get dressed before noon.

4. I will make an attempt to clean the house, wash clothes, and plan dinner before even thinking of the Web.

5. I will sit down and write a longhand letter to those unfortunate few friends and family that are Web-deprived.

6. I will call someone on the phone who I cannot contact via the Web.

7. I will read a book . . . if I still remember how.

8. I will listen to those around me talk about their needs and stop telling them to turn the TV down so I can hear the music on the Web.

9. I will not be tempted during TV commercials to check for email.

10. I will try and get out of the house at least once a week, if it is necessary or not.

11. I will remember that my bank is not forgiving if I forget to balance my cheque-book because I was too busy on the Web.

12. Last, but not least, I will remember that I must go to bed sometime . . . and the Web will always be there tomorrow!

IF RESTAURANTS FUNCTIONED LIKE MICROSOFT

Patron: Waiter!
Waiter: Hi, my name is Bill, and I'll be your Support. What seems to be the problem?
Patron: There's a fly in my soup!
Waiter: Try again, maybe the fly won't be there this time.
Patron: No, it's still there.
Waiter: Maybe it's the way you're using the soup; try eating it with a fork instead.
Patron: Even when I use the fork, the fly is still there.

Waiter:	Maybe the soup is incompatible with the bowl; what kind of bowl are you using?
Patron:	A *soup* bowl!
Waiter:	Hmmm, that should work. Maybe it's a configuration problem; how was the bowl set up?
Patron:	You brought it to me on a saucer; what has that to do with the fly in my soup?
Waiter:	Can you remember everything you did before you noticed the fly in your soup?
Patron:	I sat down and ordered the Soup of the Day!
Waiter:	Have you considered upgrading to the latest Soup of the Day?
Patron:	You have more than one Soup of the Day each day?
Waiter:	Yes, the Soup of the Day is changed every hour.
Patron:	Well, what is the Soup of the Day now?
Waiter:	The current Soup of the Day is tomato.
Patron:	Fine. Bring me the tomato soup, and the bill. I'm running late now.

Waiter leaves and returns with another bowl of soup and the bill.

Waiter:	Here you are, Sir. The soup and your bill.
Patron:	This is potato soup.
Waiter:	Yes, the tomato soup wasn't ready yet.
Patron:	Well, I'm so hungry now, I'll eat anything.

Waiter leaves.

| Patron: | Waiter! There's a gnat in my soup! |

The bill:

Soup of the Day – $5.00

Upgrade to newer Soup of the Day – $2.50

Access to support – $1.00

IS YOUR COMPUTER MALE OR FEMALE? YOU DECIDE!

The top five reasons computers must be female:

1. No-one but their creator understands their logic.
2. Even your smallest mistakes are immediately committed to memory for future reference.
3. The native language used to communicate with other computers is incomprehensible to everyone else.
4. The message, 'bad command or filename', is about as informative as 'If you don't know why I'm mad at you, then I'm certainly not going to tell you.'
5. As soon as you make a commitment to one, you find yourself spending half your pay cheque on accessories for it.

The top five reasons computers must be male:

1. They have a lot of data, but are still clueless.
2. They are supposed to help you solve problems, but half the time they *are* the problem.
3. As soon as you commit to one you realise that, if you had waited a little longer, you could have obtained a better model.
4. In order to get their attention, they have to be turned on.
5. Big power surges knock them out for the rest of the night.

ACCOUNTANTS AND THEIR ILK

Finding humour in accountants is like drawing water from a stone. Only harder. Here are a few attempts.

An accountant is having a hard time sleeping and goes to see his doctor. 'Doctor, I just can't get to sleep at night.'

'Have you tried counting sheep?'

'That's the problem. I make a mistake and then spend three hours trying to find it.'

If an accountant's wife cannot sleep, what does she say? 'Darling, could you tell me about your work?'

Three engineers and three accountants are travelling by train to a conference. At the station, the three accountants each buy a ticket and watch as the three engineers only buy one ticket.

'How are three people going to travel on only one ticket?' asks an accountant.

'Watch and you'll see,' answers an engineer.

They all board the train. The accountants take their respective seats but all three engineers cram into a rest room and close the door behind them. Shortly after the train has departed, the conductor comes around collecting tickets.

He knocks on the toilet door and says, 'Tickets, please!'

The door opens just a crack and a single arm emerges with a ticket in hand. The conductor takes it and moves on. The accountants see this and agree it is a clever idea.

So after the conference, the accountants decide to copy the engineers on the return trip and save some money. When they get to the station, they buy one ticket for the return trip. To their astonishment, the engineers don't buy a ticket at all.

'How are you going to travel without a ticket?' asks one perplexed accountant.

'Watch and you'll see,' answers an engineer.

When they board the train all three accountants cram into a toilet and the three engineers cram into another one nearby. The train departs. Shortly afterward, one of the engineers leaves his toilet and walks over to the toilet where the accountants are hiding.

He knocks on the door and says, 'Tickets, please!'

IT'S ALL IN THE MIND

I've never fully understood the difference between a psychologist, a psychiatrist and a therapist. All I know is that they're all obsessed by sex. Hey! Who isn't?

A man goes to a psychologist and says, 'I got a real problem, I can't stop thinking about sex.'

The psychologist says, 'Well let's see what we can find out.' He pulls out his ink blots. 'What is this a picture of?' he asks.

The man turns the picture upside down then turns it around and states, 'That's a man and a woman on a bed making love.'

The psychologist says, 'Very interesting,' and shows him the next picture. 'And what is this a picture of?'

The man looks and turns it in different directions and says, 'That's a man and a woman on a bed making love.'

The psychologist tries again with a third ink blot, and asks the same question, 'What is this a picture of?'

The patient again turns it in all directions and replies, 'That's a man and a woman on a bed making love.'

The psychologist states, 'Well, yes, you do seem to be obsessed with sex.'

'Me?' demands the patient. 'You're the one who keeps showing me the dirty pictures.'

A distraught man goes to see a psychologist.

'How may I help you?' the therapist asks.

'Every night I have the same dream. I'm lying in bed and a dozen women walk in and try to rip my clothes off and have wild sex with me.'

'And then what do you do?' the psychologist asks.

'I push them away,' the man says.

'Then what do you want me to do?' the psychologist asks.

'Break my arms!'

A psychiatrist is conducting a group therapy session with three young mothers and their small children.

'You all have obsessions,' he observes.

To the first mother he says, 'You are obsessed with eating. You've even named your daughter Candy.'

He turns to the second mum. 'Your obsession is money. Again, it manifests itself in your child's name, Penny.'

At this point, the third mother gets up, takes her little boy by the hand and whispers, 'Come on, Dick, let's go.'

A wife goes to see a therapist and says, 'I've got a big problem, doctor. Every time we're in bed and my husband climaxes, he lets out an ear-splitting yell.'

'My dear,' the doctor says, 'that's completely natural. I don't see what the problem is.'

'The problem is,' she complains, 'It wakes me up!'

THE BANKING SECTOR

*I only just found out that the word 'banker' is a
real term. I always thought it was rhyming slang.*

A little old lady goes into a bank one day, carrying a bag
of money. She asks to speak with the bank manager to open
an account. The staff usher her into the manager's office and the
manager asks how much she wants to deposit.

She replies, '$165 000!' and dumps the cash on his desk.

The manager is curious as to how she came by all this cash,
so he asks her, 'Ma'am, where did you get this money?'

The old lady replies, 'I make bets.'

The manager then asks, 'Bets? What kind of bets?'

The old woman says, 'Well, for example, I'll bet you
$25 000 that your balls are square.'

'Ha!' laughs the manager, 'That's a stupid bet. You can never
win that kind of bet!'

The old lady challenges, 'So, would you like to take my bet?'

'Sure,' says the manager, 'I'll bet $25 000 that my balls are not
square!'

The old lady says, 'OK, but since there is a lot of money
involved, may I bring my lawyer with me tomorrow at 10 a.m. as
a witness?'

'Sure!' replies the confident manager.

That night, he is very nervous about the bet and often checks
his balls in the mirror. The next morning, at precisely 10 a.m.,
the little old lady appears with her lawyer at the manager's
office. She introduces the lawyer to the manager and repeats the
bet, '$25 000 says the manager's balls are square.'

The manager agrees with the bet again and the old lady asks him to drop his pants so they can all see. The manager complies. The little old lady peers closely at his balls and then asks if she can feel them.

'Well, OK,' says the manager, 'I suppose $25 000 is a lot of money, so you should be absolutely sure.'

Just then, he notices that the lawyer is quietly banging his head against the wall. The manager says, 'What's wrong with your lawyer?'

She replies, 'Nothing, except I bet him $100 000 that at 10 a.m. today, I'd have the bank manager's balls in my hand!'

A guy walks into a bank and says to the teller at the window, 'I want to open a bloody cheque account.'

The teller replies, 'I beg your pardon, what did you say?'

'Listen up dammit, I said I want to open a bloody cheque account right now.'

'Sir, I'm sorry but we do not tolerate that kind of language in this bank.'

The teller leaves the window and goes over to the bank manager and tells him about her situation. They both return and the manager asks, 'What seems to be the problem here?'

'There's no damn problem,' the man says, 'I just won $50 million in the lottery and I want to open a bloody cheque account in this damn bank!'

'I see Sir,' the manager says, 'and this bitch is giving you a hard time?'

THINGS YOU WOULD NOT WANT TO SEE HAPPEN AT THE ATM

- You go to get a balance inquiry, and instead of printing out a receipt the screen says, 'Not worth wasting paper' and ejects your card.

- You insert your card, and try to get some cash, and the ATM laughs and spits out your shredded card.

- You withdraw some money to pay some bills, count it, and the screen says, 'What, you thought there was some *extra* there? Ha!' and ejects your card clear across the room.

FUNNY SIGNS SEEN IN GREAT BRITAIN

IN A LAUNDROMAT: Automatic washing machines. Please remove all your clothes when the light goes out.

IN A LONDON DEPARTMENT STORE: Bargain Basement Upstairs.

IN AN OFFICE: Would the person who took the step ladder yesterday kindly bring it back or further steps will be taken.

IN ANOTHER OFFICE: After the tea break, staff should empty the teapot and stand upside down on the draining board.

ON A CHURCH DOOR: This is the gate of heaven. Enter ye all by this door. (This door is kept locked because of the draft. Please use side entrance.)

OUTSIDE A SECOND-HAND SHOP: We exchange anything – bicycles, washing machines etc. Why not bring your wife along and get a wonderful bargain?

QUICKSAND WARNING: Quicksand. Any person passing this point will be drowned. By order of the District Council.

NOTICE IN A DRY CLEANER'S WINDOW: Anyone leaving their garments here for more than thirty days will be disposed of.

IN A HEALTH FOOD SHOP WINDOW: Closed due to illness.

SPOTTED IN A SAFARI PARK: Elephants – please stay in your car.

SEEN DURING A CONFERENCE: For anyone who has children and doesn't know it, there is a day care on the first floor.

NOTICE IN A FIELD: The farmer allows walkers to cross the field for free, but the bull charges.

MESSAGE ON A LEAFLET: If you cannot read, this leaflet will tell you how to get lessons.

ON A REPAIR SHOP DOOR: We can repair anything (Please knock hard on the door – the bell doesn't work.)

SPOTTED IN A TOILET IN A LONDON OFFICE BLOCK: Toilet out of order. Please use floor below.

THE MILITARY

We're a sick society! After all, we find humour in the subtle art of killing, maiming and bombing (so long as we're not the ones being killed, maimed and bombed).

An American soldier, serving in World War II, returns from several weeks of intense action on the German frontlines. He is granted R&R and finds himself on a train bound for London. The train is very crowded, so the soldier walks the length of the train, looking for an empty seat. The only unoccupied seat is next to a well-dressed, middle-aged woman. Actually, the seat is not technically unoccupied. It is being used by her little dog.

The war-weary soldier asks, 'Please, Ma'am, may I sit in that seat?'

The English woman looks down her nose at the soldier, sniffs and says, 'You Americans. You are such a rude class of people. Can't you see my little Fifi is using that seat?'

The soldier walks away, determined to find a place to rest, but after another trip down to the end of the train, finds himself again facing the woman with the dog.

Again he asks, 'Please, lady. May I sit there? I'm very tired.'

The English woman wrinkles her nose and snorts, 'You Americans! Not only are you rude, you are also arrogant. Imagine!'

The soldier doesn't say anything else. He just leans over, picks up the little dog, tosses it out the window of the train and sits down in the empty seat. The woman shrieks and demands that someone defends her and chastises the soldier.

An English gentleman sitting across the aisle speaks up, 'You know, Sir, you Americans do seem to have a penchant for doing the wrong thing. You eat holding the fork in the wrong hand. You drive your cars on the wrong side of the road. You boil your tea to make it hot and put ice in to make it cold, a dash of lemon to make it sour and then sugar to make it sweet. And now, Sir, you've thrown the wrong bitch out of the window.'

It's the end of the Vietnam War and some Einstein in the Pentagon decides that every decorated US Marine will be presented with a specially struck medal on the tarmac of Edwards Air Force Base. But they are three short, and to cover their embarrassment, they pretend that the final three have been singled out for a special honour. Each of them is marched into the Medical Unit and advised that Uncle Sam will give them $1000 for every centimetre which lies between any two parts of their body they choose.

The first is a hulking Indiana farmer who earns enough for a new farm from the distance between the top of his head and the soles of his feet. The second, an Iowa basketball player, buys his entire team for the stretch between his armpit and the tip of his index finger.

The third is a scrawny Arkansas cotton worker who insists 'Ah wanna be measured from mah foreskin to mah balls, man.'

'Come on, soldier,' advises the supervising medic sympathetically, 'You gotta do better than that.'

But the Marine insisted, 'Ah wanna be measured from mah foreskin to the base of mah balls.'

Not wishing to upset him, they agree, and he drops his pants with a grin. The medic looks at him in amazement.

'Where are your balls, soldier?'

'Back in Vietnam.'

I suppose,' snarls the leathery sergeant to the private, 'that when you're discharged from the army, you'll wait for me to die, just so you can spit on my grave.'

'Not me,' observes the private. 'When I get out of the army, I never want to stand in line again.'

A t the height of the Cold War, the Americans and Russians realised that if they continued in the usual manner they were going to blow up the whole world. They decided to settle the whole dispute with one dogfight. They'd have five years to breed the best fighting dog in the world and whichever side's dog won would be entitled to dominate the world. The losing side would have to lay down its arms.

The Russians found the biggest, meanest Doberman and the biggest, meanest Rottweiler in the entire world and bred them with the biggest, meanest Siberian wolves. They selected only the biggest and strongest puppy from each litter, killed his siblings, and gave him all the milk. They used steroids and trainers and after five years came up with the biggest, meanest dog the world had ever seen. Its cage needed steel bars that were 20cm thick and nobody could get near it.

When the day came for the fight, the Americans showed up with a strange animal. It was a 4m-long dachshund. Everyone felt sorry for the Americans because they knew there was no way that this dog could possibly last 10 seconds with the Russian dog.

When the cages were opened up, the dachshund came out and wrapped itself around the outside of the ring. It had the Russian dog almost completely surrounded. When the Russian dog leaned over to bite the dachshund's neck, the dachshund, in a snarling, vicious movement, reached out, opened up its enormous jaws, and consumed the Russian dog in one bite. There was nothing left of the Russian dog. The Russians shook their heads in disbelief.

'We don't understand how this could have happened. We had our best people working for five years with the meanest

Doberman and Rottweiler in the world and the biggest, meanest Siberian wolves,' they lamented.

'We looked at the problem from a different angle,' an American replied. 'We had our best plastic surgeons working for five years to make an alligator look like a Dachshund.'

A young officer was posted to a British army detachment in the desert. On his tour of the facility with the master sergeant, he noticed a group of camels.

'What are those for?' he asked.

'The men use them when they want to have sex.'

'Don't say another word, sergeant. That is the most disgusting thing I have ever heard. Get rid of those camels immediately!'

'Yes, sir.'

A few weeks went by and the young officer began to get rather horny. He called the sergeant over and asked, 'Where are the camels we used to have?'

The sergeant replied that he had sold them to a Bedouin that camped nearby.

'Take me to them, please.'

The officer and the sergeant went over to the Bedouin camp and found the camels. The officer told the sergeant to leave him alone with the camels, then picked out the most attractive one, and had sex with the camel.

On the way back to the camp, the officer asked, 'Sergeant, do the men actually enjoy sex with the camels?'

The sergeant looked at the officer in astonishment and exclaimed, 'Of course not! They use them to ride into town to where the girls are.'

A soldier serving overseas, far from home, was annoyed and upset when his girl wrote breaking off their engagement and asking for her photograph back. He went out and collected from his friends all the unwanted photographs of women that he could find. He bundled them all together and sent them to her with a note: 'Regret cannot remember which one is you. Please keep your photo and return the others.'

An army major visiting the sick soldiers in an army hospital approaches one of the patients and asks, 'What's your problem, soldier?'

'Chronic syphilis, sir!'

'What treatment are you getting?'

'Five minutes with the wire brush each day, sir!'

'What's your ambition?'

'To get back to the front lines, sir!'

'Good man!' says the major.

He goes to the next bed. 'What's your problem, soldier?'

'Chronic piles, sir!'

'What treatment are you getting?'

'Five minutes with the wire brush each day, sir!'

'What's your ambition?'

'To get back to the front lines, sir!'

'Good man!' says the major.

He goes to the next bed. 'What's your problem, soldier?'

'Chronic gum disease, sir!'

'What treatment are you getting?'

'Five minutes with the wire brush each day, sir!'

'What's your ambition?'

'To get to the front of the line and get the wire brush before the other two, sir!'

The captain called the sergeant in.

'Sarge, I just got a telegram that Private Jones' mother died yesterday. Better go tell him and send him in to see me.'

So the sergeant calls for his morning formation and lines up all the troops.

'Listen up, men,' says the sergeant. 'Johnson, step out and report to the mess hall for KP. Hoskins, step out and report for guard duty. Jones, step out and report to Personnel, your mother is dead. The rest of you are to report to the motor pool for maintenance.'

Later that day the captain called the sergeant into his office. 'Sergeant, that was a pretty cold way to inform Jones his mother died. Could you be a bit more tactful next time, please?'

'Yes, sir,' answered the sergeant.

A few months later, the captain called the sergeant in again. 'Sarge, I just got a telegram that Private McGrath's mother died. You'd better go tell him, and then send him in to see me. This time, please be more tactful.'

So the sergeant calls for his morning formation.

'OK, men, fall in and listen up. Everybody with a mother, take two steps forward. Not so fast, McGrath!'

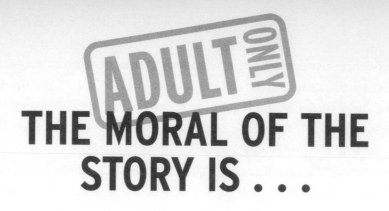

THE MORAL OF THE STORY IS . . .

Forget Satre, forget Plato, and forget Confucius. It's stories like these that teach you the real meaning of life.

A horse is stumbling home from the pub after a solid night of drinking when he falls into a huge hole by the side of the road. No matter how hard he tries, he cannot climb out. He starts to panic, knowing that Farmer Brown will be furious if he is not at work on time. Along comes a chicken.

'Hey chicken!' cries the horse. 'You have to help me. I'm pissed and I gotta get home for work or the farmer will drag me to the glue factory.'

The chick looks at the horse, then at the hole, and finally tells the horse that he is far too small to haul the horse up. He has no other choice but to leave him there. The horse suddenly has an idea.

'I've got it! Go home and get the farmer's Porsche, drive over here and tie a rope to the bumper and drag me out of this hole and home.'

The chicken agrees and sure enough, it works. A few days later, the horse is walking by the same bar and past the same hole when he finds the chicken pissed out of his head and clucking around aimlessly at the bottom of the hole.

'Hey, horse!' the chicken shouts. 'You gotta help me! I can't make it out and the farmer will chop my neck if I'm not home in the morning to give him eggs.'

The horse looks at the chicken and at the hole and admits

that although he owes him a huge favour, he couldn't possibly get down to pick him up. So the chicken tells the horse to go home and get the farmer's Porsche and come back and get him. But the horse tells the chicken that while it sounds like a great idea, he's far too big to fit in the car. The chicken starts to cry and the horse feels so badly that he begins to rack his brains to find a solution to help out the chicken, who, after all, had saved his arse. Finally, he has an idea. He stands over the hole and lets down his huge horse cock. He tells the chicken to grab on and proceeds to pull him out of the hole. The chicken gets home on time and all is well.

The moral of this story is: If you're hung like a horse; you don't need a Porsche to pick up chicks.

Two bored casino dealers are waiting at a craps table. A very attractive blonde woman arrives and bets $20 000 on a single roll of the dice. She says, 'I hope you don't mind, but I feel much luckier when I'm nude.'

With that she strips from her neck down, rolls the dice and yells, 'Mama needs new clothes!'

Then she hollers, 'Yes! Yes! I won! I won!'

She jumps up and down and hugs each of the dealers. With that she picks up her winnings and her clothes and quickly departs.

The dealers just stare at each other dumbfounded. Finally, one of them asks, 'What did she roll?'

The other answers, 'I thought *you* were watching!'

Moral of the story: Not all blondes are dumb.

In a classroom of third graders, the teacher says to the kids, 'Today, class, we will be telling stories that have a moral to them.'

She explains what a moral to a story is and asks for volunteers. Little Suzie raises her hand.

'I live on a farm and we have a chicken that laid twelve eggs, we were excited to have twelve more chickens but only six of them hatched,' she says.

'That's a good story, now what is the moral?' asks the teacher.

'Don't count your chickens before they hatch.'

'Very good Suzie, anyone else?'

'Yes teacher,' says Ralphie. 'I was carrying some eggs I bought for my mum in my bicycle basket one day and I crashed my bike and all the eggs broke.'

'That's a nice story, what is the moral?'

'Don't put all your eggs in one basket.'

'Very good Ralphie, anyone else?'

'Yes teacher,' says little Johnny. 'My Aunt Karen is in the army and when she was in the Gulf War, she parachuted down with only a gun, twenty bullets, a knife, and a six-pack of beer. On her way down, she drank the six pack. When she landed, she shot twenty Iraqis and killed ten of them with her knife.'

'Very interesting, Johnny, what is the moral to your story?'

'Don't screw with Aunt Karen when she's drunk.'

A little girl is out with her grandmother when they come across a couple of dogs mating on the sidewalk.

'What are they doing, Grandma?' asks the little girl.

The grandmother is embarrassed, so she says, 'The dog on top has hurt his paw, and the one underneath is carrying him to the doctor.'

'They're just like people, aren't they Grandma?'

'How do you mean?' asks the grandmother.

'Offer someone a helping hand,' says the little girl, 'and they screw you every time!'

ADULT ONLY

HOW MANY . . . DOES IT TAKE TO CHANGE A LIGHT BULB?

How many Californians does it take to screw in a light bulb?
None. They screw in a hot tub.

How many psychiatrists does it take to change a light bulb?
Only one, but the light bulb has to want to change.

How many male chauvinist pigs does it take to change a light bulb?
None. Let the bitch cook in the dark.

How many men does it take to change a light bulb?
Four. One to actually change it, and three friends to brag to about how he screwed it.

How many women with PMS does it take to change a light bulb?
Six.
Why?
It just does OK!

How many electrical engineers does it take to change a light bulb?
We don't know yet. They're still waiting on a part.

How many software developers does it take to change a light bulb?

The light bulb works fine on the system in my office.

How many perverts does it take to screw in a light bulb?
One, but it takes the entire staff of the emergency room to remove it.

How many actors does it take to change a light bulb?
One hundred. One to screw it in and the other ninety-nine to say 'I could've done that!'

How many Zen masters does it take to change a light bulb?
A tree in the golden forest.

How many Los Angeles policemen does it take to break a light bulb?

We did not break it. It fell down the stairs.

How many university lecturers does it take to change a light bulb?

Four. One to do it and three to co-author the paper.

How many graduate students does it take to change a light bulb?

Only one. But it takes nine years.

How many altos does it take to change a light bulb?
None. They can't get that high.

How many gods does it take to change a light bulb?
Two. One to hold the bulb and the other to rotate the planet.

How many cops does it take to change a light bulb?
None. It turned itself in.

How many authors does it take to change a light bulb?
Two. One to screw it almost in and the other to give it a surprising twist at the end.

ADULT ONLY

WE WISH YOU A MERRY CHRISTMAS

At any other time of year, the sight of a fat, hairy man wearing red clothes and putting children on his knee would involve the police and, probably, a long jail sentence. For some reason, in mid-December each year, we not only tolerate these people, we encourage them.

A young man wants to purchase a Christmas present for his new sweetheart. As they have not been dating very long, after careful consideration, he decides a pair of gloves will strike the right note: romantic but not too personal. Accompanied by his sweetheart's younger sister, he goes to a department store and buys a pair of white gloves. The sister purchases a pair of panties for herself. During the wrapping, the clerk mixes up the items and the sister gets the gloves and the sweetheart gets the panties. Without checking the contents, the young man seals the package and sends it to his sweetheart with the following note:

'I chose these because I noticed that you are not in the habit of wearing any when we go out in the evening. If it had not been for your sister, I would have chosen the long ones with the buttons but she wears short ones that are easier to remove. These are a delicate shade, but the lady I bought them from showed me the pair she had been wearing for the past three weeks and they are hardly soiled. I had her try yours on for me and she looked really smart. I wish I was there to put them on for you the first time as no doubt other hands will come in contact with them before I have a chance to see you again. When you take them off, remember to blow in them before putting them away as they will naturally be a little damp from wearing. Just think how many times I will kiss them during the coming year!

All my love.

P.S. The latest style is to wear them folded down with a little fur showing.'

Two young boys are spending the night at their grandparents the week before Christmas. At bedtime, the two boys kneel beside their beds to say their prayers when the youngest one begins praying at the top of his lungs.

'I pray for a new bicycle! I pray for a new Nintendo! I pray for a new VCR!'

His older brother leans over and nudges him, 'Why are you shouting your prayers? God isn't deaf.'

The little brother replies, 'No, but Grandma is!'

A beautiful innocent young woman wants to meet Santa Claus so she puts on a robe and stays up late on Christmas Eve. Santa arrives, climbs down the chimney, and begins filling the stockings.

He is about to leave when the woman says in a sexy voice, 'Oh Santa, please stay. Keep the chill away.'

Santa replies, 'Ho ho ho, Gotta go, gotta go. Gotta get the presents to the children, you know.'

The girl drops the robe to reveal a sexy bra and panties and says in an even sexier voice, 'Oh Santa, don't run a mile; just stay for a little while . . .'

Santa begins to sweat but replies, 'Ho ho ho, gotta go, gotta go. Gotta get the presents to the children, you know.'

The girl takes off her bra and says, 'Oh Santa. Please, stay.'

Santa wipes his brow but replies, 'Ho ho ho, gotta go, gotta go. Gotta get the presents to the children, you know.'

She loses the panties and says, 'Santa, why don't you stay?'

Santa, with sweat pouring off his brow, says, 'Hey hey hey, gotta stay, gotta stay! Can't get up the chimney with my pecker this way!'

What do you call people who are afraid of Santa Claus?
Claustrophobic.

What was so good about the neurotic doll the girl was given for Christmas?
It was wound up already.

What was wrong with the brand new electric train set that the boy received for Christmas?
Forty metres of track – all straight!

MISCELLANEOUS

Two aerials meet on a roof – fall in love – get married. The ceremony was rubbish but the reception was brilliant.

I went to the butchers the other day and I bet him 50 bucks that he couldn't reach the meat off the top shelf. And he said, 'No, the steaks are too high.'

Two cows are standing next to each other in a field. Daisy says to Dolly, 'I was artificially inseminated this morning.'
'I don't believe you,' said Dolly.
'It's true, straight up, no bull!'

Cannibal 1:   How do you make an explorer stew?
Cannibal 2:   Keep him waiting a few hours.

Once there was a boy named Odd. He was the butt of jokes his whole life, because of his name. Eventually he grew up to be a very successful fisherman and owner of three fish processing plants.
    When Odd was about to die, he said, 'People have been teasing me my whole life and I don't want them doing that after I'm dead, so don't put my name on my gravestone.'
    After Odd died, people saw his blank tombstone and said, 'That's odd.'

Two cows are in a field. One says to the other, 'So what do you think of mad cow disease?'
'What do I care? I'm a chicken.'

My friend drowned in a bowl of muesli. He was pulled in by a strong currant.

The Seven Dwarfs go to the Vatican and are granted an audience with the pope.

'Dopey, my son,' says the pope. 'What can I do for you?'

Dopey asks, 'Excuse me, Your Excellency, but are there any dwarf nuns in Rome?'

The pope wrinkles his brow at this odd question, thinks for a minute and answers, 'No Dopey there are no dwarf nuns in Rome.'

In the background a few of the dwarfs start sniggering. Dopey turns around and gives them a glare, silencing them.

Dopey turns back, 'Your Worship, are there any dwarf nuns in all of Europe?'

The pope, puzzled now, again thinks for a moment and then answers, 'No Dopey, there are no dwarf nuns in Europe.'

The other dwarfs begin to giggle.

Dopey implores the pope, 'Mr Pope, are there any dwarf nuns anywhere in the world?'

'I'm sorry, my son, there are no dwarf nuns anywhere in the world.'

The other dwarfs collapse into a heap, rolling around in laughter. They're pounding the floor and tears are rolling down their cheeks as they begin chanting, 'Dopey screwed a penguin! Dopey screwed a penguin!'

Porky was 18 years old, friendly, and eager to do things right. Unfortunately, he wasn't especially bright. He had just started his first job, as a delivery boy and general 'go-fer' at a furniture warehouse. His first task was to go out for coffee.

He walked into a nearby coffee shop carrying a large thermos. When the assistant finally noticed him, he held up the thermos.

'Is this big enough to hold six cups of coffee? he asked.

The assistant looked at the thermos, hesitated for a few seconds, then finally said, 'Yeah. It looks like about six cups to me.'

'Good,' Porky said. 'Give me two white, two black, and two decaf.'

Two hydrogen atoms walk into a bar.
'I think I've lost an electron,' says one.
'Are you sure?' asks the second.
'Yes, I'm positive.'

A jump-lead walks into a bar.
The barman says 'I'll serve you, but don't start anything.'

A man walks into a bar with a roll of tarmac under his arm.
He says 'Pint please, and one for the road.'

An ice cream man was found lying on the floor of his van covered with hundreds and thousands. Police say that he topped himself.

Apparently, one in five people in the world are Chinese. There are five people in my family, so one of them must be Chinese. It's either my mum or my dad. Or my older brother Colin. Or my younger brother Ho-Cha-Chu. But I think it is Colin.

Two fat blokes in a pub, one says to the other, 'Your round.'
'So are you, you fat bastard!'

Two prostitutes standing on a street corner, one says to the other, 'Have you ever been picked up by the fuzz?'
'No, but I've often been swung around by the boobs.'

I had a ploughman's lunch the other day. He wasn't very happy.

Two cannibals are eating a clown. One says to the other 'Does this taste funny to you?'

The phone was ringing. I picked it up, and said, 'Who's speaking please?'
  'You are,' said a voice.

I rang up my local swimming pool. I said, 'Is that the local swimming pool?'
  'It depends where you're calling from.'

Q: What's brown and sounds like a bell?
A: Dung.

An old man is eating in a truck stop when three Hells Angels bikers walk in. The first walks up to the old man, pushes his cigarette into the old man's pie and then takes a seat at the counter. The second walks up to the old man, spits into his milk and takes a seat at the counter. The third walks up to the old man, turns over his plate, and then takes a seat at the counter. Without a word of protest, the old man quietly leaves the diner.
  Shortly thereafter, one of the bikers says to the waitress, 'Humph, not much of a man, was he?'
  The waitress replies, 'Not much of a truck driver either, he just backed his big-rig over three motorcycles.'

Six guys are playing poker when Smith loses $500 on a single hand, clutches his chest and drops dead at the table. Showing respect for their fallen comrade, the other five complete their playing time standing up.

Roberts looks around and asks, 'Now, who is going to tell the wife?'

They draw straws. Rippington, who is always a loser, picks the short one. They tell him to be discreet and gentle, and not to make a bad situation any worse than it is.

'Gentlemen! Discreet? I'm the most discreet man you will ever meet. Discretion is my middle name, leave it to me.'

Rippington walks over to the Smith house and knocks on the door. The wife answers and asks what he wants.

Rippington says, 'Your husband just lost $500 playing cards.'

She hollers, 'Tell him to drop dead!'

Rippington says, 'I'll tell him.'

Jim, Joe and Harry have been going to the same pub for as long as they can remember. And never have they won anything in the monthly raffle – until now. In the latest draw, all three of them have won a prize.

Jim is the first one of the three to get his name drawn. He wins 2kg of spaghetti sauce, four boxes of noodles, and 3kg of meatballs.

Joe has his name drawn next. He gets himself a holiday on the Gold Coast, four night's accommodation at the Mermaid Inn and a pair of tickets to see the *Wilson Triplets Bikinis on Ice Show*. Joe thinks that he has died and gone to heaven.

Harry is the last one to have his name drawn, he wins a toilet brush. A month later, they compare notes on their prizes.

Jim says, 'It was fantastic. I had spaghetti for three days. It was so good, and Marge didn't have to buy food for those three days. We saved so much money.'

Joe says 'Pat was so happy when I brought home those tickets. The Gold Coast was nice, the hotel was very luxurious and the Wilson Triplets, if I didn't know better, I would swear they were sisters.'

Then Jim turns to Harry, and asks him how his prize worked out.

Harry looks at them both and says, 'That toilet brush is nice, but I think I'll go back to using paper.'

It's the spring of 1957 and Bobby goes to pick up his date. He's a pretty hip guy with his own car. When he goes to the front door, the girl's father invites him in.

'Carrie's not ready yet. Why don't you have a seat?'

Carrie's father asks Bobby what they're planning to do. Bobby replies politely that they will probably just go to the soda shop or a movie.

'Why don't you two go out and screw? I hear all the kids are doing it!'

Naturally, this comes as quite a surprise to Bobby so he asks Carrie's dad to please repeat himself.

'Yeah,' says Carrie's father, 'Carrie really likes to screw; she'll screw all night if we let her!'

A few minutes later, Carrie comes downstairs in her little poodle skirt and announces that she's ready to go. Almost breathless with anticipation, Bobby escorts his date out the front door.

About twenty minutes later, Carrie rushes back into the house, slams the door behind her, and screams at her father, 'Dad, it's called the twist!'

One morning, Mr Toad wakes up to note with alarm that his penis has turned yellow. He rushes round to the tree in which Wise Old Owl is nesting, and shows him the affected part.

'No worries,' replies the owl. 'Down the track there, second burrow to the left, you'll find Dr Rabbit. He'll fix you up.'

No sooner has the toad departed than Millie Mouse arrives under Wise Old Owl's tree with a shining pair of pink tits, and seeks the owl's advice.

'Straight down the path,' replies Owl. 'Follow the yellow-dick toad.'

A man is very rich indeed but despite having everything a man can have, he is still bored. To relieve his boredom, every year he holds an amazing party. Every year he throws a better party than the year before. But he is still bored. One year he has an idea. He fills the pool with crocodiles.

Halfway through the party, he announces, 'Anyone who can swim through my pool and get out the other side still alive can have my house.' There is silence. Then he adds, 'Anyone who can swim through my pool and get out the other side still alive can have my house and all my shares.' Still silence. Sweetening the offer he adds, 'Anyone who can swim through my pool and get out the other side still alive, can have my house, my shares and all my money.'

Suddenly, there's a loud splash. A man in the pool is fighting for his life with the crocodiles. It's a struggle, but he manages to swim across the pool. He just makes it to the other end and climbs out, half dead with one arm and one leg.

'Oh my god' says the rich man. 'That was incredible. When do you want the house?'

'I don't want the house' says the guy.

'When do you want my shares?'

'I don't want the shares.'

'When do you want all my money?'

'I don't want your money.'

So the rich guy says, 'Well what do you want then?'

'I want the bastard that pushed me in.'

A man slips on some dog poo as he walks into a bar. Moments later, a Hell's Angel does the same thing.

'I just did that,' the first man says. So the Hell's Angel hits him.

Two boys are playing football in Central Park when one is attacked by a rabid Rottweiler. Thinking quickly, the other boy rips off a board of the nearby fence, wedges it down the dog's collar and twists, breaking the dogs neck. A reporter who is strolling by sees the incident, and rushes over to interview the boy.

'Young Giants Fan Saves Friend From Vicious Animal,' he starts writing in his notebook.

'But I'm not a Giants fan,' the little hero replies.

'Sorry, since we are in New York, I just assumed you were,' says the reporter and starts again. 'Little Jets Fan Rescues Friend from Horrific Attack,' he writes.

'I'm not a Jets fan either,' the boy says.

'I assumed everyone in New York was either for the Giants or Jets. What team do you root for?' the reporter asks.

'I'm a Cowboys fan,' the child says.

The reporter starts a new sheet in his notebook and writes, 'Little Redneck Maniac Kills Beloved Family Pet.'

A white guy in a bar goes to the toilet. While he's standing there, a black guy comes in, stands beside him and whips out his massive dong. The white guy asks him how he got it.

The black guy tells him, 'Every night I tie a piece of cord round the end and pull it tight for five minutes.'

The white guy thanks him and leaves. The two meet up in the same toilets six months later.

'How are you doin' with the dick,' says the black guy.

'Excellent' says the white guy, 'look it's nearly all black.'

A woman rushes home, bursting through the front door of her house and yelling to her husband, 'Pack your bags honey, I just won the lottery! All $10 million of it. Woooo hoooo!'

'That's great, sweetie!' he replies, 'but should I pack for the beach or for the mountains?'

'Who cares?' she replies, 'Just piss off!'

A man walks into a store to buy a Barbie doll for his daughter. 'How much is that Barbie in the window?' he asks the shop assistant.

In a condescending manner she responds, 'Which Barbie? We have Barbie Goes to the Gym for $19.95, Barbie Goes to the Ball for $19.95, Barbie Goes Shopping for $19.95, Barbie Goes to the Beach for $19.95, Barbie Goes Nightclubbing for $19.95, and Divorced Barbie for $265.'

The guy asks, 'Why is Divorced Barbie $265 when all the others are only $19.95?'

'That's obvious,' the assistant states, 'Divorced Barbie comes with Ken's house, Ken's car, Ken's boat and Ken's furniture.'

B ob always wanted a pair of authentic cowboy boots. Seeing some on sale one day, he buys them and wears them home, walking proudly. He walks into the bedroom and says to his wife, 'Notice anything different, Bessie?'

Bessie looks him over, 'Nope.'

Bob says excitedly 'Come on Bessie, take a good look. Notice anything different about me?'

Bessie looks again, 'Nope.'

Frustrated, Bob storms off into the bathroom, undresses, and walks back into the room completely naked except for his boots. Again he asks, a little louder this time, 'Notice anything different?'

Bessie looks up and says, 'Bob, what's different? It's hanging down today, it was hanging down yesterday, and it'll be hanging down again tomorrow.'

Furious, Bob yells, 'And do you know why it is hanging down, Bessie? It's hanging down because it's looking at my new boots!'

Bessie replies, 'Should'a bought a hat, Bob.'

Two women are having lunch together, discussing the merits of cosmetic surgery.

The first woman says, 'I need to be honest with you, I'm getting a boob job.'

The second woman says, 'Oh that's nothing, I'm thinking of having my arsehole bleached.'

The first replies, 'Funny, I just can't picture your husband as a blonde.'

A woman has a passion for baked beans. She loves them but unfortunately they have always had a very embarrassing and somewhat lively reaction to her. Then one day she meets a guy and falls in love. When it becomes apparent that they will marry she thinks to herself, 'He is such a sweet and gentle man, I would hate to lose him. I just have to give up beans.'

Some months later her car breaks down on the way home from work. Since she lives in the country, she calls her husband and tells him that she will be late because she has to walk home. On her way she passes a small diner and the odour of the baked beans is more than she can stand. Since she still has miles to walk, she reckons that she will walk off any ill effects by the time she reaches home. So, she stops at the diner and before she knows it, she has consumed three large plates of baked beans. All the way home she farts. Upon arriving home, she feels reasonably sure she can control it.

Her husband seems excited to see her and exclaims delightedly, 'Darling, I have a surprise for dinner tonight.'

He then blindfolds her and leads her to her chair at the table. She seats herself and just as he is about to remove the blindfold from his wife, the telephone rings. He makes her promise not to touch the blindfold until he returns. He then goes to answer the phone. The baked beans she has consumed are still affecting her and the pressure is becoming almost unbearable, so while her husband is out of the room she seizes the opportunity, shifts her weight to one leg and lets it go. It is not only loud, but it smells like a fertiliser truck running over a skunk in front of a pulpwood mill. She takes her napkin and fans the air around her vigorously. Then, she shifts to the other cheek and rips three more, which remind her of cabbage cooking. Keeping her ears tuned to the conversation in the other room, she goes on like this for another ten minutes. When the phone farewells signal the end of her freedom, she fans the air a few more times with her napkin, places it on her lap and folds her hands upon it, smiling contentedly to herself. She is the picture of innocence when her husband returns. Apologizing for taking so long, he asks her if she peeked, and she assures him that she didn't. At this point, he removes the blindfold, and she is surprised.

There are twelve dinner guests seated around the table to wish her a happy birthday.

A t school, Little Johnny is told by a classmate that most adults are hiding at least one dark secret, and that this makes it very easy to blackmail them by saying, 'I know the whole truth.'

Little Johnny decides to go home and try it out. He goes home, and is greeted by his mother.

He says, 'I know the whole truth.'

His mother quickly hands him $20 and says, 'Just don't tell your father.'

Quite pleased, the boy waits for his father to get home from work, and greets him with, 'I know the whole truth.'

The father promptly hands him $40 and says, 'Please don't say a word to your mother.'

Very pleased, the boy is on his way to school the next day when he sees the mailman at his front door. The boy greets him by saying, 'I know the whole truth.'

The mailman immediately drops the mail, opens his arms, and says, 'Then come give your daddy a great big hug.'

A woman rushes into the supermarket to pick up a few items. She heads for the express line where the clerk is talking on the phone with his back turned to her.

'Excuse me,' she says, 'I'm in a hurry. Could you check me out, please?'

The clerk turns, stares at her for a second, smiles and says, 'Not bad.'

'L ook at me,' boasts the fit old man, pounding a very flat and firm stomach, having just finished 100 sit-ups before a group of young people.

'Fit as a fiddle! And you want to know why? I don't smoke, I don't drink, I don't stay up late, and I don't chase after loose women.' He smiles at them, teeth white, eyes aglitter, 'And tomorrow, I'm going to celebrate my ninetieth birthday.'

'Oh, really?' drawls one of the young onlookers, 'How?'

T wo eggs have just been married and are on their honeymoon. While they are sitting on the bed making out, the female egg pushes the male egg away and says, 'I just have to go to the bathroom. I'll be back in a minute,' and off she goes.

Five minutes later the male egg sees his sexy wife walk out in a slinky egglige, wiping her hands up and down her smooth, oval body. Instantly, the male egg slaps his hands on the top of his head, covering it completely. The female egg looks at him and asks what he is doing.

He replies, 'The last time I was this hard, someone cracked me on the head with a spoon.'

J im and Joe often go to the beach to pick up women. Unfortunately, Joe never has any luck, while Jim never fails. One day, Joe asks Jim the secret of his success. Jim promises to tell Joe, so long as Joe keeps it to himself.

After Joe agrees, Jim says, 'You see the fruit and vegetable shop over the road? Well, every time I come to the beach I buy a potato and put it in my swimming trunks. When the women see it they come running from miles around.'

Joe says, 'That's easy. I can do that.'

The next day, Joe goes over to the shop and picks out the biggest, most perfectly shaped potato he can find. He then goes into the changing room and slips it into his swimming trunks. As he walks out onto the beach he immediately notices that women begin to take notice of him.

'Its working!' he thinks.

But soon he begins to realise that they are not looking interested but rather upset, almost disgusted, by the sight of him. He rushes over to Jim and asks, 'Jim, what's the problem? Why isn't it working?'

Jim takes one look and says, 'Because you're supposed to put the potato in the front!'

A guy is walking down the road looking very pleased with himself. He bumps into his friend who asks why he looks so happy.

'I just bought a great new hearing aid. It's fantastic.'

'Are you wearing it now?' the friend asks.

'Yup. It cost me $4000. It's top of the line.'

'Wow! What kind is it?' asks the friend.

'Twelve-thirty.'

What is a dyslexic agnostic insomniac? Someone who lays awake at night wondering if there really is a dog.

One day a diver is exploring about 10m below sea level. He notices a guy at the same depth as him, but he has on no scuba gear whatsoever. The diver goes below another 10m and the other guy joins him a few minutes later. The diver goes below another 10m and minutes later the same guy joins him.

This confuses the diver, so he takes out a waterproof chalk-and-board set, and writes, 'How the hell are you able to stay under this deep without equipment?'

The guy takes the board and chalk, erases what the diver has written, and writes, 'I'm drowning, you moron!'

Prince Charles finds an ancient wine bottle in the cellar of Windsor Castle. When he opens it a genie flies out and grants him a wish. Charles is ecstatic, as just that morning he had reversed his Range Rover over the Queen's favourite corgi and squashed it flat. He asks the genie to bring the dog back to life before the Queen finds out.

The genie examines the dog which is splattered all over the drive and tells Charles that there is nothing at all he can do. The only way out is to chuck the dog in the dustbin and keep quiet. Charles then asks the genie if he can make his wife, Camilla Parker-Bowles, beautiful and sexy, so that the media will stop making nasty comments about her.

The genie thinks for a moment, scratches his head and says, 'On second thoughts get that bloody dog out of the bin.'

An explorer in the deepest Amazon suddenly finds himself surrounded by a bloodthirsty group of natives. Upon surveying the situation, he says quietly to himself, 'Oh God, I'm stuffed.'

There is a ray of light from heaven and a voice booms out, 'No you are not stuffed! Pick up that stone at your feet and bash in the head of the chief standing in front of you!'

So the explorer picks up the stone and proceeds to bash the hell out of the chief. As he stands above the lifeless body, breathing heavily and surrounded by 100 natives with a look of shock on their faces, God's voice booms out again, 'OK . . . now you're stuffed!'

Little Red Riding Hood is skipping down the road when she sees the Big Bad Wolf crouched down behind a log.

'My, what big eyes you have, Mr Wolf,' says Little Red Riding Hood.

The wolf jumps up and runs away. Further down the road Little Red Riding Hood sees the wolf again. This time he is crouched behind a tree stump.

'My, what big ears you have Mr Wolf,' says Little Red Riding Hood.

Again the wolf jumps up and runs away. Further down the track Little Red Riding Hood sees the wolf again, this time crouched down behind a road sign.

'My, what big teeth you have Mr Wolf,' taunts Little Red Riding Hood.

With that the Big Bad Wolf jumps up and screams, 'Will you piss off! I'm trying to take a shit.'

What do you get when you cross LSD with birth control? A trip without the kids.

A philosopher is doing a survey on a group of men, on the topic of happiness.

He tells them, 'I can prove to you that the amount of happiness has a relation to the amount of sex you have.'

He glances at his audience and sees a man in the right-hand corner, smiling.

'Sir, How often do you have sex?' the philosopher asks.

'Once a month.' the man answers.

Looking for another happy face, he spots a man in the middle, with a bigger smile.

He asks him, 'Sir, How often do you have sex?'

'Once a week,' the man shouts.

Trying to prove his theory further, he sees another man, laughing.

'You seem to be a very happy man. So how often do you have sex?'

'Well . . . every day,' the happy man answers.

'There, I am right. The amount of happiness is in relation to the amount of sex you have,' says the philosopher.

But far off at the end of the room, he sees a man with his hands in the air, laughing and jumping with so much happiness. So the philosopher says to him, 'You sure look like a very happy man?'

'Yes, yes, yes,' answers the very happy man.

'So how often do you get to have sex?' the philosopher asks.

The man answers, 'Once a year.'

The puzzled and embarrassed philosopher asks the man, 'What? Then why are you so happy?'

The man starts laughing and jumping and crying out, 'It's tonight, it's tonight!'

The Mafia is looking for a new man to be their bagman and collect money from all the businesses they are standing over. Feeling the heat from the police, they decide to use a deaf person for this job – if he ever gets caught, he won't be able to communicate to the police what he is doing.

On his first week, the deaf collector picks up over $50 000. But he gets greedy, decides to keep the money and stashes it in a safe place. The Mafia soon catch up with the deaf man and want to interrogate him. Unable to communicate with him, they take along a sign interpreter.

The Mafia boss says to the interpreter, 'Ask him where the money is?'

The interpreter signs, 'Where's the money?'

The deaf man replies, 'I don't know what you're talking about.'

The interpreter tells the boss, 'He says he doesn't know what you're talking about.'

The hood pulls out a .38 gun and places it in the ear of the deaf collector.

'Now ask him where the money is.'

The interpreter signs, 'Where is the money?'

The deaf man replies, 'The $50 000 is in Central Park, hidden in the third tree stump on the left from the West 78th Street gate.'

The interpreter turns to the boss, 'He says get stuffed!'

A team of archaeologists is excavating in Israel when they come upon a cave. Written on the wall of the cave are the following symbols in order of appearance:

1. A dog
2. A donkey
3. A shovel
4. A fish
5. A Star of David

They decide it is a unique find and the writings are at least 3000 years old. They chop out the piece of stone and have it brought to the museum where archaeologists from all over the world come to study the ancient symbols. They hold a huge meeting after months of conferences to discuss the meaning of the markings.

The president of their society stands up and points at the first drawing and says, 'This looks like a dog. We can judge that this was a highly intelligent race as they had animals for companionship. To prove this statement you can see that the next symbol resembles a donkey, so, they were even smart enough to use animals to till the soil. The next drawing looks like a shovel of some sort, which means they had tools. Even further proof of their high intelligence is the fish which means that when a famine hit the earth and food didn't grow, they could take to the sea for food. The last symbol appears to be the Star of David which means they were evidently Hebrews.'

The audience applauds enthusiastically and the president smiles and says, 'I'm glad to see that you are all in full agreement with our interpretations.'

Suddenly a little old Jewish man stands up in the back of the room and says, 'I object to every word. The explanation of what the writings say is quite simple. First of all, everyone knows that Hebrew isn't read from left to right, but from right to left. Now, look at the markings. It says, "Holy mackerel, dig the ass on that bitch!"'

A high-court judge is at a bar in a high-class hotel where he is a regular visitor. He drinks into the small hours of the morning. On leaving the bar he vomits down the front of his suit then staggers to his parked car, which he manages to start and drives home in a most dangerous fashion. When he arrives at his mansion in a suburb, he falls out of the car, and staggers to the door, which his wife has opened. On seeing his state she asks what happened. Despite his condition, he thinks quickly.

'I had a few civil drinks in the Shelburne hotel, and when I came out a drunk got sick all over me. But the police caught him and he's up in front of me in the morning. I'll give the swine six months in jail,' he replies.

His wife then sends him to the shower and then bed, while she makes him some food and a hot drink. Having put his soiled clothes in the wash she returns to the bedroom with his food.

'How long did you say you would give the drunk in jail?' she asks.

'Six months,' he replies.

'Well you better make it twelve because he shat in your trousers as well.'

God is looking down at earth and He sees all of the rascally behaviour that is going on. He decides to send an angel down to check it out.

When the angel returns, he tells God, 'Yes, it is bad on earth, 95% of the people are misbehaving and 5% are not.'

God thinks for a moment. 'Maybe I had better send down a second angel to get another opinion.'

So God sends another angel to earth. When the angel returns he goes to God and says, 'Yes, the earth is in decline, 95% are misbehaving and 5% are being good.'

God is not pleased. So He decides to email the 5% that are good because He wants to encourage them. Give them a little something to help them keep going.

Do you know what that email said? No? I didn't get one either.

Upon arriving home in eager anticipation of a leisurely evening, the husband is met at the door by his sobbing wife. Tearfully she explains, 'It's the pharmacist. He insulted me terribly this morning on the phone.'

Immediately, the husband drives into town to accost the pharmacist and demand an apology.

Before he can say more than a word or two, the pharmacist tells him, 'Now, just a minute – listen to my side of it. This morning the alarm failed to go off, so I was late getting up. I went without breakfast and hurried out to the car but I'll be damned if I didn't lock the house with both house and car keys inside. I had to break a window to get my keys. Driving a little too fast, I got a speeding ticket. Then, about three blocks from the store I got a flat tyre. When I finally got to the store there was a bunch of people waiting for me to open up. I got the store opened and started waiting on these people, and all the time the darn phone was ringing its head off. Then I had to break a roll of nickels against the cash register drawer to make change, and they spilled all over the floor. I got down on my hands and knees to pick up the nickels – the phone still ringing – when I came up I cracked my head on the open cash drawer, which made me stagger back against a showcase with a bunch of perfume bottles on it, and half of them hit the floor and broke. The phone was still ringing with no let up, and I finally got back to answer it.

It was your wife. She wanted to know how to use a rectal thermometer. Well, Mister, I told her!'

A man returns from the doctor and tells his wife that the doctor has told him he has only twenty-four hours to live. Given this prognosis, the man asks his wife for sex. Naturally, she agrees, and they make love.

About six hours later, the husband goes to his wife and says, 'Honey, you know I now have only eighteen hours to live. Could we please do it one more time?'

Of course, the wife agrees, and they do it again. Later, as the man gets into bed, he looks at his watch and realises that he now has only eight hours left.

He touches his wife shoulder, and asks, 'Honey, please . . . just one more time before I die.'

She says, 'Of course, Dear,' and they make love for the third time.

After this session, the wife rolls over and falls asleep. The man, however, worries about his impending death. He tosses and turns until he's down to four more hours. He taps his wife, who rouses.

'Honey, I only have four more hours. Do you think we could . . .'

At this point the wife sits up and says, 'Listen, I have to get up in the morning. You don't!'

There are several men sitting around in the locker room of a private gym after exercising. Suddenly a mobile phone on one of the benches rings. A man picks it up.

'Hello?'

'Honey, it's me. Are you at the gym?'

'Yes.'

'Great! I am at the mall two blocks from where you are. I just saw a beautiful mink coat. It's absolutely gorgeous! Can I buy it?'

'What's the price?'

'Only $1500.'

'Well, OK, go ahead and get it, if you like it that much.'

'Ahhh, and I also stopped by the Mercedes dealership and saw the 2003 models. I saw one I really liked. I spoke with the salesman, and he gave me a really good price . . . and since we need to exchange the BMW that we bought last year . . .'

'What price did he quote you?'

'Only $60 000'

'OK, but for that price I want it with all the options.'

'Great! But before we hang up, something else.'

'What?'

'It might look like a lot, but I was reconciling your bank account and I stopped by the real estate agent this morning and saw the house we had looked at last year. It's on sale! Remember? The one with a pool, an English garden, an acre of park area and a beachfront.'

'How much are they asking?'

'Only $450 000, a magnificent price, and I see that we have that much in the bank to cover it.'

'Well, then go ahead and buy it, but just bid $420 000. OK?'

'OK, sweetie, Thanks! I'll see you later! I love you!'

'Bye, I do too.'

The man hangs up, closes the phone's flap, and raises his hand and asks all those present, 'OK. Whose phone is this?'

A man enters a barber for a shave. While the barber is foaming him up, he mentions the problem he has getting a close shave around his cheeks.

'I have just the thing,' says the barber taking a small wooden ball from a nearby drawer. 'Just place this between your cheek and gum.'

The client places the ball in his mouth and begins to give the man the closest shave he has ever experienced.

After a few strokes, the client asks in garbled speech 'And what if I swallow it?'

'No problem,' says the barber. 'Just bring it back tomorrow like everyone else does!'

A woman is picking through the frozen turkeys at the grocery store, but can't find one big enough for her family.

She asks a stock boy, 'Do these turkeys get any bigger?'

The stock boy replies, 'No Ma'am, they're dead.'

A ndy wants a job as a signalman on the railways. He is told to meet the inspector at the signal box.

The inspector asks him, 'What would you do if you realised that two trains were heading for each other on the same track?'

Andy says, 'I would switch the points for one of the trains.'

'What if the lever broke?' asks the inspector.

'Then I'd dash down out of the signal box,' says Andy, 'and I'd use the manual lever over there.'

'What if the manual lever had been struck by lightning?'

'Then,' Andy continues, 'I'd run back into the signal box and phone the next signal box.'

'What if the phone was engaged?'

'Well in that case,' perseveres Andy, 'I'd rush down out of the box and use the public emergency phone at the level crossing up there.'

'What if that was vandalised?'

'Oh well then I'd run into the village and get my uncle Silas.'

This puzzles the inspector, so he asks, 'Why would you do that?'

'Because he's never seen a train crash.'

JAIL VS WORK

IN PRISON . . . you spend the majority of your time in a 3m × 3m cell.
AT WORK . . . you spend the majority of your time in a 2m × 2m cubicle.

IN PRISON . . . you get three meals a day.
AT WORK . . . you only get a break for one meal and you pay for it.

IN PRISON . . . you get time off for good behaviour
AT WORK . . . you get more work for good behaviour

IN PRISON . . . the guard locks and unlocks all the doors for you.
AT WORK . . . you must carry around a security card and open all the doors for yourself.

IN PRISON . . . you can watch TV and play games.
AT WORK . . . you get fired for watching TV and playing games.

IN PRISON . . . you get your own toilet.
AT WORK . . . you have to share with some idiot who pees on the seat.

IN PRISON . . . they allow your family and friends to visit.
AT WORK . . . you can't even speak to your family.

IN PRISON . . . the taxpayers pay all expenses with no work required.

AT WORK . . . you get to pay all the expenses to go to work and then they deduct taxes from your salary to pay for prisoners.

IN PRISON . . . you spend most of your life inside bars wanting to get out.
AT WORK . . . you spend most of your time wanting to get out and go inside bars.

IN PRISON . . . you must deal with sadistic wardens.
AT WORK . . . they are called managers.

COUNTRY FOLK

Billy-Bob and Ray were talking one afternoon.
Billy-Bob tells Ray, 'Ya know, I reckon I'm 'bout ready for a holiday. Only this year I'm gonna do it a little different. The last few years, I took your advice about where to go. Three years ago you said to go to Hawaii. I went to Hawaii and Earline got pregnant. Then two years ago, you told me to go to the Bahamas, and Earline got pregnant again. Last year you suggested Tahiti and darned if Earline didn't get pregnant again.'

'So, what you gonna do this year that's different?' asks Ray.

'This year I'm taking Earline with me.'

The first grade class gathered around the teacher for a game of 'Guess the Animal'. The first picture the teacher held up was of a cat.

'OK, boys and girls,' she said brightly, 'can anyone tell me what this is?'

'I know, I know, it's a cat!' yelled a little boy.

'Very good, Eddie. Now, who knows what this animal is called?'

'That's a dog!' piped up the same little boy.

'Right, again. And what about this animal?' she asked, holding up a picture of a deer.

Silence fell over the class. After a minute or two, the teacher said, 'I'll give you a hint, children. It's something you're mother calls your father.'

'I know, I know,' screamed Eddie. 'It's a horny bastard!'

Three dead bodies turn up at the mortuary, all with very big smiles on their faces. The coroner calls the police to tell them the causes of death.

'First body: Frenchman, 60, died of heart failure while making love to his mistress. Hence the enormous smile,' says the Coroner.

'Second body: Scotsman, 25, won a thousand dollars on the lottery, spent it all on whisky. Died of alcohol poisoning, hence the smile.'

'What of the third body?' asks the inspector.

'Ah, this is the most unusual one: Billy-Bob, the country lad from Oklahoma, 30, struck by lightning.'

'Why is he smiling then?'

'Thought he was having his picture taken.'

A nationwide search is held for the country's best poet. There is pretty stiff competition but eventually it comes down to two finalists – one a Yale graduate, the other a country lad.

The final contest is for them to write a poem in two minutes containing the word Timbuktu.

The Yale graduate recites his poem first.

Slowly across the desert sand
Trekked a lonely caravan.
Men on camels two by two
Destination Timbuktu.

The audience goes wild. They think the country lad doesn't stand a chance. Nevertheless, he stands up and recites his poem.

Me and Tim ahunting went
Met three whores in a pop-up tent
They were three and we were two
So I bucked one and Timbuktu.

THE 80S!

YOU'RE DEFINITELY AN 80S CHILD IF:

- You can remember what Michael Jackson looked like before his nose fell off.
- You wore a banana clip or one of those slap on wrist bands at some point during your youth.
- You wore French rolls on the bottom of your splatter painted jeans.
- You had slouch socks, and puff painted your own shirt at least once.
- You know the profound meaning of 'Wax on, wax off.'
- You can name at least half of the members of the elite 'Brat Pack'.
- You have seen at least 10 episodes of *Fraggle Rock*.
- You know that another name for a keyboard is a 'synthesiser'.
- You hold a special place in your heart for *Back to the Future*.
- You fell victim to 80's fashion: spandex pants and big hair, crimped and combed over to the side.
- You owned an extensive collection of Cabbage Patch Kids and Trolls.
- You wore fluorescent clothing.
- You could break dance.
- Or wished you could.
- You remember when Atari was a state-of-the-art video game system. That is, ping pong.
- You remember MC Hammer.
- You own cassettes.

- You believed that in the year 2000 we'd all be living on the moon.
- You own any of the Care-Bear glasses from Pizza Hut.
- *Poltergeist* freaked you out.
- You carried your lunch to school in a gremlins lunchbox.
- You have pondered why Smurfette was the only female smurf.
- You wanted to have an alien like Alf living in your house.
- You wore biker shorts underneath a short skirt and felt stylish.
- You wore tights under shorts and felt stylish.
- You had a Swatch watch.
- You spent countless hours trying to perfect the Care-Bear stare.
- You had Wonder Woman underwear.
- You wanted to be the Hulk for Halloween.
- You thought that Transformers were more than meets the eye.
- Partying 'like it's 1999' seemed soooo far away!

DOMESTIC TIPS

Smell gas? Locate the suspected leak by striking an ordinary match in every room in the house until a loud explosion reveals the source of the escaping gas.

To stop nose bleeds, simply place your head between your knees until your heart stops.

When you leave the house simply plug the phone into your video recorder. Not only will it record the caller's voice, but you will also get a picture of them speaking, probably.

Transform your garage into a drive-thru restaurant by sitting in your car, lowering your window and demanding that your wife brings you a cup of tea, on roller skates.

Pretend to be Welsh by putting coal dust behind your ears, talking gibberish and singing all the time.

If a small child is choking on an ice cube, don't panic. Simply pour a jug of boiling water down its throat and hey presto! The blockage is almost instantly removed.

Save electricity on freezing winter nights by simply unplugging your fridge and placing the contents of it on your doorstep.

Help the local police by popping into the mortuary every day to see if you can identify any of the bodies.

Fill a shredded wheat with pink soap and, hey presto – an inexpensive Steelo soap pad.

Save money on expensive earrings by sticking Mentos or sugared almonds to your ear with Blu-Tack.

Can't afford contact lenses? Simply cut out small circles of cling wrap and press them into your eyes.

Fumes from burning settees can be lethal, so before sitting down always look around and plan your escape route in the event of a fire.

Edge your lawn into the shape of a pair of trousers then mow it in lines so it looks like a huge pair of green corduroy trousers. Pockets can simply be added by planting small flower beds.

Townies: whenever you see country folk driving into town in their green Range Rovers to go shopping, jump up and down screaming 'Get off my land!' Then shoot their dog.

Save money on expensive personalised car number plates by simply changing your name to match the existing plate.

Avoid embarrassment after tripping in the street by repeating the same movement several times to make it look like a normal part of your behaviour.

Hey vegetarians: make your veggie burgers go further by adding a 200g of mince to them.

Stop flies landing on your dinner by placing a pile of poo on the dinner table. The flies will be so busy munching on the faeces they will leave you to enjoy your meal.

Avoid the morning-after hangover – simply stay drunk past noon.

Brighten up dull Monday mornings at work by concealing a bottle of vodka in your jacket pocket and taking swigs from it at regular intervals throughout the day.

Are you sick and tired of using the same jokes over and over? Why not send them in to be recycled. You'll be saving lots of hot air that would have otherwise effected global warming.

Housewives: When nipping out to the shops, remember to carry a stiff broom in the boot of your car. Use it to sweep the broken glass to the side of the road every time you have a minor accident.

Bomb disposal experts' wives: Keep hubby on his toes by packing his lunchbox with plasticine and an old alarm clock.

Bus drivers: Pretend you are an airline pilot by wedging your accelerator pedal down with a heavy book, securing the steering wheel with some old rope, and then strolling back along the bus chatting casually to the passengers.

X-Files fans: Create the effect of being abducted by aliens by drinking two bottles of vodka. You'll invariably wake up in a strange place the following morning, having had your memory mysteriously 'erased'.

Increase blind people's electricity bills by switching all their lights on when their guide dog isn't looking.

International Master Criminals: Tell your guards to shoot James Bond in the head at the first opportunity. Under no circumstances give him a guided tour of your base, tell him your plans for the destruction of the world, or leave him in the custody of attractive women in bikinis.

EDUCATION

A little boy returning home from his first day at school said to his mother, 'Mum, what's sex?'.

His mother, who believed in all the most modern educational theories, gave him a detailed explanation, covering all aspects of the tricky subject.

When she had finished, the little lad produced an enrolment form which he had brought home from school and said, 'Yes, but how am I going to get all that into this one little square?'.

YOU KNOW YOU ARE NO LONGER A STUDENT WHEN:

- Your potted plants stay alive.
- Shagging in a single bed seems absurd.
- You keep more food than beer in the fridge.
- You haven't seen a daytime soap opera in over a year.
- 8am is not ridiculously early.
- You hear your favourite song in the elevator at work.
- You carry an umbrella.
- Your friends marry instead of hook-up, and divorce instead of break-up.
- You go from 12 weeks of holiday a year to four.
- You go to parties that the police don't raid.
- Adults feel comfortable telling jokes about sex in front of you.
- You refer to college students as kids.
- You drink wine, scotch and martinis instead of beer, bourbon, and rum.

The children were lined up in the cafeteria of a Catholic elementary school for lunch. At the head of the table was a large pile of apples. A nun had made a note and posted it on the apple tray, 'Take only one. God is watching.'

At the other end of the table was a large pile of chocolate-chip cookies. A child had written a note, 'Take all you want. God is watching the apples.'

A nerd was walking on campus one day when his nerd friend rode up on an incredible shiny new bicycle. The first nerd was stunned and asked, 'Where did you get such a nice bike?'

'Well, yesterday I was walking home minding my own business when a beautiful woman rode up to me on this bike. She threw the bike to the ground, took off all her clothes and said, "Take what you want!".'

The first nerd nodded approvingly and said, 'Good choice. The clothes probably wouldn't have fitted.'

A professor stood before his philosophy class. Wordlessly, he picked up an empty jar and filled it with golf balls. He asked the students if the jar was full. They agreed that it was.

The professor then poured pebbles into the jar, shaking the jar lightly so they rolled into the spaces between the golf balls. He asked the students again if the jar was full. They agreed it was.

Next the professor poured sand into the jar. The sand filled up the smaller gaps. He asked once more if the jar was full. The students responded with a unanimous 'yes'.

The professor then produced two cans of beer from under the table and poured the entire contents into the jar, filling the empty spaces in the sand. The students laughed.

'Now,' said the professor, as the laughter subsided, 'This jar represents your life. The golf balls are the important things, your family, your health, your friends and your favourite passions – things that would mean something even if you lost everything else. The pebbles are things that matter a little less, like your job, your house, your car. The sand is everything else – the small stuff. Yet these things are the ones that we tend to fixate on.

'If you put the sand into the jar first,' he continued, 'there is no room for the pebbles or the golf balls. The same goes for life. If you spend all your time and energy on the small stuff, you will never have room for the things that are important to you. Pay attention to the things that are critical to your happiness. Play with your children. Take your partner out to dinner. There will always be time to clean the house and mow the lawn. Take care of the golf balls first, the things that really matter. The rest is just sand.'

One of the students raised her hand and inquired what the beer represented.

The professor smiled. 'It just goes to show you that no matter how full your life may seem, there's always room for a couple of beers.'

A confused driving student one night
Made a left by mistake at the light
Then she turned left twice more
With intent to be sure
For she knew that three wrongs make a right.

DICTIONARY OF DEFINITIONS OF TERMS COMMONLY USED IN MATH LECTURES

Briefly:	I'm running out of time, so I'll just write and talk faster.
Check for yourself:	This is the boring part of the proof, so you can do it on your own time.
Clearly:	I don't want to write down all the in-between steps.
Hint:	The hardest of several possible ways to do a proof.

It's easily shown:	Even you should be able to prove this.
Let's talk it through:	I don't want to write it on the board in case I make a mistake.
Obviously:	I hope you weren't sleeping when we discussed this earlier, because I refuse to repeat it.
Proof omitted:	Trust me, it's true.
Recall:	I shouldn't have to tell you this, but for those of you who erase your memory tapes after every test.
Similarly:	At least one line of the proof of this case is the same as the previous equation.
Trivial:	If I have to show you how to do this, you're in the wrong class.

IF YOU ARE GOING TO FAIL YOUR EXAM, YOU MIGHT AS WELL ENJOY IT

- Bring a pillow. Fall asleep (or pretend to) until the last 15 minutes. Wake up, and say 'Oh Jeez, better get cracking!'
- Talk the entire way through the exam. Read questions aloud, debate your answers with yourself out loud. If asked to stop, yell out, 'I'm so sure you can hear me thinking.'
- Arrive wearing a black cloak. After about 30 minutes, put on a white mask and start yelling, 'I'm here, the phantom of the opera,' until they drag you away.
- After you get the exam, call the instructor over, point to a question, and ask for the answer.
- Try to get people in the room to do the Mexican Wave.
- Get a copy of the exam paper and run down the hall screaming, 'Dr Evil, Dr Evil, I've got the secret documents!'
- If it's a maths or science exam, answer in essay form. If it's long answer or essay form, answer with numbers and symbols.

- Make paper aeroplanes out of the exam paper. Aim them at the instructor's left nostril.
- Walk in, get the exam, sit down. About five minutes into it, loudly say to the instructor, 'I don't understand any of this!'
- Bring a Game Boy and play with the volume at maximum level.
- Come down with a bad case of Tourette's syndrome during the exam. The louder you make the 'involuntary' sounds, the better.
- On the answer sheet find a new and interesting way to refuse to answer every question. For example, 'I refuse to answer this question on the grounds that it conflicts with my religious beliefs.'
- Fifteen minutes into the exam, stand up, rip up all the papers into very small pieces, and throw them into the air. Then calmly ask for another copy of the exam.
- Twenty minutes into it, throw your papers down violently, scream out 'Screw this!' and walk out triumphantly.
- Every five minutes, stand up, collect all your things, move to another seat, and continue with the exam.
- Turn in the exam approximately 30 minutes into it. As you walk out say loudly, 'Too easy!'

EMPLOYMENT

There are just three types of accountants: those who can count and those who can't.

Q: Why did the Auditor cross the road?
A: Because he did it last year!

Q: Who was the world's first accountant?
A: Adam. He turned a leaf and made an entry!

Q: Why does the government jail people for theft?
A: It doesn't want any competition.

Q: Why was the sailor buried at sea?
A: Because he was dead.

When Picasso was tender in years
He considered some other careers
When he read a reportage
Of an imminent shortage
Of models with eyes in their ears.

One day a farmer called up an engineer, a physicist and a mathematician and asked them to fence off the largest possible area with the least amount of fence.

The engineer made the fence in a circle and proclaimed that he had the most efficient design.

The physicist made a long, straight line and proclaimed, 'We can assume the length is infinite.' He pointed out that fencing off half of the earth was certainly the most efficient way to do it.

The mathematician built a tiny fence around himself and said 'I declare myself to be on the outside.'

Amortician who practiced in Fife
Made love to the corpse of his wife.
'How could I know, Judge?
She was cold, did not budge
Just the same as she'd acted in life.'

An engineer, an accountant, a chemist and a bureaucrat were bragging about how smart their dogs were. To settle the argument they agreed to put their dogs through their paces.

The engineer called to his dog, 'T-square, do your stuff.'

The dog took out paper and pen and drew a circle, a square and a triangle. Everyone was suitably impressed.

The accountant called, 'Taxation, do your stuff.'

The pooch went to the kitchen, got a dozen cookies and made four stacks of three. The others nodded their surprise.

So the chemist called, 'Beaker, do your stuff.'

The dog went to the fridge for a bottle of milk, got a 250ml glass and poured exactly 200ml without spilling a drop. Everyone agreed that was great.

Finally it was the bureaucrat's turn, 'Coffee-Break, do your stuff!'

Coffee-Break ate the cookies, drank the milk, chewed the paper, said he injured his mouth doing so, filed a claim for unsafe working conditions, put in for worker's compensation and took extended sick leave.

A salesman from KFC approached the pope with a brilliant offer. For a million dollars all the pope would have to do is change the Lord's Prayer from 'Give us this day our daily bread' to 'Give us this day our daily chicken.' While the salesman tried hard to convince the pope that it was an inconsequential change, His Holiness refused the offer.

Two weeks later, the salesman returned to the pope. He reiterated his offer but this time promised 10 million dollars. The pope considered it for a little longer this time, but again refused the man's generous offer.

Another week later, the man returned and offered the pope 20 million dollars to change the Lord's Prayer. After some deliberation the pope reluctantly accepted. The following day, the pope met with his council.

'I have some good news and some bad news,' he said. 'The good news is, that we have just received a cheque for 20 million dollars.'

'What is the bad news, Your Holiness?'

'The bad news is we have lost the Wonder Bread account.'

There once was a midwife of Gaul
Who had almost no business at all.
She cried, 'Hell and damnation!
There's no procreation,
God made the French penis too small.'

A bobby of Nottingham Junction
Whose organ had long ceased to function
Deceived his good wife
For the rest of her life
With the aid of his constable's truncheon.

In the prime of her career, a world-famous painter started to lose her eyesight. Fearful that she might lose her career, she went to see the best eye surgeon in the world. After several weeks of delicate surgery and therapy, her eyesight was restored.

The painter was so grateful that she decided to show her gratitude by repainting the doctor's office. Part of her mural included a gigantic eye on one wall. When she had finished her work, she held a press conference to unveil the mural.

During the press conference, one reporter noticed the eye on the wall.

'What was your first reaction upon seeing your newly painted office, especially that large eye on the wall?' he asked the doctor.

'My first thought was "Thank God I'm not a gynaecologist."'

ETHNICITY

Q: What do you say to a Kiwi bloke with a be-yooooood-i-ful woman on his arm?

A: Hey, nice tattoo.

Q: How do Kiwis practice safe sex?

A: They paint an X on the back of the sheep that kick.

A married couple on holiday in Pakistan went to a marketplace. In the far corner of the market was a dimly lit stall, with a wizened old man sitting out the front of it. As they walked past he implored them to come into his shop to see his special sandals.

'These sandals,' he said, 'have magic powers. They make the wearer wild about sex like a great desert camel.'

The wife was intrigued, but the husband, who believed himself to be the world's greatest lover, was disbelieving.

'I tell you it is true,' said the old Pakistani man. 'Try them on for yourself!'

Reluctantly the man tried on the sandals. As soon as his feet slipped into the shoes he got a wild look in his eyes – a look his wife hadn't seen in many years. Frenzied by his raw sexual power the husband rushed the Pakistani man, threw him on a table and started tearing at the guy's pants.

'You have them on the wrong feet! You have them on the wrong feet!' screamed the Pakistani.

The security forces got all of the Saddam look-alikes together and told them that they have some good news and some bad news. The good news was that Saddam survived the bombings, so they all still had jobs.

One of the look-alikes asked, 'What's the bad news?'

'He lost an arm and an eye.'

Barty was trapped in a bog and seemed a goner when Big Mick O'Reilly wandered by.

'Help!' Barty shouted, 'Oi'm sinkin'!'

'Don't worry,' assured Mick. 'Next to the Strong Muldoon, Oi'm the strongest man in Erin, and Oi'll pull ye right out o' there.'

Mick leaned out and grabbed Barty's hand and pulled and pulled to no avail.

After two more unsuccessful attempts, Mick said to Barty, 'Shure, an' Oi can't do it. The Strong Muldoon could do it alone, mebbe, but Oi'll have to get some help.'

'Mick! Mick! D'ye think it will help if Oi pull me feet out of the stirrups?

An Irishman walks into a pub and asks for three pints of Guinness. The bartender brings him three pints. The man takes alternate sips of each one until they're gone. He then orders three more.

'Sir, you don't have to order three at a time. I can keep an eye on it and when you get low I'll bring you a fresh cold one,' says the bartender.

'You don't understand,' says the Irishman. I have two brothers, one in Australia and one in the States. We made a vow to each other that every Saturday night we'd still drink together. So right now, my brothers have three Guinness stouts too, and we're drinking together.'

The bartender thought that was a wonderful tradition. And so every week the man came in and ordered three beers. Then one week he came in and ordered only two. He drank them and then ordered two more.

'I know your tradition and I'd just like to say that I'm sorry that one of your brothers died.' said the bartender.

'Oh, me brothers are fine. I just quit drinking.'

A guy goes into the store and says to the clerk, I would like some Polish sausage.

'Are you Polish?' asks the clerk.

'Well, yes I am. But if I had asked for Italian sausage would you ask me if I was Italian? Or if I had asked for German sausage, would you ask me if I was German? Or if I had asked for a taco would you ask if I was Mexican?'

'Well, no.'

'Then, why do you ask me if I'm Polish just because I ask for Polish sausage?'

'Because this is a hardware store.'

Q: Why do Greeks wear thick gold chains?
A: So they know where to stop shaving.

Q: What do you call a hot chick in Lebanon?
A: A tourist.

Q: Why didn't the Italian Olympic boxing team compete at Sydney 2000?
A: They found out you have to fight one on one.

PROOF THAT JESUS WAS JEWISH:

1. He went into his father's business.
2. He lived at home until the age of 33.
3. He was sure his mother was a virgin, and his mother was sure he was God.

PROOF THAT JESUS WAS PUERTO RICAN:

1. His first name was Jesus.
2. He was bilingual.
3. He was always being harassed by the authorities.

PROOF THAT JESUS WAS A CALIFORNIAN:

1. He never cut his hair.
2. He walked around barefoot.
3. He invented a new religion.

PROOF THAT JESUS WAS BLACK:

1. He called everybody brother.
2. He liked Gospel.
3. He couldn't get a fair trial.

The good Father was warning his listeners about the suddenness of death.

'Before another day is ended,' he thundered, 'somebody in this parish will die.'

Seated in the front row was a little old Irishman who laughed out loud at this statement.

Very angry, the priest said to the jovial old man, 'What's so funny?'

'Well,' spoke up the oldster, 'I'm not a member of this parish.'

Brothers Mike and Seamus O'Malley are the two richest men in town and complete shites, both of 'em. They swindle the church out of its property, foreclose on the orphanage and cheat widows out of their last penny. One day Seamus up and dies and Mike pays a visit to the priest.

'Father,' he says, 'my good name will be upheld in this town. You'll be givin' the eulogy for me brother and in that eulogy you are going to say "Seamus O'Malley was truly a saint".'

'I won't do such a thing,' says the priest. 'T would be a lie!'

'I know you will,' says Mike. 'I hold the mortgage on the parish school and if you don't say those words, I'll foreclose.'

The priest is over a barrel. 'And if I pledge to say those words,' he says, 'then you'll sign the note over free and clear?'

'Done,' cackles Mike and he signs over the note. Next morning at the funeral, the priest begins the eulogy.

'Seamus O'Malley was a mean-spirited, spiteful, penurious, lying, cheating, arrogant and hateful excuse for a human being,' he says. 'But compared to his brother, Mike, Seamus O'Malley was truly a saint.'

Two English ladies were discussing their holiday plans on a London street corner near an Irish lady.

'We're planning a lovely holiday in Devon this year,' said one.

'Oh you oughtn't to do that,' said the other, 'there are Irish there! It would be awful.'

'Dear me!' said the first lady. 'Well where are you going?'

'Salisbury,' she replied.

'But Salisbury is simply crawling with Irish!' the first objected.

At this point the Irish lady could no longer hold her tongue. 'Why don't ye go t' hell,' she suggested. 'There be no Irish there!'

Irish they were, and drunk for sure, and they sat in the comer of Mulligan's newly refurbished bar. Across the wall opposite was a huge mirror, 4m long and stretching from floor to ceiling. Glancing around the room Pat suddenly spotted their reflection in the mirror.

'Mick, Mick,' he whispered. 'Don't look now but there's two fellas over there the image of us!'

'In the name of God,' said Mick, spotting the reflection. 'They're wearing identical clothes and everything.'

'That does it,' said Pat. 'I'm going to buy them a drink.'

But as Pat started to rise from his seat, Mick said, 'Sit down Pat. One of them's coming over.'

Paddy and Seamus were giving a motorcycle a ride on a brisk autumn day. After a wee bit Paddy, who was sitting behind Seamus, began to holler 'Seamus, Seamus, the wind is cutting me chest out!'

'Well, Paddy me lad,' said Seamus, 'why don't you take your jacket off and turn it from front to back. That'll block the wind for you.'

So Paddy took Seamus' advice and turned his jacket from front to back. After a bit, Seamus turned to talk to Paddy and was horrified to see that Paddy wasn't there. Immediately he turned the bike around and retraced their route. After a short time he came to a turn and saw some farmers standing around Paddy who was sitting on the ground.

'Tanks be to heaven, is he alright?' Seamus asked.

'Well,' said one of the farmers, 'he was alright when we found him here but since we turned his head the right way around he hasn't said a word!'

FAMILIES

A woman in the hospital has just had twins, a boy and a girl. She had a caesarean and is in the recovery room just coming out of the anaesthetic.

The nurse comes into the room and says, 'Your brother has taken the liberty to name the children.'

'Oh no. He probably gave them stupid names.'

'Well, the girl's name is Denise.'

'That's not bad, I like it. What about the boy?'

'The boy's name is De-nephew.'

Neighbour: What are you up to there, Tim?

Tommy: My goldfish died and I've just buried him.

Neighbour: That's an awfully big hole for a goldfish, isn't it?

Tommy: That's because he's inside your stupid cat.

A woman gets on a bus with her baby. The bus driver says:
'That's the ugliest baby that I've ever seen. Ugh!'

The woman goes to the rear of the bus and sits down, fuming. She says to a man next to her: 'The driver just insulted me!'

'You go right up there and tell him off – go ahead, I'll hold your monkey for you.'

A young woman was taking an afternoon nap. When she woke up, she told her husband, 'I just dreamed that you gave me a pearl necklace for Valentine's day. What do you think it means?'

'You'll find out tonight,' he said.

That evening, the man came home with a small package and gave it to his wife. Delighted, she opened it. It was a book entitled *The Meaning of Dreams*.

Two cannibals are eating their dinner and one cannibal says to the other, 'I don't like my mother-in-law much.'
'Well, just eat your chips then.'

Husband: Shall we try a new position tonight?
Wife: Sure. You stand by the ironing board and I'll sit on the couch and drink beer and fart.

A newlywed farmer and his wife were visited by her mother, who immediately demanded an inspection of their home. The farmer had tried to be friendly to his new mother-in-law, hoping that theirs would be a non-antagonistic relationship. All to no avail. She nagged them at every opportunity, demanding changes, offering unwanted advice, and generally making life unbearable to the farmer and his new bride.

During a forced inspection of the barn, the farmer's mule suddenly reared up and kicked the mother-in-law in the head, killing her instantly. It was a shock to all, no matter what were their feelings toward her demanding ways.

At the funeral service a few days later, the farmer stood near the casket and greeted folks as they walked by. The pastor noticed that whenever a woman whispered something to the farmer, he would nod his head yes and say something. Whenever a man walked by and whispered to the farmer, however, he would shake his head no, and mumble a reply. Very curious about this bizarre behaviour, the pastor asked the farmer what was going on.

The farmer replied, 'The women say, "What a terrible tragedy" and I nod my head and say "Yes, it was." The men ask, "Can I borrow that mule?" and I shake my head and say, "I can't lend it to you. It's all booked up for a year."

A father and son went fishing one summer day. While they were out in their boat, the boy suddenly became curious about the world around him.

He asked his father, 'Dad, how does this boat float?'

'Don't rightly know son.'

'Dad, how do fish breathe underwater?'

'Don't rightly know son.'

'Dad, why is the sky blue?'

'Don't rightly know son.'

Finally, the boy asked his father, 'Dad, do you mind my asking you all of these questions?'

'Of course not, son. If you don't ask questions, you never learn nothin'.'

Little Johnny:	Mum, when I was on the bus with daddy this morning, he told me to give up my seat to a lady.
Mum:	Well, you've done the right thing.
Little Johnny:	But Mum, I was sitting on daddy's lap.

Sally:	Mummy why can't I go swimming in the sea?
Mum:	Because there are sharks in the sea.
Sally:	But mummy, daddy is swimming in the sea.
Mum:	That's different. He's insured.

A little kid gets onto a city bus and sits right behind the driver. He starts yelling, 'If my dad was a bull and my mum a cow I'd be a little bull.'

The driver starts getting mad at the noisy kid, who continues with, 'If my dad was an elephant and my mum an elephant I would be a little elephant.'

The kid goes on with several animals until the bus driver gets angry and yells at the kid, 'What if your dad was gay and your mum was a prostitute?'

The kid smiles and says, 'I would be a bus driver!'

A six-year-old boy called his mother from his friend Charlie's house and confessed he had broken a lamp when he threw a football in their living room.

'But, Mum,' he said, brightening, 'you don't have to worry about buying another one. Charlie's mother said it was irreplaceable.'

Bill and Linda decided that the only way to pull off a Sunday afternoon quickie with their 10-year-old son in the apartment was to send him out on the balcony and order him to report on all the neighbourhood activities.

The boy began his commentary as his parents put their plan into operation.

'There's a car being towed from the parking lot,' he said. 'An ambulance just drove by.'

A few moments passed.

'Looks like the Andersons have company,' he called out. 'Matt's riding a new bike and the Coopers are having sex.'

Mum and dad stop short.

'How do you know that?' the startled father asked.

'Their kid is standing out on the balcony too,' his son replied.

FISHING

Mrs Pete Monaghan came into the newsroom to pay for her husband's obituary. She was told by the kindly newsman that it was a dollar a word and he remembered Pete and wasn't it too bad about him passing away. She thanked him for his kind words and bemoaned the fact that she only had two dollars. But she wrote out the obituary, 'Pete died.'

The newsman said he thought old Pete deserved more and he'd give her three more words at no charge. Mrs Pete Monaghan thanked him profusely and rewrote the obituary: 'Pete died. Boat for sale'

If a fishing inspector and an insurance agent were both drowning and you could only save one of them, would you go to lunch or would you continue reading your paper?

Bob and Earl were two fishermen who lived for their sport. They fished at every opportunity and watched all the fishing shows on television. They pored over every magazine article on fishing and discussed tactics on how to win the major fishing competitions. They even agreed that whoever died first would try to come back and tell the other if there was fishing in heaven.

One summer night, Bob passed away in his sleep after coming in from a big day out fishing. He had had a good day and so he died happy. A few nights later, his buddy Earl awoke to the sound of Bob's voice coming from beyond.

'Bob, is that you?' Earl exclaimed. 'This is unbelievable! So tell me, is there fishing in heaven?'

'Well, I have some good news and some bad news for you. Which do you want to hear first?'

'Tell me the good news first.'

'The good news is that yes, there is fishing in heaven.'

'Oh, that is wonderful! So what could possibly be the bad news?'

'You're coming out fishing with me tomorrow night.'

I got a new rod and reel for my wife. Best trade I ever made.

Q: How can a fisherman tell if his wife is dead?
A: The sex is the same, but the dishes pile up.

Some fishermen catch their best fish by the tale.

Ben, a local fisherman, went into his favourite bar and ordered six double vodkas.

Bob, the bartender said, 'Wow, you must have had a bad day.'

'Yeah', said Ben, 'I just found out my older brother is gay.'

The next day Ben showed up and again ordered six doubles.

Bob said, 'What, more problems?'

'Damn right, I just found out that my younger brother is gay.'

The third day, the same routine again – six doubles.

'What the hell, doesn't anyone in your family like women?' asked Bob.

'Yeah,' said Ben, 'I just found out my wife does.'

A drunken fisherman stumbled upon a traditional baptismal service at the river where he fished. He walked out in the water to where the minister stood.

The minister turned to the drunk and said, 'Mister, are you ready to find Jesus?'

'Yes, reverend, I sure am.'

The minister then dunks the fellow under the water, pulls him up asking, 'Have you found Jesus?'

'No.'

So the preacher dunks him a bit longer, pulls him up and again asks, 'Did you find Jesus?'

'No.'

The minister is disgusted. He pushes the man under the water for about 30 seconds, pulls him up and asks in a harsh voice, 'Now, my good man, have you found Jesus yet?'

The old fisherman wipes his eyes, spits out some water and says to the minister, 'No. Are you sure this is where he fell in?'

A man is out in his rowboat when suddenly a passing speed boat raises huge waves and the man's oars fall overboard. He is stranded out in the middle of the lake! After about two hours, he sees another row boat going by with a man and two women in it.

The first man yells, 'Hey buddy, can I borrow one of your oars?'

The other man yells back, 'They're not whores, they're my sisters.'

An elderly fisherman was at home, dying in bed, when he smelled his favourite aroma – chocolate chip cookies baking. He wanted one last cookie before he died, so he crawled to the kitchen, reached up to the cookie sheet on the table and grasped a warm, moist chip. His wife hit his hand with a spatula and yelled, 'Leave them alone. They're for the funeral.'

This fisherman goes to the river to check an illegal fish trap that he owns. He looks around to make sure there are no fishing inspectors about and pulls the fish trap out to check it. An inspector steps out of the bushes.

'Ahha!' he says.

The fisherman spins around and yells 'Shiiiit! Oh god. Noooo! Please don't hurt me!'

'Settle down, I'm not going to hurt you. I'm the fishing inspector.'

'Thank God for that,' says the fisherman, 'I thought you were the bugger who owned this fish trap'.

A taxidermist was driving through the country when he thought he would stop at a local bar and have a beer. The locals didn't like outsiders in their bar and when he entered he was greeted with dirty stares and low mumbles. He went to the bartender and asked for a beer.

'What do you do?' asked the barman.

'I'm a taxidermist.'

'Taxidermist? What is that?'

'Well, I mount animals, birds, and fish.'

The bartender turned to the other men in the bar and said, 'It's OK boys he's one of us'.

Q: What is the difference between a fish and a piano?
A: You can't tuna fish.

A man phones home from his office and tells his wife: 'Something has just come up. I have a chance to go fishing for a week. It's the opportunity of a lifetime and we leave right away. So, honey, please pack my clothes, my fishing equipment and especially my blue silk pyjamas. I'll be home in an hour to pick them up.'

He goes home in a hurry and grabs everything and rushes off. A week later he returns.

'Did you have a good trip, dear?' asks his wife.

'Oh yes it was great. But you forgot to pack my blue silk pyjamas.'

'Oh no, I didn't. I put them in your tackle box.'

I think the only reason my husband likes to go fishing so much is that it's the only time he hears someone tell him, 'Wow, that's a big one!'

A fisherman came home one evening to find his eight-year-old son riding a new 10-speed bike.

'Boy', he yelled, 'where did you get the money for that bike? It must have cost $300!'

'Dad, I earned it hiking,' said his son. 'Every other night, while you've been fishing, Mr Green from the bait shop came to see Ma.

'He'd give me $20 and tell me to go take a hike.'

Q: What is the difference between a fairy tale and a fish story?
A: A fairy tale begins with 'Once upon a time,' a fish story begins with 'This ain't no bullshit.'

A fisherman's wife gave birth to twin boys. When the babies were side by side, they always looked in opposite directions, so they were named Forward and Away.

Years later the fisherman took his sons fishing, but they didn't return. Months passed, and the wife finally spotted her husband plodding sadly up the beach. He explained to her that during their trip, Forward had hooked an enormous fish. He had struggled for hours, when suddenly the fish pulled Forward into the water and they never saw him again.

'That's just terrible!' his wife cried.

'It was terrible all right. But you should have seen the one that got Away!'

A woman is in bed with her lover who also happens to be her husband's best friend. After they make love, the phone rings. Since it is the woman's house, she picks up the receiver. Her lover looks over at her and listens, only hearing her side of the conversation.

'Hello? Oh, hi. I'm so glad that you called,' she says speaking in a cheery voice.

'Really? That's wonderful. I am so happy for you, that sounds terrific.'

'Great!'

'Thanks.'

'OK.'

'Bye.'

She hangs up the telephone and her lover asks, 'Who was that?'

'That was my husband telling me all about the wonderful time he's having on his fishing trip with you.'

M other's advice to daughter: Feed a man a fish and he'll eat for a day. But teach a man to fish and you get rid of him for the whole weekend.

T wo men were walking down the street with two salmon each under their arms. Two Irishmen were walking in the opposite direction.

'How did you catch those?' asked the first Irishman.

'Well it's like this. Michael here holds my legs over the bridge, and I grab the salmon as they swim up the river. We got four salmon. A great day's fishing!'

So the fishless pair agreed to give it a try.

They got to the bridge and Sean called to his friend, 'Hold my legs now Paddy.'

After he had been hanging upside down for 30 minutes he cried, 'Pull me up! Pull me up!'

Paddy asked, 'Do you have a fish Sean?'
'No, there's a bloody train coming!'

A country priest loves to fly fish. It's an obsession. So far this year the weather has been so bad that he hasn't had a chance to get his beloved wadders on and his favourite flies out of their box. Strangely though, every Sunday the weather has been good, but of course Sunday is the day he has to go to work.

The weather forecast for Sunday is good again so he calls a fellow priest, claiming to have lost his voice with the flu. He asks him to take over his sermon and on Sunday, the fly-fishing priest drives 100km to a river near the coast so that no one will recognise him.

An angel up in heaven is keeping watch and sees what the priest is doing. He tells God, who decides to do something about it.

With the first cast of the priest's line, a huge fish mouth gulps down the fly. For over an hour the priest runs up and down the river bank fighting the fish. At the end, when he finally lands the monster-sized fish, it turns out to be a world-record salmon.

Confused the angel asks God, 'Why did you let him catch that huge fish? I thought you were going to teach him a lesson.'

'I did. Who do you think he's going to tell?'

J oe and Bob are out fishing. A funeral service passes over the bridge they're fishing by, and Bob takes off his hat and puts it over his heart. He keeps it there until the funeral service has passed by.

'Gee Bob,' says Joe. 'I didn't know you had it in you.'

'It's the least I could do. After all I was married to her for 30 years.'

Steve was out on morning walk when he passed Ole's house and saw a sign that said 'Boat for Sale'. This confused Steve because he knew that Ole didn't own a boat, so he went in to ask Ole about it.

'Hey Ole,' said Steve, 'I noticed da sign in your yard dat says "Boat for Sale," but ya ain't ever been fishun and don't even have a boat. All ya have is your old John Deere tractor and combine harvester.'

'Yup, and they're boat for sale.'

Q: Where do you find most of the fish?
A Between the head and the tail.

Q: What swims and is highly dangerous?
A: A trout with a hand grenade.

Q: What side of a fish has the most scales?
A: The outside.

Q: What can fly under the water?
A: A bird in a submarine.

First guy: You have no idea what I had to do to be able to come out fishing this weekend. I had to promise my wife that I will paint every room in the house next weekend.

Second guy: That's nothing, I had to promise my wife that I will build her a new deck for the pool.

Third guy: Man, you both have it easy! I had to promise my wife that I will remodel the kitchen for her.

Fourth guy: Why did you go to all that trouble? I just set my alarm for 5:30am and when it went off I gave my wife a nudge and said, 'Fishing or sex?' and she said, 'Don't forget your sweater.'

OFFICE, BUSINESS AND TECHNOLOGY

ANSWERING MACHINE MESSAGES

Twinkle, twinkle little star
How we wonder who you are.
Leave a message at the beep.
We'll call back before you sleep.
Twinkle, twinkle little star,
Betcha you're wondering where we are.

Now I lay me down to sleep;
Leave a message at the beep.
  If I should die before I wake,
  Remember to erase the tape.

No, No! Not that! Anything but that! Not the beep! No! Please!
Not the beep! Anything but the beep!
AAAAIIIIEEEEEEEEEEEE!

Hi! John's answering machine is broken. This is his refrigerator.
Please speak very slowly, and I'll stick your message to
myself with one of these magnets.

Hello, this is Ron's toaster. Ron's new answering machine is in
the shop for repairs, so please leave your message when the
toast is done.

Hi. Now you say something.

If you are a burglar, then we're probably at home cleaning our weapons right now and can't come to the phone. Otherwise, we aren't home, and it's safe to leave a message.

Greetings, you have reached the Sixth Sense Detective Agency. We know who you are and what you want, so at the sound of the tone, just hang up.

(In a Darth Vader voice) Speak, worm!

10 EXCUSES TO USE WHEN CAUGHT NAPPING AT YOUR DESK

1. . . . in the Lord Jesus' name, Amen.
2. They told me at the blood bank this might happen.
3. Damn! Why did you interrupt me? I had almost worked out a solution to our biggest problem.
4. I was doing Yoga exercises to relieve work-related stress.
5. Someone must've put decaf in the wrong pot.
6. I was testing my keyboard for drool resistance.
7. This is just a 15-minute powernap, as described in that time management course you sent me.
8. I wasn't sleeping! I was meditating on the mission statement and envisioning a new paradigm.
9. The coffee machine is broken.
10. Whew! Guess I left the top off the Liquid Paper! You got here just in time!

A site foreman had 10 very lazy men working for him, so one day he decided to trick them into doing some work for a change.

'I've got a really easy job today for the laziest one among you,' he announced. 'Will the laziest man please put his hand up?'

Nine hands went up.

'Why didn't you put your hand up?' he asked the 10th man.

'Too much trouble,' came the reply.

YOU WORK IN A GLOBAL CORPORATION IF:

- You sat at the same desk for four years and worked for three different companies.
- You worked for the same company for four years and sat at more than 10 different desks.
- You've been in the same job for four years and have had 10 different managers.
- You see a good-looking person and know it is a visitor.
- You order your business cards in 'half-orders' instead of whole boxes.
- When someone asks what you do for a living, you can't explain it in one sentence.
- You get really excited about a 2% pay raise.
- You use acronyms in your sentences.
- Art involves a white board.
- Your biggest loss from a system crash is that you lose your best jokes.
- You sit in a cubicle smaller than your bedroom closet.
- Weekends are those days your significant other makes you stay home.
- It's dark when you drive to and from work.
- Fun is when issues are assigned to someone else.
- The word 'opportunity' makes you shiver in fear.
- Free food leftover from meetings is your main staple.

- Being sick is defined as 'can't walk or admitted to hospital'.
- You're already late on the assignment you just got.
- Dilbert cartoons hang outside every cube and are read by your co-workers only.
- Your boss' favourite lines are 'when you get a few minutes' or 'when you're freed up'.
- You read this entire list and understood it all.

Aman was eating in a restaurant and he dropped his spoon. The waiter was immediately at his table and took another spoon out of his pocket and gave it to the man. The man thanked him, and took a sip of his soup and then asked,

'Excuse me, but why do all the waiters have spoons in their pockets?'

The waiter said, 'Well sir, a time and motion survey in our restaurant showed that one in four customers drop their spoon just like you, so we always have a spare spoon on hand so we can give it to the customer so that he is not eating with the dirty one. It saves time as the waiter does not have to go back to the kitchen to retrieve a clean spoon. The management prides itself in the efficiency of the staff.'

Just as the waiter was about to walk back to the kitchen, the man noticed that there was a string hanging from his fly and the man said, 'Excuse me but why do you, and all the other waiters have a string hanging out of your flies?'

The waiter said, 'Well sir, a survey in our restaurant showed that the waiters can save time and serve more customers, if we do not wash our hands after using the toilet. So we use the string tied to our penises to pull it out of our trousers so we don't get our hands dirty.'

Then the man took another sip of his soup and replied, 'That's all very well, but how do you get it back in again?'

'Well I don't know about the others,' replied the waiter, 'But personally, I use the spoon.'

A man walks up to a woman in his office and tells her that her hair smells nice. The woman immediately goes into her supervisor's office and tells him that she wants to file a sexual harassment suit and explains why.

The supervisor is puzzled and says, 'What's wrong with your co-worker telling you that your hair smells nice.'

The woman replies, 'He's a midget.'

A blonde, a brunette, and a redhead all work at the same office for a female boss who always goes home early.

'Hey, girls,' says the brunette, 'let's go home early tomorrow. She'll never know.'

So the next day, they all leave right after the boss does. The brunette gets some extra gardening done, the redhead goes to a bar, and the blonde goes home to find her husband having sex with the female boss! She quietly sneaks out of the house and comes back at her normal time.

'That was fun,' says the brunette. 'We should do it again sometime.'

'No way,' says the blonde. 'I almost got caught.'

HOW TO ANNOY THE HELL OUT OF EVERYONE ELSE AT YOUR WORKPLACE

- Page yourself over the intercom. Don't disguise your voice.
- Find out where your boss shops and buy exactly the same outfits. Wear them one day after you boss does. This is especially effective if your boss is of a different gender than you.
- Make up nicknames for all your co-workers and refer to them only by these names, eg 'That's a good point, Sparky,' or 'No, I'm sorry, but I'm going to have to disagree with you there, Cha-Cha.'
- Highlight your shoes. Tell people you haven't lost them as much since you did this.

- Hang mosquito netting around your cubicle. When you emerge to get a coffee or a printout or whatever, slap yourself randomly the whole way.
- Put a chair facing a printer. Sit there all day and tell people you're waiting for your document.
- Every time someone asks you to do something, anything, ask them if they want fries with that.
- Encourage your colleagues to join you in a little synchronised chair-dancing.
- Feign an unnatural and hysterical fear of staplers.
- Send email messages saying there's free pizza or cake in the lunchroom. When people drift back to work complaining that they found none, lean back, pat your stomach and say, 'Oh you've got to be faster than that!'

An engineer had an exceptional gift for fixing all things mechanical. After serving his company loyally for over 30 years, he happily retired. A few years later the company contacted him regarding an impossible problem they were having with one of their multi-million dollar machines. They had tried everything and everyone else to get the machine fixed, but to no avail.

In desperation, they called on the retired engineer who had solved so many of their problems in the past. The engineer reluctantly took the challenge. He spent a day studying the huge machine.

At the end of the day, he marked a small 'x' in chalk on a particular component of the machine and proudly stated, 'This is where your problem is'.

The part was replaced and the machine worked perfectly again. The company received a bill for $50,000 from the engineer for his service. They demanded an itemised accounting of his charges. The engineer responded briefly: One chalk mark: $1. Knowing where to put it: $49,999.

It was paid in full and the engineer retired again in peace.

POLITICS

A secretary for a foreign embassy was entertaining a wealthy ambassador during lunch at a very expensive restaurant in uptown New York. The ambassador was so enthralled by the beauty and presence of this secretary that he asked her to marry him.

The secretary was startled, but remembered that her boss told her never to insult foreign dignitaries, so she decided to let him down easy.

'I'll only marry you under three conditions,' she said.

'Anything, anything,' said the ambassador.

'First, you must buy me a 14-carat gold wedding band with a 72-carat diamond, along with a 70cm studded matching necklace for our engagement.'

Without hesitation, the ambassador picked up his cellular phone, called his personal accountant, told him the instructions, and said, 'Yes, yes, I buy, I buy!'

The secretary thought that her first request was too easy, so she thought of a more difficult situation.

'Second, I want you to build me a 58-acre mansion in the richest part of the Poconos along with a 40-acre summer home in the sweetest vineyards of France.'

The ambassador picked up his phone, called his personal broker in New York, then called another broker in France, and after a quick conversation, he said, 'Yes, yes, I build, I build!'

The secretary was very startled, and knew she must think of a final request that would be impossible to live up to.

'Finally,' she said. 'I'll only marry you if you have a 25cm penis.'

A sad face befell the ambassador, and he cupped his face in his hands. After weeping in his native language for a few minutes, the ambassador slowly lifted his head and said, 'Ok, ok, I cut, I cut!'

The CIA were conducting a job interview for only highly qualified people. After all the background checks, interviews and testing were done, there were three finalists: two men and a woman.

For the final test, the CIA agents took one of the men to a large metal door and handed him a gun.

'We must know that you will follow your instructions, no matter what the circumstances,' said the agent.

'Inside this room, you will find your wife sitting in a chair. Kill her!'

The man said, 'You can't be serious. I could never shoot my wife.'

'Then you're not the right man for this job. Take your wife and go home.'

The second man was given the same instructions. He took the gun and went into the room. All was quiet for about five minutes.

Then the man came out with tears in his eyes. 'I tried, but I can't kill my wife.'

'You don't have what it takes. Take your wife and go home.'

Finally, it was the woman's turn. She was given the same instructions to kill her husband. She took the gun and went into the room. Shots were heard, one shot after another. They heard screaming, crashing, banging on the walls.

After a few minutes, all was quiet. The door opened slowly and there stood the woman. She wiped the sweat from her brow.

'This gun is loaded with blanks,' she said. 'I had to beat him to death with the chair.'

President George W Bush was visiting an elementary school. After the typical civics presentation, he announced, 'All right, boys and girls, you can ask me questions now.'

A little boy named Bobby raised his hand and said, 'Mr President, I have three questions. First, how did you win the election with fewer votes than Gore? Second, why are you using the US Patriot Act to limit Americans' civil liberties? And third, why hasn't the US caught Osama Bin Laden yet?'

The president said, 'Well, Bobby –'

But suddenly, the bell sounded, everything came to a halt, and all the kids ran out to the playground. After lunch the kids were back in class and the president said, 'I'm sorry we were interrupted by the bell. Now, where were we. Oh, yes, you can ask me questions.'

A little girl raised her hand and said, 'Mr President, I have five questions. First, how did you win the election with fewer votes than Gore? Second, why are you using the US Patriot Act to limit Americans' civil liberties? Third, why hasn't the US caught Osama Bin Laden yet? Fourth, why did the bell go off 20 minutes early? And fifth, where's Bobby?'

Acolonel on his way home from work at the pentagon came to a dead halt in traffic and thought to himself, 'Wow, this traffic seems worse than usual. Nothing's even moving.'

He noticed a police officer walking back and forth between the lines of cars so he rolled down his window and asked, 'Excuse me, officer, what's the hold up?'

The officer replies, 'President Bush is just so depressed about being behind in the polls that he stopped his motorcade in the middle of the highway. He says he can't find donators to give him money for his campaign and he's threatening to douse himself in gasoline and set himself on fire. I'm walking around taking up a collection for him.'

'Oh really? How much have you collected so far?'

'So far only about three hundred gallons, but I've got a lot of folks still siphoning!'

Defence Secretary Donald Rumsfeld still believes we will find weapons of mass destruction in Iraq – and Santa at the North Pole.

Many years after Bill Clinton had been president of the United States a famous biographer was interviewing him.

'Bill, what were your best and worst decisions during the presidency?' he asked.

Bill thought deeply and then said, 'Monica Lewinsky! I'd have to say Monica was my best, as well as my worst, decision.'

'How could that be?' asked the surprised biographer.

Bill smiled and shook his head, 'I'd have to say she was both my best and my worst decision for the same reason.'

'And what was that reason?'

Bill squirmed in his chair and answered, 'Monica had a big mouth.'

Said Bill Clinton to young Ms Lewinsky
We don't want to leave clues like Kaczynski,
Since you look such a mess,
Use the hem of your dress
And wipe that stuff off of your chinsky.

'Miss Jones,' Clinton said with affection,
Be so kind as to check my erection.'
But Paula, so silly
Misunderstood Billy,
And thought he said, 'Wreck my election.'

Tony and Cherie Blair are on a trip back to their old home town. They're almost out of fuel, so Tony pulls into a service station on the outskirts of town. The attendant runs out of the station to serve them when Cherie realises it's an old boyfriend from school. She and the attendant chat as he puts petrol in their car and cleans the windows. Then they all say good-bye.

As Tony pulls the car onto the road, he turns to Cherie and says, 'Now aren't you glad you married me and not him? You could've been the wife of a grease monkey!'

To which Cherie replies, 'No, Tony. If I had married him, you'd be pumping gas and he would be prime minister.'

Saddam Hussein and George W Bush meet up in Baghdad for a round of talks in a new peace process. When George sits down, he notices three buttons on the side of Saddam's chair.

They begin talking and after about five minutes Saddam presses the first button. A boxing glove springs out of a box on the desk and punches Bush on the face. Confused, Bush carries on talking, as Saddam falls about laughing. A few minutes later he presses the second button, and this time a big boot comes out and kicks Bush in the shin. Again, Saddam laughs, and again Bush carries on talking, not wanting to be put off the bigger issue.

But when Saddam presses the third button and another boot comes out and kicks Bush in the privates, he's finally had enough.

'I'm going back home!' he tells the Iraqi. 'We'll finish these talks in two weeks – on my territory!'

A fortnight passes and Saddam flies to the States for talks. As the two men sit down, Hussein notices three buttons on Bush's chair and prepares himself for the Yank's revenge.

They begin talking and Bush presses the first button. Saddam ducks, but nothing happens. Bush snickers. A few seconds later, he presses the second button. Saddam jumps up, but again nothing happens. Bush roars with laughter. When he presses the third button, Saddam jumps up again, and again nothing happens. Bush falls on the floor in a fit of hysterics.

'Sod this,' says Saddam. 'I'm going back to Baghdad.'

Bush says through tears of laughter, 'What Baghdad?'

During a recent publicity outing, Cherie Blair sneaked off to visit a fortune teller of some local repute. In a dark and hazy room, peering into a crystal ball, the mystic delivered grave news.

'There's no easy way to say this, so I'll just be blunt: Prepare yourself to be a widow. Your husband will die a violent and horrible death this year.'

Visibly shaken, Cherie stared at the woman's lined face, then at the single flickering candle, then down at her hands. She took a few deep breaths to compose herself. But she drew herself up to ask the important question. She simply had to know. She met the fortune teller's gaze, steadied her voice, and asked, 'Will I be acquitted?'

The mistress of a big English house called her Irish maid and pointed out the dust still on top of the piano.

'Mary,' she said, 'I could write my name in this dust.'

'Isn't education a grand thing, ma'am?' said Mary.

'Capital punishment is our society's recognition of the sanctity of human life.'

– Orrin Hatch, Senator from Utah, explaining his support of the death penalty.

'I stand by all the mis-statements.'

– Dan Quayle, defending himself against criticism for making verbal gaffes.

'**O**utside of the killings, Washington DC has one of the lowest crime rates in the country.'
  – Mayor Marion Barry, Washington DC

'**T**his is the worst disaster in California since I was elected.'
  – California Governor Pat Brown, discussing a local flood.

'**F**acts are stupid things.'
  – Ronald Reagan

A Canadian, Osama bin Laden and George W Bush are out walking together one day. They come across a lantern. A genie pops out of it, granting each man one wish.

The Canadian says, 'I'm a farmer, my dad was a farmer, and my son will also farm. I want the land to be forever fertile in Canada.'

With a blink of the genie's eye, poof! the land in Canada is made forever fertile for farming.

Bin Laden is amazed, so he says, 'I want a wall around Afghanistan, so that no infidels, Jews or Americans can come into our precious state.'

Again, with a blink of the genie's eye, poof! there is a huge wall around Afghanistan.

George W Bush, says, 'I'm very curious, please tell me more about this wall.'

The Genie explains, 'Well, it's about 15,000 feet high, 500 feet thick and completely surrounds the country; nothing can get in or out – it's virtually impenetrable.'

George W Bush says, 'Fill it with water.'

Nelson Mandela, Bill Gates, and David Suzuki were all killed in a horrific aeroplane crash. They arrived at the gates of heaven and were greeted by God sitting on a great golden throne.

God addressed David Suzuki first. 'David, what do you believe in?'

Suzuki replied, 'I believe that man has destroyed the earth with his rampant greed and lust for industrialisation. If we are to continue to survive we must begin to respect the environment and learn to live in harmony with our surroundings.'

God was impressed and asked Suzuki to sit on his left. He then turned to Nelson Mandela and asked what he believes in.

Mandela replied, 'I believe in the equality of all men and women – be they black or white. I believe in fighting vehemently for your ideals, no matter what the personal sacrifice is.'

God was equally impressed and invited Mandela to sit on his right side.

God then addressed Bill Gates.

'Bill, what do you believe in?'

Bill Gates said, 'I believe you're in my chair.'

The president was out walking on a beautiful snowy day, when he saw that somebody had urinated on the white house lawn. In large loopy letters it spelt out 'the president sucks.'

Infuriated, he called on the secret service to work out who had done it. In a few hours, they came to him and told him that there was some bad news and some worse news.

'Give me the bad news first,' said the president.

'The bad news is that the urine is the vice president's.'

'How could he do this to me? What could be worse than that?'

'The handwriting is the first lady's.'

On one of his first nights in the white house George Dubya is woken by the ghost of George Washington. Bush is frightened, but asks, 'George, what is the best thing I could do to help the country?'

Washington advises him, 'Be honest above all else and set an honourable example, just as I did.'

This makes Bush somewhat uncomfortable but he manages to get back to sleep. The next night, the ghost of Thomas Jefferson moves through the dark bedroom.

'Tom,' Dubya asks, 'what is the best thing I could do to help the country?'

Jefferson replies, 'Throw away your prepared remarks and speak eloquently and extemporaneously from your heart.'

Bush isn't sleeping well at all the next night, and sees another figure moving in the shadows. It's Abraham Lincoln's ghost.

'A right winger, finally!' Dubya thinks, 'At last I'll get some advice that I can use.'

So he asks the ghost, 'Abe, what is the best thing I could do to help the country?'

Abe answers, 'Go see a play.'

Chelsea Clinton burst into the room shouting, 'Dad! Mom! I have some great news! Nick asked me to marry him. We are getting married next month.'

Bill takes Chelsea in the back and says, 'As you might have heard, I have been known to fool around with other women on occasions. Your boyfriend Nick happens to be the product of one of my liaisons. He is my son and is your half-brother.'

Chelsea runs out of the office screaming, 'Not another brother!'

She rushes to her mother's side, telling her all about dad's shameful behaviour and how every man she dates turns out to be one of her father's illegitimate sons.

Hillary begins to laugh and says, 'Don't pay any attention to him. He isn't really your father anyway.'

Two terrorists are chatting. One of them opens his wallet and flips through pictures.

'You see, this is my oldest. He's a martyr. Here's my second son. He's a martyr, too.'

The second terrorist says, gently, 'Ah, they blow up so fast, don't they?'

A son asked his father, 'What can you tell me about politics? I have to learn about it for school tomorrow.'

The father thought a little and said, 'OK, son, the best way I can describe politics is to use an analogy. Let's say that I'm a capitalist because I'm the breadwinner. Your mother will be the government because she controls everything. Our maid will be the working class because she works for us. You will be the people because you answer to us. And your baby brother will be the future. Docs that help any?'

The little boy said, 'Well, dad, I don't know, but I'll think about what you said.'

Later that night, after everyone had gone to bed, the little boy was awoken by his baby brother's crying. He went to his brother and realised that he had a dirty nappy. So he went down the hall to his parent's bedroom to tell his parents.

His father's side of the bed was empty, and try as he could his mother wouldn't wake up. He then saw a light on in the guest room down the hall, and through the crack in the door he saw that his father was in bed with the maid.

The son then turned and went back to bed. The next morning, he said to his father at the breakfast table, 'Dad, I think I understand politics much better now.'

'Excellent, my boy,' he answered, 'What have you learned?'

The little boy thought for a minute and said, 'I learned that capitalism is screwing the working class, government is sound asleep ignoring the people, and the future's full of crap.'

While visiting England, George Bush is invited to tea with the Queen. He asks her what her leadership philosophy is.

She says that it is to surround herself with intelligent people. Bush asks how she knows if they're intelligent.

'I know by asking them the right questions,' says the Queen. 'Allow me to demonstrate.'

Bush watches as the Queen phones Tony Blair and says, 'Mr Prime Minister, please answer this question: your mother has a child, and your father has a child, and this child is not your brother or sister. Who is it?'

Tony Blair responds, 'It's me, ma'am.'

'Correct. Thank you and good-bye, sir,' says the Queen. She hangs up and says, 'Did you get that, Mr Bush?'

Bush nods: 'Yes ma'am. Thanks a lot. I'll definitely be using that!'

Bush, upon returning to Washington, decides he'd better put the chairman of the senate foreign relations committee to the test. Bush summons Jesse Helms to the white house and says, 'Senator Helms, I wonder if you can answer a question for me.'

'Why, of course, sir. What's on your mind?'

Bush poses the question: 'Uhh, your mother has a child, and your father has a child, and this child is not your brother or your sister. Who is it?'

Helms ponders this and finally asks, 'Can I think about it and get back to you?'

Bush agrees, and Helms leaves. He immediately calls a meeting of other senior right wing senators, and they puzzle over the question for several hours, but nobody can come up with an answer. Finally, in desperation, Helms calls Colin Powell at the state department and explains his problem.

'Now lookee here, son, your mother has a child, and your father has a child, and this child is not your brother or your sister. Who is it?'

Powell answers immediately, 'It's me, of course.'

Much relieved, Helms rushes back to the white house, finds George Bush, and exclaims, 'I know the answer, sir! I know who it is! It's Colin Powell!'

And Bush replies in disgust, 'Wrong, you dumb shit, it's Tony Blair!'

The president was woken one night by an urgent call from the pentagon.

'Mr President,' said the four-star general, barely able to contain himself, 'There's good news and bad news.'

'Oh, no,' muttered the president, 'Well, let me have the bad news first.'

'The bad news, sir, is that we've been invaded by creatures from another planet.'

'Gosh, and the good news?'

'The good news, sir, is that they eat reporters and piss oil.'

Einstein dies and goes to heaven. At the pearly gates, St Peter tells him, 'You look like Einstein, but you have no idea the lengths that some people will go to in order to sneak into heaven. Can you prove who you really are?'

Einstein ponders for a few seconds and asks, 'Could I have a blackboard and some chalk?'

St Peter snaps his fingers and a blackboard and chalk instantly appear. Einstein describes with arcane mathematics and symbols his theory of relativity. St Peter is suitably impressed.

'You really are Einstein!' he says. 'Welcome to heaven!'

The next to arrive is Picasso. Once again, St Peter asks for credentials.

Picasso asks, 'Mind if I use that blackboard and chalk?'

St Peter says, 'Go ahead.'

Picasso erases Einstein's equations and sketches a truly stunning mural with just a few strokes of chalk. St Peter claps.

'Surely you are the great artist you claim to be!' he says. 'Come on in!'

Then St Peter looks up and sees George W Bush.

St Peter scratches his head and says, 'Einstein and Picasso

both managed to prove their identity. How can you prove yours?'

George W looks bewildered and says, 'Who are Einstein and Picasso?'

St Peter sighs and says, 'Come on in, George.'

Monica Lewinsky was taking some of her clothes to the dry-cleaners. The man behind the counter was hard of hearing. She was holding a dress up and pointing at stains on the front of it, when she realised that the man was looking confused.

The old man put a hand up to his ear, and said, 'Come again?'

'No,' said Monica, 'It's red wine this time!'

Cherie Blair dies and goes to heaven. She is standing outside the pearly gates when she notices a wall of clocks behind St Peter. Curious she asks him why he has so many

'Ah,' he says, 'They are truth clocks. Every person has their own clock, and whenever they tell a lie the hands on their clock moves forward one minute.'

Cherie looks up and sees Pope John Paul II's clock. The time on his clock shows one minute past twelve, meaning that he has only told one lie in his entire life.

She then sees Mother Teresa's clock. Amazingly the hands on her clock are unmoved. She has never told a lie, or even a fib!

Cherie then starts to wonder where her husband's clock is. She asks St Peter to point it out to her. St Peter looks a little uncomfortable as he says, 'It's hanging in Jesus' office. He's using it as a ceiling fan.'

While on a state visit to England, George Bush met the queen. He said to her, 'Your Majesty, I think you are onto something here. As I'm the president, I'm thinking of changing how my great country is referred to, and I'm thinking that it should become a kingdom.'

The queen replied, 'I'm sorry Mr Bush, but to be a kingdom, you have to have a king in charge – and you're not a king.'

George Bush thought about this for a while and then said, 'How about a principality then?'

The queen replied, 'Again, to be a principality your head of state must be a prince – and you're not a prince, Mr Bush.'

Bush thought long and hard and came up with, 'How about an empire then?'

The queen, getting a little annoyed by now, replied, 'Sorry again, Mr Bush, but to be an empire you must have an emperor in charge – and you are not an emperor.'

Before George Bush could utter another word, the queen said: 'I think you're doing quite nicely as a country.'

PRESIDENT GEORGE W BUSH

There was one kind of embarrassing moment when President Bush was asked if he ever went AWOL and he said, 'No, we have EarthLink.'

Bush made the declaration, 'I'm a war president.' It's a pity that he didn't tell the American public that back in 2000 before they voted him in.

Remember the good old days when the only thing the president was trying to cover up was a stain?

President Bush was asked if his commission investigating Iraq was bipartisan. He replied, 'A person's sexuality should play no role in this.'

Bush the younger has two things going for him that his father never had. One – an easy charm with regular people; and two – the power to make them disappear without a trial.

George Bush sent his warmest regards to ex-president, Ronald Reagan, on his 93rd birthday and asked if he wanted to be on his committee looking in on intelligence failures. Oh, and Reagan has Alzheimer's.

President Bush's approval rating is now down under 50 percent. So now what he's going to have to do is let Saddam go so we can capture him again.

President Bush has appointed a commission to answer one big question about pre-war Iraq: how did American oil get under their sand?

This Iraqi intelligence scandal is growing. Americans are asking, 'What did President Bush not know?' and 'When did he mispronounce it?'

Critics are now saying that his dad got him out of going to Vietnam. However, his dad did get him to go to Iraq.

A reporter asked George W Bush if he was a deserter. Bush answered, 'No, I skip the pie and the ice cream. I'm not a big deserter.'

Who cares if Bush didn't do his job in the National Guard 30 years ago? Personally, I'm more afraid of the job he's doing now.

In the same week an issue of Time magazine asked if President Bush has a credibility problem and the cover of the Newsweek magazine asked who really killed Jesus. And in both cases, it proved the same thing – it's hard to get good intelligence in the Middle East.

Clinton, Dole and Perot are on a long flight in Air Force One. Perot pulls out a $100 bill and says 'I'm going to throw this $100 bill out and make someone down below happy.'

Dole, not wanting to be outdone, says, 'If that was my $100 bill, I would split it into two $50 bills and make two people down below happy.'

Of course Clinton doesn't want these two candidates to outdo him, so he pipes in, 'I would instead take 100 $1 bills and throw them out to make 100 people just a little happier.'

At this point the pilot, who has overheard all this bragging and can't stand it anymore, comes out and says, 'I think I'll throw all three of you out of this plane and make 250 million people happy.'

George W Bush and his driver were heading for Air Force One and were passing a farm. A pig jumped out in the road suddenly. The driver tried to get out of the way, but he hit him.

He went in the farm to explain what had happened. He came out with a beer, a cigar, and tons of money.

Bush saw this and said, 'My God, what did you tell them?'

The driver replied, 'I told them that I'm George W Bush's driver and I just killed the pig.'

JANET JACKSON'S BREAST

As a result of Janet Jackson's performance at the Super Bowl, the Grammys were on a five-minute delay so they can take out any mistakes. Dick Cheney wants to use this technology on Bush's speeches.

GEORGE W BUSH & THE NATIONAL GUARD

The Ninja were Japanese warriors who could make themselves invisible whenever there was a war. Kind of like George W Bush.

The white house has now released military documents that 'prove' George Bush met his requirements for the National Guard. Big deal, there's documents that prove Al Gore won the election.

QUOTES

'**H**ere we are in the Holy Land of Israel – a Mecca for tourists.'
– BBC

'**I**n a sense it's a one-man shown, except there are two men involved – Hartson and Berkovic, and a third man, the goalkeeper.'
– BBC 1

'**I**'d be surprised if all 22 players are on the field at the end of the game – one's already been sent off.'
– Sky Sports

'**L**iz Taylor is recovering in hospital after having had a benign tuna removed from just behind her right ear.'
– Capital Radio

Peter Snow: In a sense, Deng Xiaoping's death was inevitable, wasn't it?
Expert: Yes.
– Channel 4 News

'**A**s Phil de Glanville said, each game is unique, and this one is no different to any other.'
– BBC1

'**I**t's like learning to play golf. Just when you think you've cracked it, they move the goalposts.'
– Southern Counties Radio

*...an idea someone picks up and runs with, only to find they've painted themselves into a corner.'
- BBC1

Cystitis is a living death, it really is. Nobody ever talks about it, but if I was faced with a choice between having my arms removed and getting cystitis, I'd wave goodbye to my arms quite happily.'
- Q Magazine

Well, you gave the horse a wonderful ride, everyone saw that.'
- BBC

Julian Dicks is everywhere. It's like they've got eleven Dicks on the field.'
- Metro Radio

Morcelli has the four fastest 1500m times ever. And all those times are at 1500m.'
- BBC1

| Listener: | My most embarrassing moment was when my artificial leg fell off at the altar on my wedding day. |
| Simon Fanshawe: | How awful! Do you still have an artificial leg? |

- Talk radio

| Interviewer: | So did you see which train crashed into which train first? |
| 15-year-old: | No, they both ran into each other at the same time. |

- Radio 4

'The lack of money is evident but you've got 12,000 volunteers who'll break their back to make sure it's a success.'
– Today Program (on the Paralympics)

'You weigh up the pros and cons and try to put them in chronological order.'
– Radio 5 Live

REDNECKS

HILLBILLY STATE RESIDENCY APPLICATION

Name (tick appropriate box):

☐ Billy-Bob   ☐ Billy-Mae
☐ Billy-Joe   ☐ Billy-Jack
☐ Billy-Ray   ☐ Billy-Cart
☐ Billy-Sue

Age: _____

Sex: ☐ M ☐ F ☐ N/A

Shoe Size:
Left _____
Right _____

Occupation:
☐ Farmer   ☐ Hairdresser
☐ Mechanic   ☐ Unemployed

Spouse's Name: _____

Relationship with spouse:
☐ Sister   ☐ Mother
☐ Brother   ☐ Father
☐ Aunt   ☐ Son
☐ Uncle   ☐ Daughter
☐ Cousin   ☐ Pet

Number of children living in household: _____
Number that are yours: _____

Mother's Name: _____
Father's Name: _____
(If not sure, leave blank)

Education: 1 2 3 4 (Circle highest grade completed)

Do you ☐ own or ☐ rent your mobile home? (Check appropriate box)

Total number of vehicles you own _____
Number of vchicles that still crank _____
Number of vehicles in front yard _____
Number of vehicles in back yard _____
Number of vehicles on cement blocks _____
Total number of firearms you own _____
Number of firearms in truck _____
Number of firearms in bedroom _____
Number of firearms in bathroom _____
Number of firearms in kitchen _____
Number of firearms in shed _____

Model and year of your pickup: _____194__

Number of times you've seen a UFO _____
Number of times you've seen Elvis _____
Number of times you've seen Elvis in a UFO _____

How often do you bathe?
☐ Weekly   ☐ Monthly   ☐ Not Applicable

Colour of teeth:
- [ ] Yellow
- [ ] Brownish-Yellow
- [ ] Brown
- [ ] Black
- [ ] N/A

Brand of chewing tobacco you prefer: _____

How far is your home from a paved road? _____
Have you ever seen a paved road? _____

RIDDLES

Q: What do you call a beautiful, sunny day that comes after two cloudy, rainy ones?

A: Monday.

Q: Why did the chicken lawyer cross the road?

A: To get to the car accident on the other side.

Q: Why do birds fly south?

A: Because it's too far to walk.

Q: What is the difference between a cat and a comma?

A: One has the paws before the claws and the other has the clause before the pause.

Q: What has four legs and an arm?

A: A happy pit bull.

Q: What colour is a hiccup?

A: Burple.

Q: Why did the cannibal live on his own?

A: He'd had his fill of other people.

Q: What is the difference between a Rottweiler and a social worker?

A: It is easier to get your kids back from a Rottweiler!

Q: Why did the salmon cross the road?
A: Because it was tied to the chicken.

Q: Why do women have breasts?
A: So men will talk to them!

Q: Did you hear about the idiot who walked around the world?
A: He drowned.

Q: What's the difference between Monica Lewinsky and the rest of us?
A: When we want some dick in the white house, we just vote.

Q: What is the difference between a statistician and an accountant?
A: A statistician is someone who is good with numbers but lacks the personality to be an accountant.

TELEPHONE TALES

ANSWERING SERVICE AT A MENTAL INSTITUTE

Hello, and welcome to the mental health hotline.
If you are obsessive-compulsive, press one repeatedly.

If you are co-dependent, please ask someone to press two for you.

If you have multiple personalities, press three, four, five and six.

If you are paranoid, we know who you are and what you want. Stay on the line so we can trace your call.

If you are delusional, press seven and your call will be transferred to the mother ship.

If you are schizophrenic, listen carefully and a small voice will tell you which number to press.

If you are manic depressive, it doesn't matter which number you press, no one will answer.

If you have a nervous disorder, please fidget with the hash key until someone comes on the line.

If you are dyslexic, press 6969696969.

If you have amnesia, press eight and state your name, address, phone number, date of birth, social security number, and your mother's maiden name.

If you have post-traumatic-stress disorder, slowly and carefully press 000.

If you have bipolar disorder, please leave a message after the beep, or before the beep, or after the beep. Please wait for the beep.

If you have short-term memory loss, press nine. If you have short term memory loss, press nine. If you have short term memory loss, press nine. If you have short term memory loss, press nine.

If you have low self esteem, please hang up. All our operators are too busy to talk to you.

TELEMARKETER TORTURE 2004

What to do when your dinner is interrupted by a keen telemarketer on the phone:

Go absolutely silent.

Breather slowly and heavily into the phone.

Mumble: 'I like to watch.'

Pretend that this is a call that you are expecting from the child psychologist in relation to your troubled and disruptive teenage son.

Ask them if they are selling beer.

Start speaking in another language.

Tell them the person they want doesn't live here anymore. Give them the number of a phone sex line and tell them that it is the new number.

Tell them that you're not here right now.

Start selling them something else.

Tell them you're poor and ask for money.

Start preaching your religion to them.

Try to hypnotise them.

Put on some really annoying music and put the phone up to the stereo.

Ask the telemarketer if s/he is single. Then try hitting on him/her. Be sure to mention your various medical problems and your fascination with odd smells.

Use a voice changer to disguise your voice.

Rap all your replies to the telemarketer's questions.

Ask the telemarketer if s/he minds if you talk to him/her on the toilet. Then take a plastic sauce bottle and squeeze out sauce repeatedly.

Try to rhyme with everything the telemarketer says.

Sell them on the 'value of high colonics'. Explain your 'dedication to good health' in your most convincing, passionate voice.

Start talking about your many medical ailments and don't allow the telemarketer to get a word in.

TOILET HUMOUR

SOME THINGS TO PONDER ON THE LOO

- If all the world is a stage, where is the audience sitting?
- If all is not lost, where is it?
- If God dropped acid, would he see people?
- What's the speed of dark?
- If you're in hell and mad at someone, where do you tell them to go?
- What happens if you were scared half to death twice?
- How is it possible to have a civil war?
- If only the good die young, what does that say about senior citizens?
- How can you be alone with someone?
- If corn oil comes from corn, where does baby oil come from?
- What do sheep count when they can't get to sleep?
- If it's tourist season, why can't we shoot them?
- Why do they call it instant credit, when it actually means instant debt?
- If we're not supposed to eat late-night snacks, why is there a light in the refrigerator?
- Why is it called a TV set, when you only get one?
- Did God create man before woman, because He didn't want any advice?
- Isn't it scary that doctors call what they do 'practice'?
- Why do they sterilise needles for a lethal injection?
- Can a blonde play an AM radio in the evening?
- Why are they called 'apartments', when they're all stuck together?

- Does a heavy voice on the phone mean I should not go to bed with that person?
- How come wrong numbers are never busy?
- If a word in the dictionary was misspelled, how would we know?
- If space is a vacuum, who changes the bags?
- Where do they keep daylight savings time?
- Why do banks charge you an 'insufficient funds' fee when they know you don't have any funds?
- If the No 2 pencil is the most popular why is it still No 2?
- Can a stupid person be a smart-arse?
- Why is the time of day with the slowest traffic called rush hour?
- Since Australians throw rice at weddings, do Asians throw meat pies?
- When God rested on the seventh day, what did He do?
- And if He played golf, did he set a course record?
- If man evolved from monkeys and apes, why are there still monkeys and apes?
- Do they give pilots crash courses in flight school?
- Is killing time a crime?
- When I erase a word with a pencil, where does it go?
- How do you get off a non-stop flight?
- If you're sending someone Styrofoam, what do you pack it in?
- How do you write zero in Roman numerals?
- Can you buy a full chess set in a pawn shop?
- Why is the third hand on a watch called the second hand?
- Why don't people in Australia call the rest of the world 'up over'?
- If all those psychics know the winning lottery numbers, why are they still working for a living?
- How did a fool and his money get together in the first place?
- Why doesn't the fattest man in the world become a goalie?
- How can someone draw a blank?

- Before they invented drawing boards, what did they go back to?
- How come Superman can stop a bullet with his chest but always ducks when someone throws a gun at him?
- Why do we wait till a pig is dead before we cure it?
- When everything is coming your way, are you in the wrong lane?
- If tin whistles are made out of tin, what are fog horns made out of?
- Can vegetarians eat animal crackers?
- Is Santa always jolly because he knows where all the bad girls live?

MORE THINGS TO PONDER ON THE LOO

- All those who believe in psychokinesis raise my hand.
- Ambition is a poor excuse for not having enough sense to be lazy.
- Beauty is in the eye of the beer holder.
- Black holes are where God divided by zero.
- Corduroy pillows – they're making headlines!
- Drink 'til she's cute, but stop before the wedding.
- Eagles may soar, but weasels don't get sucked into jet engines.
- Energizer Bunny arrested, charged with battery.
- Everyone has a photographic memory, but some don't have any film.
- Excuses are like arses – everyone's got em and they all stink.
- For Sale: Parachute. Only used once, never opened, small stain.
- Give a man a free hand and he'll run it all over you.
- How do you tell when you run out of invisible ink?
- I almost had a psychic girlfriend but she left me before we met.
- I couldn't repair your brakes, so I made your horn louder.
- I drive way too fast to worry about cholesterol.
- I intend to live forever – so far, so good.
- I love defenceless animals, especially in good gravy.
- I poured Spot remover on my dog. Now he's gone.

- I used to have an open mind but my brains kept falling out.
- If Barbie is so popular, why do you have to buy her friends?
- If everything seems to be going well, you have obviously overlooked something.
- If I worked as much as others, I would do as little as they do.
- If you ain't making waves, you ain't kicking hard enough!
- If you choke a Smurf, what colour does it turn?
- Join the army, meet interesting people, kill them.
- Laughing stock – cattle with a sense of humour.
- Many people quit looking for work when they find a job.
- Quantum Mechanics – The dreams stuff is made of.
- Shin – a device for finding furniture in the dark.
- Support bacteria – they're the only culture some people have.
- The early bird gets the worm, but the second mouse gets the cheese.
- The only substitute for good manners is fast reflexes.
- Wear short sleeves – support your right to bare arms!
- When I'm not in my right mind, my left mind gets pretty crowded.
- Who is General Failure and why is he reading my hard disk?
- Why do psychics have to ask you for your name?

EVEN MORE THINGS TO PONDER ON THE LOO

- A planetarium puts on all-star shows.
- A plastic surgeon's office is the only place where no one gets offended when you pick your nose.
- If a cow laughed, would milk come out her nose?
- If a no-armed man has a gun, is he armed?
- If a shop is open 24 hours a day, 365 days a year, why are there locks on the doors?
- If a turtle doesn't have a shell, is he homeless or naked?
- If nothing ever sticks to Teflon, how do they make Teflon stick to the pan?

- If swimming is so good for the figure, how then do you explain whales?
- If you cross a four-leaf clover with poison ivy, would you get a rash of good luck?
- If you crossed an electric blanket with a toaster, would you pop out of bed quicker in the morning?
- If you feed gunpowder to a chicken do you get an eggsplosion?
- If you get into a taxi and the driver starts driving backwards, does s/he owe you money?
- If you tied buttered toast to the back of a cat and dropped it from a height, which way would it end up?
- Is it is bad luck to be superstitious?
- Is it OK to use your AM radio in the afternoon?
- Is it true that cannibals won't eat clowns because they taste funny?
- Is there another word for synonym?
- Smoking kills, and if you're killed, you've lost a very important part of your life.
- The trouble with most referees is that they don't care who wins.
- What do people in China call their best plates?
- What do you call a male ladybird?
- What was the best thing before sliced bread?
- When dog food is new and improved, who tested it?
- Who says nothing is impossible? Some people do it every day.
- Why didn't Noah swat those two mosquitoes?
- Why doesn't glue stick to the inside of the bottle?
- Why is a carrot more orange than an orange?
- Why is abbreviated such a long word?
- Why is it that when a door is open, it's ajar, yet when a jar is open, it's not a door?
- Why isn't phonetic spelled the way it sounds?
- Why isn't there mouse-flavoured cat food?
- Would a fly without wings be called a walk?

As the elevator car left our floor,
Big Sue caught her tits in the door;
  She yelled a good deal,
  But had they been real,
  She'd have yelled considerably more.

Three lunatics were walking down the road when they came across a huge pile of shit.
  The first loony put his eye in it and said, 'Look's like shit'.
  The next one put his nose in it and said, 'Smell's like shit.'
  The last one put his tongue in it and said, 'Taste's like shit.'
  They all looked at each other and said, 'Lucky we did not stand in it!'

DIFFERENT TYPES OF POO

Clean poo:	The kind you poo out, and see it in the toilet, but there is nothing on the toilet paper.
Corn poo:	Self explanatory.
Gassy poo:	It's so noisy, everyone within earshot is giggling.
Gee-I-wish-I-could-poo-poo:	The kind where you know you want to poo but all you can muster are a few farts.
Ghost poo:	The kind where you feel the poo come out, you hear the splash but there is no trace of the poo in the toilet.
Log pooh:	The kind of poo that is so huge you are afraid to flush it for fear of blocking the S-bend.
Mexican poo:	It smells so bad that even you gag.
Pop-a-vein-in-your-forehead-poo:	The kind where you strain so much to get it out, you practically have a stroke.

Second-wave poo:	This happens when you think you are all done, you've pulled up your pants and then you realise that there is an encore.
Surprise poo:	You didn't even know that you wanted to poo! You were just here on other business.
Upper-class poo:	The kind that doesn't smell at all.
Wet cheeks poo:	The power dump! The kind that propels itself out with such force that the splash hits your cheeks. On your face.
Wet poo:	The kind where you wipe your bottom 50 times and it still ain't clean.

Two beggars, Seamus and Niall, were walking along the road at dusk. Being the more amateur of the two, Niall complained loudly, 'I'm famished! How will we get something to eat this night?'

'Worry not,' said Seamus, 'I'll show you how it's done.'

As they approached a farmhouse, he picked up a dried cow pat from the field and went to the door. He knocked on the door, and the missus answered.

'Yes?' she said.

'Forgive me missus,' begged Seamus, 'I am but a humble beggar with nought to eat but this dried old cow pat. Could I trouble you for some salt to go with it?'

'Why that's no fit meal for a man,' the woman exclaimed. 'Come in here and sit down, I'll feed you proper.'

A half hour later, Seamus emerged from the house stuffed with lamb and potatoes and smiling ear to ear.

'Wow,' shouted Niall, 'I can do that!'

He ran to the next farmhouse, grabbing his own cow pat along the way. He knocked on the door, and the missus answered.

'Forgive me missus,' he begged, 'I am but a humble beggar with nought to eat but 'this dried-up old cow pat. Could I trouble you for some salt to go with it?

'Sakes alive,' she cried 'that's no fit meal for a man. That things all horrible and dried up. Go on out back and get yourself a fresh one.'

THE ART OF THE FART

A sparkling young farter from Sparta,
His fart for no money would barter.
He could roar from his rear
Any scene from Shakespeare,
Or Gilbert and Sullivan's Mikado.

Q: Why do farts smell?
A: So that deaf people can appreciate them as well.

A very attractive young lady was sitting in a fine restaurant one night. She was waiting for her special date and she wanted to make sure everything was perfect. As she bent down in her chair to get the mirror from her purse, she accidentally farted quite loudly just as the waiter walked by. She sat upright, embarrassed and red faced, knowing that everyone in the place had heard her.

To cover her embarrassment she turned to the waiter and demanded loudly, 'Stop that!'

'Sure lady, which way is it headed?' said the waiter.

Q: Did you hear the joke about the fart?
A: It stinks.

A man has a serious problem. Every time he takes a step, he farts. He goes to the doctor and when he walks in, 'Parp! Fumph! Toot! Poop!' go his bowels.

He sits down and the doctor tells him to walk across the room. He walks across the room and again his arse explodes with each stride, 'Parp! Fumph! Toot! Poop!' He walks back to his seat, 'Toot! Fumph! Parp! Poop! Rumble.'

'I know what I'm going to do!' says the doctor.

He goes to his cupboard and brings out a giant pole with a great big hook on the end of it.

The fellow looks in horror and says, 'Jeez, Doc, what the hell are you gonna do with that?'

'I'm going to open the window, of course. This place stinks!'

MUMMY!

Woman: Your son is terribly spoiled.
Mother: How dare you. He's not spoiled at all.
Woman: Yes he is. He just got hit by a bus.

Mummy, mummy, why can't we give Grandma a proper burial?
Shut up and keep flushing.

Mummy, mummy, daddy's on fire.
Hurry up and get the marshmallows.

Mummy, mummy, my head hurts.
Shut up and get away from the dart board.

Mummy, mummy, why can't we buy a garbage disposal unit?
Shut up and keep chewing.

Mummy, mummy, dad's going out.
Shut up and throw some more petrol on him.

Mummy, mummy, daddy's hammering on the roof again.
Shut up and drive a bit faster.

CONFUCIUS SAY . . .

- Woman who wear G-string, high on crack!
- Woman who pounce on dead rooster go down on limp cock.
- Woman who cooks carrots and peas in same pot is unsanitary.
- While others are inside sitting down, you will be outstanding.
- War doesn't determine who's right, war determines who's left.
- Virgin like balloon. One prick, all gone.
- Secretary not permanent until screwed on desk.
- Put rooster in freezer to get a stiff cock.
- Penis put in vacuum cleaner get sucked off.
- Panties not best thing on earth, but next to it.
- OK for shit to happen. It will decompose.
- Never eat yellow snow.
- Naked man fears no pick pocket.
- Man with one chopstick go hungry.
- Man with no legs bums around.
- Man with hole in pocket feels cocky all day.
- Man with hand in pocket is having a ball.
- Man with an unchecked parachute will jump to conclusion.
- Man who tell one too many light bulb jokes soon burn out.
- Man who stand on toilet is high on pot.
- Man who speaks with forked tongue should not kiss balloons.
- Man who sneezes without tissue takes matters into his own hands.
- Man who smoke pot choke on handle.
- Man who sit on tack get point.
- Man who sink into woman's arms soon have arms in woman's sink.

- Man who scratches ass should not bite fingernails.
- Man who put head on railroad track to listen for train likely to end up with splitting headache.
- Man who put face in punchbowl gets punch in nose.
- Man who piss into wind get wet.
- Man who paints on toilet door is a shithouse painter.
- Man who masturbate only screwing himself.
- Man who masturbate into cash register, soon come into money.
- Man who keep feet firmly on ground have trouble putting on pants.
- Man who go to bed with diarrhoea wake up in deep shit.
- Man who fart in church sit in own pew.
- Man who eat many prunes get good run for money.
- Man who drop watch in toilet have shitty time.
- Man who drive like hell bound to get there.
- Man who chase cars will soon get exhausted.
- Man who bounce woman on bedspring this spring have offspring next spring.
- Man trapped in sewer, eat shit and die.
- It takes many nails to build crib, but one screw to fill it.
- Is good to learn how to masturbate, may come in handy.
- Hockey player on ice have big stick.
- He who stands in corner with hands in pocket doesn't feel crazy, feels nuts.
- He who sleeps with itchy bum, will wake with smelly thumb.
- He who sits on an upturned tack shall surely rise.
- He who lives in glasshouse dresses in basement.
- He who eats crackers in bed gets crummy sleep.
- He who crosses the ocean twice without washing is a dirty double crosser.
- Girl laid in tomb may soon become mummy.
- Fly who sit on toilet seat get pissed off.
- Butcher who back into meat grinder get a little behind in his orders.

- Boy who go to bed with sex problem wake up with solution in hand.
- Best way to prevent hangover is to stay drunk.
- Baseball is wrong. Man with four balls can't walk!
- Baby conceived on back seat of car with automatic transmission grow up to be shiftless bastard.
- A bird in hand makes hard to blow nose.

BEST JOKES IN THE WORLD . . . DEBATABLE!

We've left the best until last. Two recent world-wide competitions found that the following two jokes were the funniest in the world.

Sherlock Holmes and Dr Watson go camping, and pitch their tent under the stars.

During the night, Holmes wakes his companion and says, 'Watson, look up at the stars, and tell me what you deduce.'

Watson says, 'I see millions of stars, and even if a few of those have planets, it's quite likely there are some planets like earth, and if there are a few planets like earth out there, there might also be life.'

Holmes replies, 'Watson, you idiot. Somebody stole our tent.'

Two hunters are out in the woods when one of them collapses. He doesn't seem to be breathing and his eyes are glazed. The other guy whips out his mobile phone and calls the emergency services.

He gasps, 'My friend is dead! What can I do?'

The operator says, 'Calm down, I can help. First, let's make sure he's dead.'

There's a silence, then a shot is heard.

Back on the phone, the guy says, 'OK, now what?'